THE HEART-CENTERED HABIT:

"Perceiving through the Heart of the Matter"

A 22 Day Journey of Remembrance
- ♥ Remembering your authentic nature
- ♥ Remembering the heart-centered you
- ♥ Remembering your Divine essence
- ♥ Remembering your true infinite nature
- ♥ Remembering your soul purpose
- ♥ Remembering your innocent nature
- ♥ Remembering a love that has no opposite
- ♥ Remembering the joy of being

Acknowledgements

"It is better to live your own life imperfectly than to imitate someone else's perfectly."

–Elizabeth Gilbert

Every person who has ever crossed my path, and every person whose path I have crossed, has a special part in the writing of this book. I acknowledge and thank everything and everyone throughout my life for being the perfect role I needed at each twist and turn along the journey of returning home to the presence of pure love in my heart.

I thank my parents, Larry and Linda Miller, for never giving me the answers to my big questions in life, and allowing me to find my own way. You both provided me the freedom to discover the glowing presence of pure love within my own heart. Thank you, Dad for giving me the most powerful words a father could give to their young daughter, "You can do whatever you set your mind to do!" You didn't tell me who I was at a young age. Instead, you allowed me to discover the infinite potential that lies within my own heart. Thank you, Mom for being an infinitely loving, compassionate, and faithful being. Your love for the underdogs of the world carried me through many dark nights of the soul. Because of you I never stopped believing in the underdog I felt I was. Thank you for seeing me through the heart of the chaos in my life. I love you!

I thank my sister, Melanie Stuckrath. Even though you are my sister by blood, I consider you to be my soul sister. Thank you for the loving support your presence has provided me throughout the writing of this book. You inspire me in so many ways to be the real, authentic, and unique me. Thank you for truly seeing the real me despite what I have been through or the way I have appeared in the past! I love you!

I thank my husband, Joshua. Even though you do not understand my highly sensitive nature, you have always believed in me and encouraged me to shine brightly. Thank you for allowing me to be unique and honor my gifts. I love you!

I thank my children, Jaden and Josiah Best. Thank you for accepting and loving me the way I am. Jaden, your presence awoke within me a creativity I had forgotten since I was a child. Thank you for reminding me of the infinite creative being that I am. Josiah, your presence awoke within me my true innocent nature. Thank you for reminding me of my innocent loving voice. Jaden and Josiah, in so many ways you have been my spirit guides reminding me of the truth that I am. You have reminded me to listen to the intuition in my heart over what my environment says is the "right" thing to do. You inspire me every day to live in a heart-centered way! I love you!

"The gift is knowing that your past has been your spiritual classroom."

– Paul Williams and Tracey Jackson

CONTENTS

Preface

Returning Home

"You have to stop trying to find a way out to discover the way in." -Lisa Best

When I was a child I felt so satisfied, fulfilled, free, and open to all of life. I loved exploring the world and imagining myself as anything and everything. I was growing and evolving in a world where every individual seemed to have a solid sense of self, firm beliefs in wrong, and very specific points of view. I remember thinking, *Something must be wrong with me because God didn't give me a solid identity or any beliefs in wrong.*

In an effort to fit in with this world of knowns, I began to act as if I had an identity. I used my open, empathic, and sensitive nature to blend in with my environment. As an empath, I could walk into a room and feel everybody's judgments, feelings, and beliefs right away even before I spoke with them. I noticed most people acted in ways which didn't resonate with what they truly felt under the surface. Nobody seemed to be bothered that their inner experience was different than the way they acted in the external world. Nobody talked about these inner feelings that I was experiencing under the surface. Therefore, I kept them to myself and became a social chameleon, which I call the head-centered habit of me. The head-centered me matched, conformed, and mimicked what I sensed from the world around me. I did this on a mental level and as I continued to react this way in my relationships to the world, this habit became an automatic subconscious response. I had no boundaries. I didn't know where I stopped and another began. Their ideas, perspectives, judgments, thoughts, emotions, and beliefs became mine. I could become best friends with anybody because I knew them to their core. It was like being an actress and the world was my stage.

I realized early on that everybody lived by their own unique belief system of right and wrong. They blended with other likeminded people, but each individual had a uniqueness to their belief system, based upon past experiences. Two people can have similar past experiences, but they are not exactly identical. For instance, individuals in a family usually had similar beliefs but were still slightly unique, as well as individuals in religious, political, cultural, societal, residential, sports-related groups, and communities. I noticed that people bonded through their systems of belief. I was scared to death that I would never be able to bond with another human being because I had no set beliefs. Beliefs for me came and went. They didn't stay for too long. I felt like such an outcast because every time I placed my faith in a particular belief, I felt fake and superficial. All perspectives felt relevant to me, but none felt like my home. I couldn't fit my entire being into a specific belief. Therefore, I didn't stick to any belief for long. I had an inner knowing that I was so much more than what I thought or believed myself to be, which kept me from resonating with a likeminded group of people for long periods of time. Everybody I knew appeared to have a home or a group they fit in with apart from me.

Once I went to elementary school, the infinite reality I experienced as a child began to fade, and a limited reality formed in my perception of reality. I became distracted by sensing into other people's experiences of reality. Instead of exploring the physical world, I began to explore other people's inner belief world. I observed how tuning into other people's energy made them feel connected to me and provided us both with a sense of safety and security. I thought this was how I was supposed to help people feel better. However, this was extremely exhausting because I didn't only do this with my family and friends, but with everyone; the homeless person on the corner, the grocery store clerk, my teachers, and everyone in my presence.

Often, complete strangers would come up to me saying, "Don't I know you?" Or "I feel like we've met before." I had never physically met them, but on a deeper level I knew them. By the time I reached high school I felt lost in the head-centered habit. I was spending more time being head-centered out in the world than giving attention to the inner knowing I sensed in my heart. I was becoming more unhealthy, unconscious, and reckless. I grew extremely despondent by the time I entered college. I had no passion, joy, or peace in my life. I escaped into alcohol, food, and partying to numb my experience of dullness. I tried so hard to fit in with the status quo of my relationships, but no matter how much I acted like I fit in and felt like I fit into the "inner circle" of my relationships, I continued to feel lost and miserable. I felt like the light I had as a child was dimming. I did not understand this world and I didn't want to physically live anymore because I felt dead on the inside.

When I was 23 years old, I knew I needed to rediscover the light I remembered as a child or else I wouldn't live much longer. My heart was calling the head-centered me inward to the full remembrance of my authentic infinite nature. I had a yearning to step out from the norms of society and defy the status quo to create my own unique path. I had a burning question that fueled my desire for change: "What have I come here to do with my life and who am I really?" These questions fueled my journey of self-awareness to become aware of what was happening within me.

I first began to change the patterns in my health. I began to exercise and eat healthy whole foods. I stopped partying and focused on feeling better in my body. My path took a turn toward the positive because I started hanging out with a group of personal health trainers. I joined their group and became a personal trainer. I stopped escaping into substances and began escaping into self-righteousness. I started attending church and became a spiritual seeker. I was searching for the "right" belief system in health and religion, which I thought would bring an inner sense of home or freedom. I became extremely involved in helping other people become healthy. I thought that being a personal trainer was how I was supposed to help people. I had many clients from all walks of life with whom I deeply bonded. However, I was still unconscious to being the social chameleon head-centered me. I wasn't helping people any more than before I was a personal trainer. I simply had a new platform. I was doing the same head-centered habit to help my clients momentarily feel better. I would tap into their energy, which made them feel safe, and they would open up to me about all of their worries, troubles, and stresses. I unconsciously absorbed their unresolved emotions and experienced them as if they were my own. During my own physical training I would work out my clients' unresolved emotions. At the time, I didn't know this is what I was doing. I had become a band aid that momentarily made my clients feel better. In truth, I could never truly help them through being the head-centered me. However, now I was becoming aware that serving others as a personal trainer wasn't the way. An intuitive sense said, "This isn't it. Keep going." Since I couldn't heal my clients, I decided to try to help others through religion. I worked as a youth minister in a Christian church and once again I failed at helping others heal. I felt like I was missing something. My intuition said, "This isn't it. Keep going."

The head-centered me couldn't truly help others because I wasn't being the unique and authentic ever-expanding expression that was the real me. I was scared to stand out like a sore thumb because during moments when I did, I was wrongly accused and judged. My intentions for being real and genuine were perceived through a lens of fear in my relationships. I felt like such a failure. So, I spent the next sixteen years searching for the truth in religion, spirituality, metaphysics, family traditions, cultural traditions, science, and quantum physics. I loved researching everything considered spiritual.

I became a sort of hermit and began writing to express my authentic voice. I was too scared to be real, genuine, unique, different, and truthful in my relationships, but paper seemed to absorb my authentic expression. I wanted to find that one relationship or group that would accept, love, and validate the real me. I refused to stand out in my uniqueness in the world until I found that relationship where I felt like I fit in. Finally, after many years of searching, I found the soul mate relationship I was looking for. My writing and journaling became a communication tool between my head and my heart, which was within me the whole time. My head was searching for the presence of truth and pure love that existed in my heart, and it finally found its place to rest there.

I became aware of the head-centered me, which wasn't the real me at all. Instead, it was a sense of self rooted in surviving my relationships. A sense of self that was not genuine because it feared what others thought about me. Every belief I tried on and discarded became another moment of failure, which led to my head's surrender to the Truth I sensed within my heart. I realized that my quests to find myself through my relationships to the world always led me to the same dead end. Not one single belief system in right and wrong resonated the peace, fulfillment, unconditional love, and joy I remembered as a child. I continued to wake up out of the head-centered me and into my inner knowing of innocence until I was 40 years old.

I feel like I have lived a thousand lifetimes in this one lifetime because I have felt and perceived reality through so many different perspectives, beliefs, and judgments. I have harmonized with so many different kinds of people, life situations, religions, cultures, and belief systems that I feel one with all of them. However, I don't feel that any one way is who I am. I never found the true authentic me from my relationships to the world. However, I did fully realize the infinite being I AM always was, and always will be. I realized God or Truth is infinite. Therefore, Truth expresses itself in an infinite number of ways. This awareness resonated so deeply with my experiences. Every time I grasped a particular way or belief system from my relationships as the Truth, I felt finite and limited. However, when I didn't try to fit into an identity or belief system, I felt open, free, infinite, and fulfilled.

As a child I was completely satisfied having no sense of self or point of reference. I loved harmonizing with all of life, not only one particular way of life. So I went back to being the heart-centered me. The deeper sense of me, which has no solid identity, belief system, or reference point. The deeper sense of me who flows with life and welcomes change. I feel a deep infinite love for every person I have ever met. I don't perceive their uniqueness as wrong or bad. Instead, I perceive them as the one identity that I finally discovered within my own heart. That one identity is what we all truly are at our core; infinite life. I realized I was never meant to conform, I was meant to shine as a bright, unique, authentically fresh, and ever-expanding expression of creativity or life!

This book is the result of allowing my inner experience of reality to have a voice. My inner experience is an intuitive, still, small voice that arises from deep within my heart. It feels like the part of me that is infinitely wise and loving. It has become my guide, light, and way. I share my experiences of the past sixteen years, which were filled with experiences of realigning, attuning, and harmonizing the finite head-centered me with the infinite heart-centered me. Through my experience of uniting the thinking part of me and the feeling part of me, a new habit formed called the heart-centered habit. The masculine go getter, figure-it-out-for-myself, driven, fixer upper, doer in me – and the feminine nurturer, gentle, patient, intuitive, wise, teacher in me – have merged into one infinite, creative, unique expression of Divine being through the heart-centered habit. The negative pessimist and the positive optimist have become one state of relaxation through the heart-centered habit. The heart-centered habit is a simple habit that my mind used to harmonize with my authentic, loving, and infinite nature. The heart centered-habit reminded my head that its true infinite source of love, acceptance, and approval, comes only from within. The heart-centered habit allowed all of me to return home to the innocence I remembered as a child. Now that still, small, infinitely wise voice that comes from deep within me is all there is in my experience. The search is over. I found the Truth; the real, authentic, genuine me. I found the place I fit in, and it was within me all along.

Sixteen years ago, when I began this journey, I thought God was out there somewhere. Now I can clearly see that all of the prayers I prayed and conversations I had with God were happening between my head and my heart...within me the whole time. My head was the lost sinner and my heart was the Savior. I was wandering the wilderness searching for the Promised Land and it was within me all along. I realized my heart is like a well of infinite wisdom that pours through me and quenches my thirst, satisfying my hunger for Truth, guidance, and wisdom. Writing this book has been the greatest gift I could ever receive because it is a product of allowing the well of wisdom to flow through me as me for the first time in this lifetime. Every time I sat down to write this book, I had to stop doing and just be, which is the greatest gift I could ever give myself. I will now share my journey of awakening with you. I hope it inspires you to return home to the innocence in your own heart. May this book be a guide that lights your path back to that still small voice within your own heart so you may realize the freedom to just be!

To get home, all you have to do is turn around and allow yourself to be.

INTRODUCTION

<u>Head-centered Consciousness</u>

Head-centered consciousness is an awareness of who we think we should be based upon external standards that do not resonate with our internal awareness within our heart. We learn from our external environment to not stand out in our uniqueness because at times when we did, we were rejected and judged as being different. Being different is not valued as being good because of the pain past generations have endured for being so. Therefore, standards are set in place to protect us from being ridiculed, rejected, and misjudged. These standards are made known by the way our family, education, society, friendships, religion, and community relates to us. The adults in our life wanted to protect us and did the best they knew how at the time. If they knew a better way to guide us, they most definitely would have done it. They were taught by the adults in their upbringing and guided us through the only way they knew. In an effort to protect us they felt the need to constantly tell us what to do, such as, "You need to do this." "You need to behave this way." "You need to perform like this." "Be more like so and so." "This is how you speak to others." "This is who you are." "You need to carry on this tradition." Words have power and all we hear when we are children is, "You aren't enough." "Your purpose in life is to make us proud." "You were born to please others." "Don't stand out too much because you make others uncomfortable." "You don't know yourself and we're here to tell you who you're supposed to be." "You're innately ignorant and we're here to teach you all of what you should and shouldn't do to ensure your safety." We learn early on what the boundaries are to the way we should choose to express the life we are.

A word often used to describe head-centered consciousness is ego. Ego stands for Energy Going Out. From the moment we are born we can feel our relationships to the physical world pulling at our energy or awareness. The external world is pulling on our energy and desiring to form and mold us into the likeness of a way of being, which is an interpretation of reality. People's interpretations of reality are rooted in beliefs of what is right and what is wrong. Families, friends, teachers, society, and all other relationships are pulling on our energy to conform to their beliefs in right and wrong, so that they won't feel alone and isolated. Aloneness and isolation is death to an ego. The ego is a false interpretation of reality that we define and squeeze our infinite nature into as a way to feel important and special. However, an ego can only gain a sense of separate self at the expense of manufacturing negative stories of wrong about reality. These stories of wrong create an inner sense that something is missing or wrong within us, which feels like a force that opposes God, love, and goodness.

Conforming to the standards of right and wrong in our relationships becomes the safest way to be in a world that fears uniqueness. In an effort to escape the pain of rejection and being wrongly accused, we become totally distracted by what we experience in our physical relationships and we begin to forget what we feel within our heart. Our rational mind focuses on the information it gathers from its experiences to the physical world to figure out the right way to be. Our head becomes an information center that receives its information from the outside-in. If we attach awareness to this information, then it becomes a solid belief system that is held prisoner in our subconscious mind. Belief systems make up the meanings, labels, names, definitions, interpretations, stories, and judgments of every culture, religion, tradition, group, and family. These belief systems can be very old and stem from our ancestors.

Ancestral beliefs get passed down from generation to generation as a way of creating a form of identification. Identification creates a false sense of safety and security. "If I know and understand you that means you are safe." The greatest threat to belief systems that are passed down generation to generation is change. When one individual in the family lives in a unique way, the family identity feels threatened.

When we are authentic, we become a unique expression of life that has never been known before. A person who perceives through head-centered consciousness cannot understand unique and different expressions. All expressions unknown to a head-centered being are perceived through a lens of fear. Therefore, head-centered individuals misperceive unique expressions of life, love, and divinity as wrong, bad, or evil.

When we are attached to a particular group of individuals, our bond is a belief system from the past. Group consciousness is an awareness shared by a group of like-minded people, which provides a connection to the past in our heads and not from deep within our heart, which is our direct connection to Divine wisdom or present moment awareness. When we misperceive reality through head-centered consciousness, we perceive our uniqueness as wrong. Therefore, head-centered consciousness is rooted in a belief that "something is wrong with me." This belief is an unconscious secret we hide from our relationships. We do this by unconsciously staying busy to fit into the inner circle of a group by maintaining their standards of belief.

Head-centered consciousness projects God, truth, dreams, purpose, passion, love, wisdom, happiness, and source of life to something outside of us because we feel a void inside. We feel disconnected to the very source of God within us because we focus more on pleasing others than listening to our intuitive feelings of Divine wisdom. Therefore, this void is an internal sense of suffering due to a dissonance between how we appear in the world and what we uniquely feel we really are from within our heart. This creates an inner sense of separation and division between the thinking aspect and the feeling aspect of our being. The thinking aspect becomes over-stimulated in the left side of our rational brain because the intuitive, spiritual, creative, and emotional right side of our brain is ignored. Our head is so distracted by trying to fit in and pleasing others that our intuitive feelings within are disregarded. Intuition is creative energy, which arises from the infinite field of existence within our being. When the head does not acknowledge the information within, the energy is repressed causing dense emotions. This causes an imbalance of energy between our relationships to the external physical world and our relationship to the inner spiritual world. This disharmony is sensed through negative emotions that build up, and when we are triggered by the unwanted change, they explode through us. When this happens, we feel vulnerable because the secret of our negative inner experience has been exposed. Instead of embracing these negative emotions, we blame either ourselves or the event or person that triggered our explosion. Stories of blame repress these negative emotions back down inside us, only to explode and become exposed over and over again through unwanted, inconvenient, painful, and uncomfortable experiences of change.

Our brain continues to misperceive reality, by projecting the inner division we feel between our head and heart onto our external environment. We believe something outside of us is causing our inner discomfort. This psychological threat creates an over-stimulated nervous system that is always on guard to protect itself from a projected enemy. An over-stimulated nervous system is the result of an over-stimulation of the "fight" or "flight" mechanism of survival wired in our brains from long ago. This leads to inflammation in the mind (fearful and anxious thoughts), emotions (negative emotions), and body (physical dis-ease). Our mind is always on hyper alert with a constant dialogue of misinterpretation about unknown experiences. We feel there is always something or someone to fight and something or someone to escape. As long as we are running from someone or something outside of us, we will veer toward addictive habits. Then we blame ourselves for our addictive habits, which we feel we have no control to change. Therefore, head-centered consciousness creates an overall experience of suffering, stress, pain, division, separation, and limitation.

Head-centered consciousness sets up a false sense of self that rests upon an unstable foundation of stagnant beliefs in the head. We feel conflict and war with those who have different foundations of belief. Our beliefs are meant to change and evolve like the rest of the natural world. But when we are head-centered, we believe change brings death to our identity or solid sense of self, so we won't let go of our reasons of "wrong." Head-centered consciousness believes, "These are my beliefs and they define me." "I am my beliefs." "I am my thoughts." This creates a fear of change. Head-centered consciousness hates change because change is death to the identification of "my beliefs." When we identify with "my beliefs," our head creates false stories of possession, victimhood, destitution, and self-righteousness. These false stories in the head create higher and lower pitfalls along our path, which creates an inner sense of restlessness keeping our awareness focused on the appearances of reality, instead of our feelings from within. This superficial focus keeps the head on an endless journey of struggling to maintain an appearance that conforms to our environments standards of right and good.

Head-centered consciousness functions through comparison, expectation, manipulation, judgment, and control to maintain an appearance of "goodness" in relation to the standards set forth by our external environment. These are the head's unconscious habits, which limits the mind from expanding into new self-realizations. The mind remains narrow and focused on particular groups to fit into, which excludes the majority of humanity. The truth is, our head is stuck in the past, and our heart dwells in the present. Some of us are still carrying old stagnant beliefs from our ancestors and past experiences that are no longer valid in the present. We have experienced major technological advances in the past fifty years. But when we are head-centered, our beliefs in who we are, God, and reality can stay the same for an entire lifetime. If technology can rapidly advance in one lifetime, then our beliefs about reality can too.

Even now, in the year 2016, the majority of humanity perceives reality through head-centered consciousness. Stress, lack, limitation, pain, and suffering are all symptoms of this division between the information stored in our head and the new information coming through our heart. The head is running like crazy from this new information arising from within. At the same time, it projects a movie of characters in its external reality, to blame for its inner sense of division. Therefore, the head-centered "me" is an illusion. It isn't real; instead it is an image formed by unconscious stagnant beliefs, which are programmed in our subconscious mind. This doesn't mean we have done anything wrong. We have been ignorant and nobody is to blame. Our ancestors, family, society, culture, and religion are not to blame for our ignorance. We didn't know any better. We just followed in the footsteps of people we admired and loved. Our family and ancestors didn't know any better either.

When we function from stagnant beliefs from the past, we are unable to be good stewards of the planet, nor can we feel equanimity, oneness, and peace with humanity as a whole. The greatest stagnant belief is that we can only be right by making others wrong, which creates an opposing force to the sense of goodness we feel within our heart. When this stagnant belief is the foundation to the way we perceive reality, we will always believe we have an enemy. There will always be a hero and a villain. There will always be a Heaven and a Hell. There will always be God and Devil. We are the only ones who can resolve this stagnant belief within our own perception of reality. When a person chooses to perceive through heart-centered consciousness, awakening from this stagnant belief occurs and a new reality is observed, of freedom, fulfillment, and peace.

Right now the human species is experiencing more diversity than ever before in history. We are living in different timelines of belief systems. Some of us have opened our minds to experiencing ourselves in new ways. We are all at different stages of the evolution of beliefs. Therefore, we are living in different realities of belief. If we could release these stagnant beliefs and align with the present moment awareness of Divine wisdom that arises from within our hearts, we could exist in the same reality of love, peace, harmony, and abundance. This doesn't mean we will all appear, speak, and create in the same way. Instead, we will all sense a reality of freedom from within that inspires each of us to express the divinity that we are through infinite creative ways of diversity. Even though our ways appear different, they all resonate love, peace, and harmony. There would be no hierarchy and no higher or lower. Present moment awareness is a valuable resource available to every single human right now because we all have a direct connection to it through our own heart.

If we truly desire to be free and live in peace then we will have to awaken from the nightmare of wrong, evil, and bad that we project onto our self, others, and reality. Awakening from our own projections of wrong requires us to shift our perception of reality. We have to perceive the wrong through heart-centered consciousness, which perceives through a single lens of oneness, love, life, and divinity. Through the single lens of the heart, all experiences, including those which the mind judges as wrong, are perceived as the same pure light of divinity. Perceiving all of reality as the life we are, is the only way to awaken out of our manufactured nightmares of problems, issues, conflicts, wars, separation, divisions, and limitations. When we fully forget all of our perceptions of wrong through perceiving them as the one power of pure goodness; suffering, lack, and dis-ease will vanish from our experience of reality.

The good news is that now we are waking up and awareness is the first step that can guide us out of ignorance and into freedom. Are you ready to align your head with the information of this present moment, which is arising from within your heart? If so, your Divine nature will save, heal, and restore you by unraveling and releasing all stagnant beliefs that keep you stuck in the past. The heart will meet your head halfway, but your head has to be willing to step into the void within. This requires faith and an openness to feel without identification. This means your head has to learn a new way of being. The new way is a habit of surrender. What the head was never meant to fix and change, the heart of present moment awareness will do in an instant!

Heart-centered Consciousness

Heart-centered consciousness is an ever-expanding perception of reality that relies upon grace. Grace is a free gift we receive when our head is tapped into the intuition of the heart. It is an endless journey into infinite realms of realization. Many beings throughout history and living today have awakened out of head-centered consciousness. All religions and spiritual philosophies were created to worship these heart-centered beings. However, instead of worshipping heart-centered beings, how about becoming one of them?

Heart-centered consciousness is an inside-out perception, which is generated by the head or thinking mind acknowledging, honoring, and following the intuitive information that comes from the still small voice, which is more like an intuitive feeling from within the heart. The head or mind abides with the information that arises from within the unknown heart space, without being distracted by the information from its external environment. This requires faith because the information coming from within the heart is brand new and has not been made known. We become the first place this intuitive information is made known because we become the first to celebrate our uniqueness. The new fresh perspective is born as our thoughts form around the intuitive feelings that arise from within the heart. Then our words, expression, and creativity form around these intuitive ideas. And our choices, actions, relationships, roles, and reality form around our creative expression of the unborn truth that is being celebrated and made known through us as us.

When the mind abides in the flow of the intuition flowing through the heart, it remains in a state of surrender and no longer possesses or takes credit and ownership for anything expressed through itself. Therefore, the mind does not identify, grasp, or hold onto any insight, thought, idea, or expression. In this way the mind is able to remain an open and clear channel for infinite information to flow through continuously. If the mind closes in on any part of the process of intuitive information going from the formless to a form of expression, it closes and inhibits the flow of infinite insight. When the mind closes in this way, we immediately experience this as pain, suffering, and limitation.

The union between the heart and head generates a reality based upon Divine will. Heart-centered consciousness is a direct connection to our infinite essence, which is the very nature of God or divinity. Our infinite essence is an unlimited energy field of information. The symptom of perceiving reality through heart-centered consciousness is an expansion of feelings or experiences, such as pure love, peace, stillness, serenity, fulfillment, abundance, joy, gratitude, goodness, and infinite beauty. Heart-centered consciousness creates an inner sense of lightness and freedom. Instead of trying to connect to God through some outside source or belief system, which is a limited field of information, we can connect to our Divine heart, which is always present, new, fresh, and relevant. Present moment awareness is wisdom that spontaneously arises from within us through intuition. This inner wisdom allows us to merge and align with the natural flow of life, which is always changing, evolving, and expanding.

Imagine taking a journey into your body. Enter into a cell. Go deeper into the atoms of that cell. At the core of the atom is a field of formless infinite energy, which is connected to the core of every other atom throughout the entire universe. This is the control center of all of existence. Divine will arises from this space within your being. Orders or Divine information is sent out into every form from this infinite center to bring about harmony and balance to the whole of existence.

This infinite center is the heart. It isn't our physical heart, but our spiritual center of information. Our atoms and cells pick up the information from this spiritual center like an antennae. We feel it as an intuitive feeling or insight, which forms into thoughts, words, actions, and reality. This is how we can live from the inside-out, which is called heart- centered consciousness.

Heart-centered consciousness is a perception that wants, chooses, and perceives Divine light, love, and life throughout all experiences of change. Heart-centered consciousness embraces the unfamiliar, uncomfortable, and unwanted circumstances of reality. Heart-centered consciousness is a constant reminder to our being, reality, and the world that it is all enough as it is. Heart-centered consciousness is the loving voice we offer all experiences of reality. It is our authentic voice of affirmation, always affirming that everything is enough, abundant, free, pure love, goodness, pure life, healthy, wealthy, Divine, inspiring, fulfillment, peace, infinite, magical, innocent, healed, and light! How does it perceive reality in this way? Because it doesn't perceive reality through a past experience of right and wrong. Therefore, it is not a perception that perceives wrong at all. What the head-centered me perceives as wrong, the heart-centered me perceives as a gift. This is because when we feel limitation, stress, or pain our experience is revealing to us that we are stuck in a limited perception. The gift offered is self-awareness and an opportunity to expand our perception of reality.

Our mind is like a camera lens. The lens on a camera can expand the view out or close it into a narrow view. The mind has the same ability and our awareness guides it to expand or narrow. When we feel limited, we know the mind is becoming narrow because it is focusing in on a thought, feeling, or experience of reality. Truth can only be perceived throughout all experiences of reality when our mind remains expanded and no longer narrows its view by perceiving through any particular thought or experience of reality. When we fully remember our infinite nature is not defined by any experience of mind and body, our awareness expands to limitless boundaries of mind. When the mind narrows in it is attaching itself to a limited point of view through a particular experience and we feel limited. Honesty is the first step to becoming self-aware. Therefore, being honest and acknowledging when we feel limited is the first step to expanding our awareness. When we feel abundant and joyous, we know our mind is expanding. When the mind expands out into the new intuitive information that is arising from an unknown space within us, we feel infinite. How we feel in our inner experience of reality provides our awareness feedback, so we can continually readjust our mind to tuning in with the infinite flow of information from within our heart. Therefore, we haven't done anything wrong if we feel limited, and nobody has wronged us. Feelings are spirit guides. Therefore, we can adopt a new relationship with our inner experience of feelings. We can welcome, honor, and respect the feedback they provide us. All experiences provide us feedback to our state of mind. Our mind is either closed or open, and the feelings in our bodies provide us that feedback. This requires us to be completely honest with how we truly feel. Most of us were taught that if you don't feel good then something is wrong with you and you need to get it fixed. Therefore, we learned to hide our true feelings. If we desire to expand our perception we must be honest about our inner experience of reality.

Our perception dictates our experience. Therefore, it is very simple. If we feel limited then we are perceiving through a limited lens. Through the heart-centered habit, we have the power to open our mind back up, so it may realign with the expanded perception of the heart. Therefore, we don't have to blame ourselves for doing something "wrong" or find reasons "why" we are being wronged or create false stories as to "why" this isn't fair. We also don't have to struggle to find an answer, fix a problem or resolve an issue. In truth we do not have any problems or issues to begin with. We simply have an unconscious habit of closing or narrowing our mind. Therefore, we can create a new habit of keeping the mind open by abiding in heart-centered consciousness.

Being a unique expression of pure Love does not fit into the limited paradigms of right and wrong because heart-centered consciousness does not perceive reality through the lens of judgment, division, and separation. Therefore, heart-centered beings never become inflamed in response to any experience because all experiences are perceived as divinity. We are all the same in that we are infinite spiritual beings but we are individual expressions of that one essence: special, unique, and authentic. We are all one infinite essence of Love appearing as brand new expressions, varieties, and diversities. Our unique expression (soul signature) of our one Divine and pure loving nature is unfamiliar because it does not have a high or low, good or bad, right or wrong reference point from which our perspective is derived. This is because when we are perceiving through heart-centered consciousness we are not perceiving from a point of reference at all. Instead, we are perceiving directly from the pure formless pointless love that we are.

When Divine will, which we sense as an intuitive feeling from within our heart, guides our thoughts, actions, perceptions, careers, roles, and relationships, we don't have to even think about how to be loving, fulfilled, and peaceful beings. We will just be peace, love, and fulfillment spontaneously and naturally without needing to think about it. Imagine no longer needing to worry whether you are being the right way or making the right choice or doing the right thing. Imagine being the unique expression of pure love that you are without worry, doubt, anxiety, or fear. This is the reality that exists within your heart.

When we align our voice with heart-centered consciousness we become a loving master, parent, and teacher toward every experience we encounter, no matter how it appears or feels. Humanity is heading inward toward sensing into the heart of our true nature as a whole. We are on the verge of implementing a new way of being, a new habit of being me, centered within the heart. There are many names for this spiritual core because it is formless and name-less. When the left and right brain are joined in holy matrimony, they work together to create new names, expressions, and ways to point to the formless Truth that we are. Some other names which have been used to refer to our nameless spiritual essence are God, Divine Source, Truth, Spirit, Holy Spirit, Soul, or Buddha nature. In Truth, everything in nature, every expression, and every appearance is pointing to our one spiritual essence of love. We perceive this Truth through heart-centered consciousness. Therefore, the heart-centered me has no solid sense of self and enjoys new experiences without being defined by any experience.

The heart-centered me is spontaneously known in the present moment without attaching to any part of the moment, so that it may experience itself fully and infinitely. The heart-centered me is not one way or one particular experience. Instead, our heart-centered nature loves the spontaneity of the unknown and enjoys the adventure and exploration of every experience, regardless of how it appears or feels. The heart-centered me is the spacious presence of pure indiscriminate love and the peace that surpasses our rational understanding of it.

The Two Become One

Holy Matrimony

When we notice we are feeling an uncomfortable emotion due to unwanted change or inconvenience we can adopt a new habit that will transform the story of separation in our head. The head can choose to love, unite, and harmonize with the heart through the heart-centered habit. The heart-centered habit guides the head to surrender all of its information to the heart. The heart receives it fully, as it is, and transmutes all experiences into the expanded energy of pure love, thereby allowing a holy marriage to occur between our head and heart. This creates a way for all uncomfortable emotions, stories of separation, and repressed memories to return to their true nature of pure spacious love. Saying an internal 'yes' to all experiences allows the head-centered me to align with the heart-centered me. Instead of being the limited character of the story in our head, which feels bound by the judgment of right and wrong, the character is released from the prison of isolation and set free to flow in a new way, which merges with the essence of life, no longer feeling limited or separate by the appearances and circumstances at the surface. Instead, free to be in the universal flow of pure consciousness or pure indiscriminate love. Not the love that the head is used to, which depends on similar belief systems; a love that perceives everything and everyone as a beautiful expression of divinity, God, and life! The head no longer has to struggle to create, manifest, and fix reality on its own. It can surrender, trust, and have faith in the power of the infinite Divine heart to flow through it as it.

By shifting the way we perceive and relate to all experiences from a head- centered to a heart-centered way, we become the voice of the one loving pure light of divinity. We become the voice that reprograms our own subconscious mind to perceive the Light of Truth throughout every encounter and experience. This reprogramming rewires our brains to be an instrument of the light of God. This reprogramming allows the right and left hemispheres of the brain to function in equilibrium, partnership, and unity. Then we become a living embodiment of Truth. The exciting part is, we become a unique, fresh, and authentic expression of the embodiment of the one eternal Truth of God.

As your head and heart become one opening of pure love, you will experience yourself as a new being. You will become the fulfillment of your heart's desire. As the head and heart merge into one expression, you will discover your authentic unique expression of pure love! The heart is one essence of pure love that connects every heart throughout existence. When the head turns around to embrace the heart, it perceives this one essence of pure love in a unique way. Nobody else in existence will ever be able to express the pure love that we all are as you do! Therefore, we will all live by our own unique expression that is supported by the one formless essence of love that we all are! As we individually become unified, harmonized, and balanced within our own being, our Divine expression adds a depth and dimension to sensing into the formless or spiritual realm of Heaven. Therefore, the more we individually step into our unique Divine expression, the more we sense Heaven on Earth as a whole. Your unique expression as the embodiment of our one Divine nature is one puzzle piece in the awe-inspiring picture of Heaven that all of humanity is piecing together here on Earth. Pretty miraculous, right?

Holy Trinity

Even though I no longer identify myself with any one particular religion, I perceive religion as symbols and stories that can be used to remind us of our Divine nature. The Holy Trinity is a symbol used in Christianity. It represents the Christian Godhead as one God in three persons; Father, Son, and Holy Spirit. The Holy Trinity is a symbol of unity. When my head (thinking self) and heart (feeling self) merged into an eternal marriage through the heart-centered habit, my entire being was flooded with infinite wisdom, energy, and love. In my experience this is the Holy Trinity, the embodiment of God or divinity through three aspects; Head, Heart, and Spirit of eternal Love.

The head's (thinking self) Divine role is to honor, respect, trust, and be faithful with its true soul-mate, the feeling self or heart. This allows the heart to open and share its connection with Divine source or wisdom. In turn, the heart shares this Divine information with the head, which expands the mind. When these two aspects of our being bond in a loving relationship, they become one; both aspects of our being become intertwined into an open channel of infinite insight. This oneness allows Divine information to flow through freely from the inside out. When the head and heart are bonded by infinite love, this unity creates an attunement, alignment, and harmonization with our true spiritual nature of indiscriminate love.

These three aspects make up the Holy Trinity of God. The Father represents the head (thinking self), the Son represents the heart of innocence (feeling self), and the Holy Spirit represents the spirit of pure love that unites the two. When the head honors, respects, values, embraces, trusts, and loves the heart, the essence of pure Love awakens and becomes the head's teacher, guide, and source of life and wisdom. The son represents the innocent heart, which is open to feeling anything and everything. The Father in the Holy Trinity represents the thinking self that has the faith to express the infinite love that it feels from the innocent heart.

The Trinity is like an energetic circuit of Divine energy that flows through our entire being. Imagine a triangle. The point at the top of the triangle is pure love. The other two points of the triangle at the bottom are head and heart. When pure love is the guide between the head and the heart, then the true nature of God or divinity is activated in your being, and you become the embodiment of God, divinity or pure love. However, when the head is distracted by trying to fit into a left-brained thinking dominated world, it ignores its better half, breaking the relational bond with the heart and unable to activate the trinity within its whole being. This cuts off our experience from the source of eternal life. The heart-centered habit reminds the head of its Divine role within the relationship with the heart.

When pure love is given and received within ourselves between our head and our heart, our sense of need vanishes. We will no longer crave, thirst, and hunger for love, validation, or nourishment from our physical relationships to the external world. Instead we will be healed, fulfilled, abundant, and enlightened from the inside-out. We will feel the deity of God. Deity means to lack nothing. Lack, separation, limitation, struggle, stress, suffering, and division will no longer be our inner experience of reality when the trinity of God comes together in perfect union within your own being. When your inner life has been resolved because the head and heart have merged into oneness, you will perceive resolution in your outer world. Your inner atmosphere determines the way you perceive your outer atmosphere. When the head and heart fully merge into one union, abundant energy fills our entire being and fulfillment is experienced. A surge of new energy enters into our experience, like nothing we have ever experienced before in life. This is the coming of the Kingdom of Heaven. Your mind and body become the territory of God. The head sits on the king's throne and the heart sits on the queen's throne. They rule with equanimity and pure love. The heart receives Divine wisdom that she shares with the king, and the king carries out the law of pure love throughout the kingdom of your being. The body becomes the first physical place that experiences this beautiful, harmonious, loving union. One does not dominate over the other because love is their guide. True fulfillment, abundance, and peace can only occur through this union within you. May your head and heart join in holy matrimony and take their rightful place in the Holy Trinity.

How To Get the Most Out of this Book:

22-Day Journey

This book guides you on a 22-day journey of embracing, honoring, respecting, and loving all aspects of yourself, possibly like you never have before. You most likely spend so much time helping, honoring, and cherishing the lives of others. Now it is time to love and cherish yourself so much that your entire being becomes infused with Divine Light and love that you truly are from the inside-out. This Light will shine through you so brightly it will inspire others to return to the Light within *their* heart. The Divine Light in me calls forth the Divine Light in you, and the Divine Light in you calls forth the Divine Light in your relationships. Right now, the Divine Light is spreading like wildfire in the hearts of many!

"To conquer oneself is a greater task than conquering others. You cannot travel the path until you have become the path itself. The only real failure in life is not to be true to the best one knows. No one saves us but ourselves. No one can and no one may. We ourselves must walk the path."
-Buddhism

Without practicing, the truth we know does us no good. Therefore, the heart-centered habit is a practice of being the Truth. The heart-centered habit is a habit for our head, which functions to welcome, support, serve, and validate every experience in existence by remaining detached from the momentary experience itself. Being honest about what we feel within, acknowledging that the head does not know how to create the life the heart desires, breathing in every experience, loving every experience that arises, and thanking every experience in existence is the head's ONLY role, habit, job, and way of being. This is how the head surrenders to the Divine will within the heart, which is the creative power of the Universe that creates through our being and as our being in the present moment.

The heart-centered habit functions from the pure loving presence of heart-centered consciousness that says an "inner YES" to all experiences. The heart-centered habit is the habit of remaining centered, balanced, and harmonized with life. It is not dependent on the ebbs and flows of our external reality. Our inner experience is not controlled by the way our outer experience appears or feels. Instead, our inner attitude, quality of experience, and sense of reality is dependent upon Divine heart-centered consciousness, which is an infinite perception of pure love, and allows all experiences of reality the freedom to be as they are by receiving them as a Divine gift! Divine heart-centered consciousness needs and opposes nothing!

The heart-centered habit guides the head to perceiving uncomfortable experiences as opportunities or doorways to reunite with the heart; the information center of Divine wisdom. These uncomfortable experiences have been programmed as wrong, bad, and evil within your subconscious mind. Instead of fighting or trying to escape these uncomfortable experiences, the head will be guided to embrace them and allow them to speak openly in the privacy of your own being, training your head to surrender to what is arising within you and learning to be still as these uncomfortable experiences flow through you. Eventually, the sting of all beliefs in wrong that you held to be true will set awareness free to flow with Divine intuition. The head and heart will reunite as one ever-expanding unique expression of pure love and abundant life.

Research shows it takes twenty-one or so days to train our subconscious mind to program a new habit. Therefore, over the next twenty-two days, you will be guided to opening your mind and heart. Read one chapter per day for 22 days. Your mind will want to either not read it all or read the whole book at once. Allow yourself to slow down and only read one chapter per day. Let the words, information, and energy sink into your awareness. This will allow your awareness to guide your mind. Instead of your mind guiding your awareness. Each day you will be guided in the following ways:

Shared Experiences

My intention for sharing my personal experiences is to provide you a sense that nothing is wrong with you. You may have felt the same feelings as I have my entire life. Knowing that there are other people in the world who validate your experiences in a world that judges them as weird, peculiar, crazy, or wrong can provide a confidence to validate your experiences for yourself. The truth is, I am not normal and neither are you! Being peculiar, unique, and authentic is the new normal! My passion is to stand in the brightness of the Divine Light that shines through my heart and to celebrate the ever-expanding way it comes through me. My passion is to inspire you to do the same. We have a choice; we can either be a part of the dis-ease or be a part of the cure in the world. I choose to be a part of the cure. How about you?

Mirror Work

At the start of each day, your head will be guided to opening up to your inner experiences. Love opens the door in toward your heart. Therefore, you will be guided to speak to your heart in the mirror. I know that may sound crazy to you, but transformation requires you to step outside your comfort zone. Your head has been in charge and it will not want to say what you are guided to say in the mirror each day. Do it anyway! Read one sentence at a time, then repeat the sentence as you look at yourself in the mirror. Your subconscious mind will not be used to your head talking to itself this way. So in the beginning you may feel nothing. However, as each day passes, you will become more sensitive to your feelings, which are the doorway into your heart.

Different Perspectives

After you have initiated the opening of your heart by speaking loving and encouraging words to yourself, you will be guided to read different perspectives that point to the Truth of our one Divine essence, helping to open your head (thinking self) or limited mind. At first, you may become aware of your stagnant beliefs because you will find yourself judging and resisting the different perspectives. This is good because you can become aware of limitations, boundaries, and judgments that have been lying hidden below your conscious awareness for years. Opening your mind allows awareness to begin to question old stagnant beliefs from the past. Questioning beliefs is like bringing "a breath of fresh air" into your head or limited mind. As we question our old beliefs, we can begin to see that their meanings and interpretations are no longer valid in the present moment. Allowing our beliefs to change and evolve is an aspect of self-love.

Also, reading different perspectives that are generated from sensing into the infinite reality in the heart opens your mind to wonder, "How would I describe the same infinite reality through my own direct experience of it within me?" Instead of following somebody else's expression, your head can sink into a direct experience by merging with the heart and becoming a tool to create a new fresh perspective of our one true infinite nature. As you tune in with what you feel within your heart; feelings, thoughts, and words will form through you as you. This infinite power will ignite, nourish, and satisfy every aspect of your being. It feels like home!

What is the Heart-centered Habit?

Heart-centered Habit

Each day you will be guided to practice aligning your head with your true infinite nature that perceives only God, divinity, goodness, life, and pure love through all experiences of mind and body that were once perceived as wrong, evil, and bad. Our subconscious mind has been programmed or conditioned to respond to uncomfortable, unfamiliar, unique, different, unwanted, painful, and inconvenient experiences through either fighting or escaping the experience. This is a paradigm that is programmed within our mind from the time we are born, and it is what creates an inner atmosphere within us of separation, division, limitation, stress, inflammation, pain, and suffering. This creates an inner sense that something is wrong, which creates a sense of void. The heart-centered habit reprograms the subconscious mind to no longer fight or escape any experience of reality. Instead, the heart-centered habit guides the head that is not aligned with the infinite nature of our being to receive all experiences it has labeled as wrong, bad, or evil. These parts of ourselves, or the reality that our head has defined as wrong, bad, or evil are experiences that arose within us in the past that were judged as something other than the Divine perfection they truly are. Therefore, we can establish a new habit of total allowance and self-acceptance by yielding to the power of our authentic heart-centered nature, which will receive these wrong beliefs on our head's behalf.

Repetitive patterns of negative feelings and experiences are indicators that we are identified with stagnant beliefs in wrong, which do not resonate with the Truth in our heart. Therefore, in an effort to harmonize with the Truth in our heart, we have to be courageous enough to feel all uncomfortable experiences triggered by life. These negative emotions are not created from the outside-in. Instead, they have been a part of our experience for a long time. They are the inner experiences that are the result of fighting or escaping reality from the past. We fought or tried to escape these past experiences because they did not resonate the infinite love we feel within our heart. These uncomfortable, painful, unwanted, and inconvenient experiences are here to provide you opportunities to step into your authentic infinite power of pure love. A love that welcomes, honors, respects, and embraces every experience just as it is. A love that has no preferences, needs, or demands toward any part of existence. A love that affirms that these negative feelings and experiences are included in the one perception of infinite love.

When repetitive patterns of negative emotions become triggered by external factors; let love be your strength. Love yourself more and more each day as you welcome, embrace, and validate the presence of these negative patterns. The heart-centered habit offers the guidance and support to learn a new way to relate to these unwanted patterns in your life. If you truly desire to be free, you have to be completely honest about the existence of your inner experience of darkness, void, limitation, suffering, depression, pain, and negative emotions when they are triggered through external circumstances. Honesty can feel vulnerable because we have been conditioned to deny the way we feel or complain about the way we feel and seek escape. We either become the voice of self-righteousness or the voice of a victim. When we feel deeper into the uncomfortable emotions we have been taught to deny or escape, such as fear, anxiety, hatred, anger, rage, shame, guilt, frustration, confusion, jealousy, and envy, we are digging deeper to expose the stagnant beliefs that limit our perception that holds them in place. Then, by faith we can acknowledge and ask that the pure love we are will teach us to receive these negative feelings. When we receive more of our experiences, our perception expands and we awaken the mind to realize its true infinite nature. This happens between your head and your heart. This is what Jesus meant when he said, "Confess your sins to God." God is within you. Therefore, you do not need to go around sharing your darkness with others. Instead, be the first one in line who listens, honors, welcomes, and receives them for yourself.

Remember, sin is a misperception of reality. Sin does not mean you have done anything wrong. Sin is a word that points to describing your limited view of self, God, and reality. Sin is the misperception that your head is in control of your destiny, and that your head needs to know how to create your destiny. When you practice the heart-centered habit, your mind will awaken to the Truth by acknowledging that it is not in control. The mind will awaken to the Truth by allowing every experience to be exactly as it is, without needing to change, fight, or deny it. The mind will awaken to the

Truth by asking the heart to resolve, harmonize, heal, and unify all experiences of inner division.

The heart-centered habit guides the head to remembering, "I am more than my feelings, thoughts, beliefs, perceptions, body, roles, and relationships. I am an infinite being that is not defined by any experience. Therefore, I receive all experiences just as they are." The head hands every experience over to the heart, relinquishing its control over what we should do, how we should think, and how we should feel. Then the heart of our authentic nature guides our thoughts, feelings, and actions. When the head awakens to its true role of being the heart-centered habit it discovers the freedom to enjoy the infinite diverse experiences of life.

When our perception expands, our subconscious mind will feel empty because we have become more aware of the space between thoughts than the thoughts themselves. This will feel different, almost like a spaciousness. Our subconscious mind has been conditioned to store past beliefs rooted in "wrong" or "no," so when it is empty of meanings, interpretations, and judgments of what is wrong, it can feel awkward. Just like when you begin to eat less food every day and your stomach is used to maintaining a certain level of fullness, it will take time to get used to the empty feeling in your stomach. Eventually, you will get used to the empty feeling and then it won't feel like emptiness anymore. The same is true for your subconscious mind. When your perception expands, the beliefs you viewed as reality are no longer in view. It will take about 22 days for your subconscious mind to adapt to abiding in an open expanded state, which is a never-ending journey.

Throughout the next 22 days, you may experience your subconscious mind falling back into old ways of identifying with thoughts, feelings, or beliefs in wrong. As soon as you feel limited, use the heart-centered habit to guide awareness into the infinite perception of your heart. Continue to persevere in training your subconscious mind to becoming heart-centered (infinitely expanding) instead of head-centered (finitely closing).

Eventually, your subconscious mind will do the heart-centered habit for you, and as soon as your perception feels limited, it will autocorrect spontaneously. When the heart-centered habit becomes automatic, divinity will guide your perceptions of reality. Instead of being stuck in negative patterns of beliefs in wrong, infinite realizations of pure goodness will be the river of life that will take your mind to perceiving the infinite realms of Heaven here on Earth.

The breath is a tool we can use to infuse love into any experience. Breathing love into your own experience of heart and mind fills the space with the infinite essence that flows through your heart. Saying thank you to these signs and symptoms of discomfort, allows the mind to remember that every experience is here to expand your perception of reality. Every experience is a symbol of Divine Light pointing you home toward your infinite heart. Everything is here to help, benefit, and guide you into an infinite expression of divinity. The heart-centered habit is a new way for your head to work with the intuition of the heart and it occurs within you, igniting the abundant energy of your soul and living as an embodiment of God; the infinite one in all.

The heart-centered habit is a communication tool that can be used between your head and your heart. The head communicates all of its stories in wrong and shares its fears with the heart. The heart receives these limited and stagnant beliefs just as they are and shares Divine wisdom and pure love with the head. As our head and heart continue to communicate with one another, they begin to merge into one infinite expression of wisdom. When perception, awareness, and consciousness expands, our attitude, mood, emotions, and inner atmosphere expands too. This feels like an explosion of abundant energy, pure love, security, fulfillment, infinite wellbeing, safety, peace, joy, and relaxation, creating an inner sense of home, unity, and oneness with all of existence.

How to Use the Heart-centered Habit?
H-honesty
A-acknowledge, allow, and ask
B-breathe
I-I love you!
T-thank you

H- Honesty

The first step to shift our perception from the outside-in to the inside-out is to confess the limited experience we are feeling in the moment. We don't have to hide or deny our feelings from ourselves. Nor do we have to complain to others about the limited feelings we experience. We can just be honest with our self. Honesty is the first step to opening up communication between our head and our heart. Honesty is also the first step toward self-awareness, which is necessary to awaken from the illusion of wrong.

"I fully feel _____."

A-Acknowledge, allow, ask

We can acknowledge the limitations and wrong that we feel without needing to figure out where to place the blame. Blame strengthens the experience of wrong and uses unnecessary mental energy to figure out how to fix the wrong. Stories of blame only create mental distractions, which keeps awareness from sinking in toward the direct path of authentic self-realization. What the mind truly desires is freedom and relaxation. There is only one direction it can go to realize its infinite nature of freedom; within. To go deeper within, the mind has to stop going out into further avenues of thinking how it is right or how it has been wronged, so it can tune in with the infinite heart of intuition.

"I acknowledge that it is safe and okay to feel this way. I embrace this feeling fully as it is because I know it is showing me the way into my heart. As I embrace this feeling fully, I ask it to consume all of the past meanings, interpretations, beliefs, and judgments I thought were true, but are not valid in this present moment. Therefore, I acknowledge this limited feeling as a gift, guide, and opening toward the infinite perception in my heart. I acknowledge its Divine role in helping me expand awareness into the depths of infinite knowing."

Allow the uncomfortable experience to have a voice. Do not believe what it is saying, but instead be a loving presence that offers a deeper level of safety, comfort, and acknowledgment than the experience has ever received from you before, thereby being the heart-centered practice of detachment, allowance, pure love, and space.

Ask: "Divine heart, please teach me how to receive the stagnant beliefs that created this inner sense of division, separation, disharmony, and imbalance, so my perception can expand and align with the flow of infinite information." And so it is (Amen).

B-Breathe

Deep conscious breaths allow us to experience what we think and feel, and expand the experience into our heart, breathing and remembering that all is life, including this experience that was once labeled wrong, uncomfortable, or bad. Acknowledging this emotion as worthy to be experienced, awareness sinks deeper into the heart or core of our being, bringing the experience of thought or emotion deeper into our heart where it is no longer opposed and free to be just as it is.

Breathe in the uncomfortable experience, mentally saying, "*I receive you as life*"*),* and exhale mentally saying, (*"You are free to be"*).

I-I love you!

The deeper awareness sinks into the depths of our being, the emptier the head feels. The head is used to being filled with thoughts of the past, so it needs to be filled. Saying, "I love you" fills the space with pure love, reminding the head that everything it needs is already here within. Love creates an environment of relaxation, safety, and security. Therefore, the mind doesn't need to fill itself from the outside-in anymore.

Place your hands over your heart. Say, "*I love you! All is an expression of one life. I validate this limited experience within me. It is an experience from my past that was not validated by my relationships to the world. Therefore, I choose to be the presence of love that provides this experience the resonation of love that it has never received. May I be all the affirmation that this limited experience needs to remember it is an infinite expression of divinity, so it may fully awaken from the illusion of limitation. I love you!*"

"*I am abundant, wise, infinite, and free!*"

T- Thank you

Thank the uncomfortable experience, and the relationship, circumstance, or event that triggered it in your body for giving you another opportunity to remember your connection to the ever-expanding unique expression of your authentic infinite nature.

"Thank you for helping me to remember my authentic voice of pure love."

Intention

After practicing the heart-centered habit, you will be given an intention. Intentions are like seeds that the head can use to plant into the subconscious mind, which will expand over time and create a beautiful garden that bears fruit of love, peace, fulfillment, abundance, and joy. Intentions are like directions that we can offer our mind to return home to the infinite heart. Say these intentions aloud. Feel free to create your own daily intentions!

Affirmation

Lastly, you will be given an affirmation that you can use throughout the day. The affirmation is a quick reminder to your subconscious mind. Affirmations help the subconscious mind to focus in on the Truth in your heart, instead of getting distracted by what feels and appears to be true out in the world. Your words have power, and the more you align your words with the Truth you feel in your heart, the more you participate in the will of the Divine. Feel free to create your own daily affirmations!

Final Note

The heart-centered habit is not the way. *You* are the way. The information, reality, and sense within your own heart is the way. Therefore, use the heart-centered habit as a way to align with your authentic nature of pure love, which opposes nothing and perceives God throughout all experiences in existence. If you are feeling called to live a life of fulfillment, freedom, abundance, and peace; then provide the time, energy, and focus to establish a new way to love yourself. When your head realigns and merges with the sense of Truth in your heart, your life will transform from the inside-out. You will never be able to create a life of fulfillment from the outside-in. It is impossible because your heart is the entry point of divinity. The higher power that has no name resides in your heart. The entire Universe was created from the infinite, eternal, and abundant energy that exists in your heart. Depending on your culture, religion, and family traditions, you have your own name for it: God, divinity, heart-centered consciousness, universal energy, Buddha nature, chi, prana, Christ consciousness, Kingdom of Heaven, Soul, Spirit, Holy Spirit, Divine consciousness, Divine will, great "I am," God mind, Jesus, unity consciousness, one essence, pure love, peace, innocence, tao, narrow path, Divine Light, great way, unified field of infinite energy... Whatever name you give the higher power, which existed before language, doesn't matter. We don't have to call it the same name. But I know you know it, you feel it, and it is calling you home. Your head has been wandering lost in the world for long enough. It is time to come home!

Allow whatever you experience as you read each day. Be with your experience and welcome it through the heart-centered habit. There is not a right way to experience this 22-day journey. You do not have to understand the Truth this book is pointing toward. You just have to remain with your experiences and know they are all valid. Whether it is rational, intuitive, comfortable, uncomfortable, wanted, unwanted, negative, positive, good, bad, blissful, painful, convenient, or inconvenient, this book is intended to guide the parts of you that have forgotten their infinite nature into remembrance. Your head and heart will join in holy matrimony. Your human nature and your spiritual nature will be joined in a unified relationship of pure love. May all of your experiences of mind and body fully open into the eternal presence that is already here now in your heart! When your head and heart reunite, you will discover that you have been the way, the Truth, and the Light the whole time!

Intention: *(say aloud)*

"Today, I choose to align with all uncomfortable experiences. So that I may fully remember my heart-centered nature that embraces every experience just as it is!"

Affirmation: *(say aloud)*

Say aloud throughout today:

"My entire being is the Truth because I am the Truth!"

Day 1

Metamorphosis

"Higher, deeper, innermost, abides another life."
-Bhagavad Gita

Mirror Work

Say Aloud: (looking into your eyes in a mirror):
> Good morning, infinite one. You are safe to feel. I always want to know how you are feeling. You are the soul-mate that I have been looking for my entire life. You matter, and you are enough. You are worthy of being seen and heard. I see you, and I am here to listen to you. There is a good reason you are here; you are Divine perfection. Today, I join you in celebrating your ever-expanding unique expression. I am open to receiving new information and new ways of being by choosing to receive all uncomfortable, unfamiliar, painful, inconvenient, and unwanted experiences as a Divine gift from you, my infinite heart. I love all of you! I really love all of you. (your name), I really love all of you. (Feel free to write your own love statement).

When I began my journey of becoming more aware of what I was feeling rather than what others thought about me, I experienced the same patterns of change. I noticed that the head-centered me, which was a reflection of the world, had three distinct patterns. The first was an aggressive need to desire, want, and consume something. This pattern was all about feeding a vision of what I wanted to become. It focused on the future. The second pattern was a fear of change. As I got closer to the goal of what I wanted in the future, I noticed the change it was creating in my surroundings. I would then become fearful and begin to doubt and worry about the change that becoming something new was creating in my relationships to the world. The third pattern was a sense of momentary achievement, satisfaction or arrival to a state of being I had desired.

I noticed that all three patterns were transitory. Each pattern came and went. I noticed that the head-centered me preferred the third pattern, which was a sense that I had arrived at some future destination where I was desirable. The only problem was, this sense of achievement didn't last because change was just around the corner. Then I would find myself back in the pattern of wanting, desiring, and consuming again. The head-centered me was always identified with one of these three stages. It was always trying, struggling, and striving to get back to the stage where it felt like it had arrived. It also struggled to maintain that pattern of achievement, because it didn't last.

As I practiced the heart-centered habit, I observed that the real me wasn't a pattern, identity, or belief at all. Instead, I experienced being the presence that observed these patterns of change. I noticed that I wasn't the character in charge of these patterns. I couldn't speed up one pattern and prolong another. These patterns of change were a part of a greater reality of coexistence with all of life. I wasn't a separate character in charge of creating change or stopping the change in my reality. Life was spontaneously happening through me as me.

The heart-centered habit guided awareness to take its seat in pure consciousness. The familiar transformed into the unfamiliar and my subconscious mind became more comfortable with the unknown. I was no longer the character in the head that was transforming, becoming, and changing. Instead, I was the heart space where transformation occurred for all experiences, emotions, and thoughts. Transformation can be seen throughout nature. If we can stop long enough and smell the roses, we might feel the intuitive messages that nature can teach us. For instance, the metamorphosis of a caterpillar into a butterfly points to the transformative cycle of all experiences.

This unwanted experience is a gift.
You are welcome here.
You are enough!
How may I serve you?

Caterpillar

When a caterpillar is born, it is extremely small. When it starts eating, it instantly starts growing and expanding. The caterpillar has one job: eat, eat, eat, eat. It consumes the leaves in its environment and it doesn't stop to enjoy what it is eating. It is on a rampage of more, more, more; must eat more, until it reaches its limit and cannot take another bite.

The caterpillar reminds me of one the patterns of identification that the head-centered me can get lost in. As humans, we have taken on the same task of accumulating knowledge from our environment, or wanting nonstop, or desiring life to be a certain way. When we identify ourselves with this pattern of wanting, needing, and desiring, we forget we are more than our needs, wants, and desires. When we are identified with what we think we need, want, and desire, we forget our true nature, which is always relaxed, fulfilled, and satisfied. Instead of being grateful and fulfilled in the moment, we focus on the future and deny the present moment. We also deny what we feel and become lost in our heads through incessant thinking. We feel lost in the momentum of doing, working, striving, becoming, seeking, learning, consuming, thinking, obsessing, desiring, wanting, needing, expecting, controlling, and can't stop for long enough to notice how we feel in our bodies. We can't stop for long enough to relax. We can't stop for long enough to listen to our hearts and the hearts of others. We think that we can't lose momentum because if we do, we will slide backward.

The nature of existence is in a continual cycle of birth, expansion, death, and rebirth. Our physical body is a good example of this. The body's cells are constantly dividing, regenerating, and dying. If the body did not allow cells to die and new ones to be born, we would not grow from an infant into a toddler and into an adult, and would have a very short physical lifespan!

The same holds true for all ideas, thoughts, feelings, and emotions. We don't have to identify with the desires, wants, and needs that we feel. We can remain heart-centered by allowing them to be birthed within us without identifying with them. Love is the power of creation. If we can remember to relax and love all wants, needs, and desires, then if they are meant to be, they will flourish as we remain centered in our heart. We don't have to identify with them and think about them incessantly, as this only drains our energy and disconnects awareness from the heart of the matter.

The head-centered habit identifies with experiences, which keeps us feeling stuck in life. However, the heart-centered habit allows all experiences to be in the natural flow of life because it is a perception that does not cling onto particular experiences or stages of life. When we perceive the nature of reality through the heart, all experiences of our inner and outer lives – such as thoughts, emotions, feelings, beliefs, perceptions, and experiences in the physical world – are in this cycle of birth, expansion, and death. Freedom is experienced when we become aware that this is natural and good. We don't have to attach or hold onto any experience. We can remain as the awareness or space that this natural flow of life happens within. Our inner

52

experience of beliefs, judgments, thoughts, emotions, and feelings can easily go through the natural cycle of metamorphosis in a moment when we don't step in and try to control or attach to it as "my identity." We can go with the flow of change; the natural way of existence. Let all experiences be as they are!

This uncomfortable experience is a gift.
You are welcome here.
You are enough!
How may I serve you?

<u>Chrysalis</u>

When the caterpillar stuffs itself to its capacity, it forms a chrysalis. From the outside it may appear that the caterpillar is resting, but on the inside, it's rapidly changing. The body of the caterpillar is dissolving into a goopy mess. Imaginal cells that were dormant in its body awaken and form new tissue, organs, and body. The head-centered habit can keep a person feeling stuck in this stage of the natural cycle of existence when one analyzes his or her experiences, trying to understand why the character appears to be deteriorating. Why is what I envisioned for my life not happening? Why can't I have the life I dreamed of? Why can't I overcome this disease, illness, or sickness? Why is life so unfair? Why can't I live an authentic life? Why am I aging so fast? Why don't I have the motivation to live as I used to? The more we analyze and try to figure out this pattern of life, the longer we prolong its natural healing powers because of undue mental suffering.

If your life appears to be falling apart, it's okay; all is well. You are going through an intense remodel, healing, and renewal. The old is dying to make way for the new way of being. The heart-centered habit will guide awareness into loving those parts and pieces of yourself that are dying off. It is okay as it is their time to go. Allow what was familiar to become unfamiliar. If you remain in the head-centered habit, it will be very difficult to let go of what was familiar, and you will suffer. You will be unable to put the broken pieces of the familiar back together again. The more you struggle to let go of the familiar, the more you will try to fix something that is not supposed to be fixed. It would be like moving from Florida, which experiences warm temperatures year round, to New Hampshire, which experiences all four seasons. When the season changes from summer to fall in New Hampshire, you freak out because summer had been the familiar and comfortable condition that you experienced in Florida. So you run outside and begin gluing the leaves back on the trees. No matter how hard you try, the leaves are all going to fade away.

This is how the head-centered habit functions. It becomes accustomed and comfortable in one mental setting, and then when life changes its setting, the mind fights the change trying to hold onto the past comfortable condition. Silly, right? This is exactly what the head-centered me does during times of great change. The head-centered habit hates this pattern of change the most and tries to fight or escape it at all costs.

In this stage the subconscious mind is undergoing a massive reorientation. The familiar, known, comfortable, and convenient ways you were used to are disintegrating into the unfamiliar, unknown, uncomfortable, and inconvenient. When you reprogram your subconscious mind to be just as okay with the uncomfortable and unfamiliar as the comfortable and familiar, your subconscious mind will expand into new realms of possibilities. You will realize new horizons and inner potentials that were brewing within you. When your reality appears to be experiencing a death, life is giving you an opportunity to reprogram your subconscious mind into receiving new ways to express yourself. So that new imaginal cells may become active within your heart and reshape your reality into a new expression, which creates new horizons, experiences, and opportunities for you to enjoy!

This painful experience is a gift.
You are welcome here.
You are enough!
How may I serve you?

Butterfly

The old has gone and the new has come. The butterfly breaks free of the darkness from within the chrysalis. It joins with the natural flow of the wind as it soars effortlessly through the air. The butterfly isn't concerned with consuming its environment. The butterfly is on the lookout to reproduce. Its purpose is to usher in a new cycle of rebirth. The head-centered habit loves this stage the most because it feels a temporary sense of accomplishment. The head-centered habit doesn't know true peace and relaxation because it believes that peace has to do with a life void of change. Its limited perception, which is based upon the outer experience lining up with what it wants, thinks that arriving at a goal will provide the peace and happiness for which it longs. The problem is, this stage doesn't last like the other two. Therefore, the head-centered habit, which is always pushing away change and pulling the arrival of a goal toward itself, can prolong our suffering through the winds of change. The older you become, and the more accomplishments you attain, the head-centered habit becomes more dismayed because it fears the change that is around the corner. You can offer wisdom to the head's perception by reminding it that life is an ever-expanding adventure of change. The only constant is the love that dwells in your heart, which can become the gift that you offer every moment of change.

Maybe your head identifies with the caterpillar, in being the character that is constantly consuming its environment to gain more knowledge, or a puffed up ego or spiritual ego. Maybe your head identifies with the chrysalis stage, where you feel totally dissatisfied with your life because it appears to be falling apart! Or maybe your head identifies with the butterfly stage, where you feel attached to reproducing your life. So, you think of ways you can create something new in your environment, such as a new business, new diet, new lifestyle, new home, new decorating style, new wardrobe, new relationship, new information, new role ... Regardless of the pattern or stage your find yourself in, there is a peace that surpasses the identification with any of the stages of metamorphosis. Your head's perception longs to join with the peace it remembers from your childhood. Peace is a symptom of heart-centered consciousness, perceiving through the expanded view of the heart and soul.

The heart-centered habit expands your head's perception to include the whole cycle of metamorphosis. Your mind can open and become a space of pure love that enjoys the entire cycle of birth, expansion, death, and rebirth. The heart-centered habit is a way of being that allows life to flow naturally without judging the way it appears, grows, or disappears. Emotions are energy in this constant flow of birth, expansion, and death. You experience emotions associated with each stage of metamorphosis. A heart-centered perception of your reality will bring the remembrance to honor and respect every emotion associated with the cycle of life. You do not have to be head-centered and identify with the energy that is in motion. Instead, you can be the space that welcomes the emotion, acknowledges it as a Divine part of life, and allows it to dissolve within your awareness. This is the one Divine nature, which functions to support and serve all forms of experience.

The heart-centered habit embraces the unknown just as much as the known. Therefore, it doesn't identify with any stage within the natural cycle of life, so that it can continually enjoy the natural flow of change. You can enjoy observing the changes that nature is undergoing and nurture every aspect of yourself with love by being heart-centered.

This unfamiliar experience is a gift.
You are welcome here.
You are enough!
How may I serve you?

Reflection

Are you willing to perceive through your infinite nature and allow your mind to become a safe place for all thoughts, feelings, ideas, emotions, desires, wants, needs, beliefs, perceptions, and experiences to be born, expand (grow), and die, without attaching to any phase of its metamorphosis?

What if you approached every experience with the mantra, "This too shall pass, so I will enjoy it while it is here?"

Reprogramming the subconscious mind

Be still and know that overwhelm, fatigue, stress, and exhaustion is God, a part of your true authentic nature.

Practicing the heart-centered habit: (Example)

Have you ever felt overwhelmed, fatigued, stressed, and exhausted?

Welcome these experiences as a part of consciousness (You):

H-Honesty

"I fully feel the parts of me that have felt overwhelm, fatigue, stress, and exhaustion."

A-Acknowledge, allow, ask

"I acknowledge that it is safe and okay to feel this limited experience. I embrace these feelings fully as they are because I know they are here to show me the way into my heart. As I embrace these feelings fully, I ask them to bring with them all of the past meanings, interpretations, beliefs, and judgments that I thought were true, but are not valid in this present moment, so that I may receive them as a gift, guide, and opening toward the infinite perception in my heart. I acknowledge their Divine role in helping me expand awareness into the depths of infinite knowing."

Allow the uncomfortable experience to have a voice. Do not believe what it is saying, but instead be a loving presence that offers a deeper level of safety, comfort, and acknowledgment than the experience has ever received from you before, thereby being the practice of detachment, allowance, pure love, and space.

Ask: "Divine heart, I accept that I don't know how to detach from old stagnant beliefs. Therefore, I ask that you detach awareness from perceiving overwhelm, stress, fatigue, and exhaustion as wrong, bad, and evil experiences. Welcome, embrace, honor, and validate these experiences for me, through me, as I am now, healing the inner division within me, so that my perception can expand and align with the flow of infinite information." And so it is (Amen).

B- Breathe

Breathe in these feelings (*"I receive you as life!)"* then exhale (*"You are free to be"*). Be one with the breath. *"The breath is the truth, answer, way, and light that I have been seeking for all my life."*

I-I love you!

Place your hands over your heart. Say, *"I love you! All is an expression of one life. I validate this limited experience within me. It is an experience from my past that was not validated by my relationships to the world. Therefore, I choose to be the presence of love that provides this experience the resonation of love that it has never received. May I be all the affirmation that this limited experience needs to remember that it is an infinite expression of divinity, so that it may fully awaken from the illusion of limitation. I love you!"*

"I am abundant, wise, infinite, and free!"

T-Thank you

Thank the experience for helping you remember that you are an ever-expanding unique expression of the Truth. Thank the circumstance, story, or relationship that triggered these feelings in your body, so your entire being could awaken to your innocent nature of authentic freedom that can enjoy all experiences.

> *"Thank you for helping me to align and attune with my heart's ever-expanding unique expression of infinite wisdom and pure love! Thank you for helping me to remember the power of life that I am!"*

Intention: *(say aloud)*

"Today I choose to allow the transformation of all experiences, thereby, remaining in the full remembrance of harmony, peace, and joy throughout all changing conditions."

Affirmation: *(say aloud)*

Say aloud throughout today:

"All experiences are Divine because I am Divine!"

DAY 2

Tree of Knowledge of Good and Evil

"Your beliefs become your thoughts,
Your thoughts become your words,
Your words become your actions,
Your actions become your habits,
Your habits become your values,
Your values become your destiny."
-Gandhi

Mirror Work

Say Aloud: (looking into your eyes in a mirror):
Good morning, infinite one. You are safe to feel. I always want to know how you are feeling. You are the soul-mate that I have been looking for my entire life. You matter, and you are enough. You are worthy of being seen and heard. I see you and I am here to listen to you. There is a good reason you are here; you are Divine perfection. Today, I join you in celebrating your ever-expanding unique expression. I am open to receiving new information and new ways of being by choosing to receive all uncomfortable, unfamiliar, painful, inconvenient, and unwanted experiences as a Divine gift from you, my infinite heart. I love all of you! I really love all of you. (your name), I really love all of you. (Feel free to write your own love statement).

I grew up in the Christian religion. I loved attending Wonderful Wednesdays at the Methodist Church, which my parents took us to when I was a child. When I got older, we moved further away from the church and didn't go as often. In my twenties I began to ask the existential questions, 'Who am I really? Why am I here? What is my purpose? What is the meaning to life?' These questions guided me back into Christianity when I became an adult. I joined a Christian ministry on campus at Florida State University. I loved reading about Jesus. I thought he was so radical, loving, powerful, fearless, and wise. I began to study his life for myself throughout my twenties. His life resonated so deeply within my heart. However, I noticed that religion can become a belief system that separates humanity into different groups. This feels head-centered to me because by perceiving others through our religious beliefs we judge other religions for not being the "Truth." I experienced firsthand the separation that can be caused by attaching to a specific way or religion about God.

Religion is made up of stories and experiences of heart-centered beings that point to our true authentic spiritual nature. But as soon as we attach to their expression of God or Truth, we become head-centered and perceive everything that feels or appears unfamiliar through a lens of fear. This judgment toward other people with different beliefs, ways, and expressions about God, Truth, or reality did not resonate with my heart nor did it resonate with the way Jesus lived. Perceiving Truth through a lens of fear sets up a world paradigm where individuals do not have the freedom to be a unique authentic expression of God or Divinity.

Jesus did not label himself as a part of a certain religion. He didn't identify with Judaism or Christianity. He traveled all over the region he was born and reached out to anyone and everyone regardless of their religious or cultural beliefs. This is what made him so radical and infuriated the Pharisees and Sadducees, who were the teachers of the religious Law. They hated him because they feared him. They feared him because he did not live by their knowledge of the truth. Rather Jesus lived as an embodiment of the Truth, pure indiscriminate unconditional love; a love that surpasses our understanding of what love is. It is a love that moves toward fear. It is a love that moves toward pain. It is a love that moves toward the storms and chaos in our lives. It is a love that is our true spiritual nature. Jesus lived his life as this love, and he shared this love with everyone. He was not interested in having them adopt a belief system about love. Instead, he was only interested in helping them remember their true spiritual nature of this pure love that exists as the unified core of all. He was my first example of how to live by this Divine wisdom of accepting the unknown and unfamiliar aspects of infinite Love.

In my late twenties I learned to study the Bible. I am forever thankful to Beth Moore and Kay Arthur, who were female teachers that showed women how to study the Bible for themselves by using a concordance. A concordance is a Bible translation tool to look up the Greek, Aramaic, and Hebrew meanings of words that have been translated into English. I studied the Book of Genesis and I saw the story about the Garden of Eden differently than my Christian religious colleagues. God told Adam and Eve they could eat from any tree in the garden. Two different kinds of trees were mentioned: the tree of life, and the tree of knowledge of good and evil. God warned them that if they ate from the tree of knowledge of good and evil, they would surely die. Well, that doesn't sound too pleasant. Regardless of God's warning they ate from it and immediately they felt that their vulnerable and innocent nature needed to be covered up. They were also cursed with a life of struggle. What happened? They were in the garden enjoying the goodness of all life, then they ate from a tree and they began to feel like they had to cover up their true nature of goodness. They felt ashamed of what God created as goodness. This felt a lot like my journey here on Earth.

I am not a Bible scholar and can only speak of my direct experiences. So like any story I investigate that points to the Truth, I go within to my direct experience. This action of Adam and Eve eating from the tree of knowledge of good and evil appears to point to a lesson of when we disobey God, we are punished; the lesson taught in most Christian churches. However, when I studied this scripture, intuition guided my awareness to a very different message. Not one of punishment and judgment, but instead about how to shine in the goodness of our true nature by perceiving only LIFE! I sensed a deeper Truth when I looked at moments when I felt like I needed to cover up my innocent and vulnerable nature. I noticed that when I perceived from the head-centered me, which believes in wrong, darkness, and bad that I literally felt like death on the inside. This is because I felt separate from my true authentic spiritual nature, which knows nothing about darkness, bad, wrong, or evil. Instead, I was placing my faith in a story of right and wrong in my head. Then I noticed I would project blame onto either myself, someone, or something for the limited feeling I was experiencing. Just like when Adam blamed Eve for giving him the forbidden fruit.

Believing in a knowledge of good and evil made me feel disconnected from God. I only believed in wrong because I thought there was something wrong with me because my unique expression of love was different from anything that I experienced in this world. Therefore, I felt ashamed of my vulnerable, innocent, and pure nature. I thought my true authentic nature was wrong or bad because it was different, unique, and unfamiliar within all of my relationships to the physical world. The longer I stayed in my head, the longer the story of good and evil played on, and the more limited I felt, which created negative thinking. The voice in my head reflected this sense of limitation and would criticize and judge myself, others, and reality. Then I noticed that I would fight to change unfamiliar or unwanted circumstances. OR I would want to escape my head, which created a dependency upon a specific habit to make me feel better. The only thing I was truly fighting and escaping from was the real, true, genuine, authentic, unique, and unfamiliar me; which did not fit in with the world's standards of right, good, and true. This was my own internal hell, where I felt separate from pure love, God, peace, life, abundance, authentic nature of goodness, and Divine Light. Just like Adam and Eve, I too was eating from the knowledge of good and evil, which produced a misperception of wrong, darkness, evil, and limitation. What I perceive, I believe, and what I believe, I feel. Therefore, if I perceive wrong and evil, I believe in wrong and evil, and I will feel wrong and evil. This is how I covered up my true authentic infinite nature of pure life and love!

The tree of knowledge of good and evil symbolizes a limited perception that you can choose by perceiving your experience of reality through the eyes of your head, which believes in what you feel and see from the outside-in. When you perceive from the outside-in, you are misperceiving reality because you are not perceiving through the lens of Truth that you directly feel from within your heart. Instead, you will believe in the evidence of an opposing force to your true nature of pure love, saying no to certain experiences and creating a sense of separation within you through limited beliefs or two opposing realities called:

Good	Evil
Right	Wrong
Acceptable	Unacceptable
God	Devil
Comfortable	Uncomfortable
Want	Unwanted
Love	Hate
Good	Bad
Should	Should not

These two opposing realities are at war within your head's perception of reality. They are polarized ideas that continually oppose each other within your head's consciousness. This is the war you feel within that is expressed in your relationships to the external world. These become the incessant voices in our head, which distracts us from sensing the peace that exists underneath. If you resolve this war within you by tuning into what you sense within your heart and perceive both sides as one expression of divinity, then you will be the peace that you wish to see in the world.

I studied many other religions that pointed to the same Truth, including Taoism. In the 49th verse of Tao Te Ching, Lao-tzu describes the behavior of a wise man:

"Those who are good he (wise man) treats with goodness. Those who are bad he also treats with goodness, because the nature of his being is good."

If you believe in a knowledge of the Truth that points to good and bad then you believe you have a good nature and a bad nature. You have to be aware that the only nature that truly exists is goodness, and then you can also be wise like Jesus and many other enlightened, spiritually awake beings. Every religion points to this Truth that when we perceive separation or two opposing realities we will suffer. Awareness is waking up out of our stories in the head of right and wrong that we have maintained in our rational minds. We are remembering that we are all diverse expressions of one life! We are all different versions of goodness! There is no one right way to be and no one right way to express the love we feel in our heart! Now is the time to return back to your vulnerable, innocent, pure loving authentic good nature. You will not witness only life or goodness in the news or within our physical world until your internal world has reconciled every labeled experience of wrong, bad, evil, uncomfortable, not wanted, mental "no," shouldn't, can't, limitation, separation, division.... into the remembrance that all is life. This requires faith and a remembrance that you are more than what you think about reality... you are the infinite reality of goodness itself!

"This unwanted experience is a gift."
You are welcome here.
You are enough!
How may I serve you?

Sin/ Virtual Reality

When you believe in the separation of life because you believe more in the evidence of wrong that you see and feel from the outer world, you are programming your brain to perceive your own sense of self as two selves, good natured and bad natured. We have all been born into sin. Sin simply means to miss the mark or misperceive reality, Truth, God, pure love, or our authentic good nature. Another way to describe misperception is to misunderstand. You misperceive your true nature of goodness because you think you need to understand or comprehend it. We cannot understand our true nature. Our true nature is infinite. How can finite understanding comprehend infinity? The head-centered me believes you need to understand everything, people, and reality. This is futile because your need to understand causes division and conflict. What if you could know without understanding? What if you could know another person without needing to understand them? The heart-centered me senses oneness in all diverse expressions. The head-centered me senses separation and tries to use its limited understanding to connect to another. There are infinite understandings about reality, but only one essence. Therefore, wouldn't it be easier to connect to another through our one essence of goodness, instead of through our limited personal understanding of right and wrong?

We have unconsciously programmed our brain to believe in what we are taught by society, which is based upon a foundation of perceiving reality through a specific lens called "my knowledge" or "my understanding" of good and evil. From the moment we were born our physical senses have been permeated with a sense of no. The n stands for need: need to know, need to understand, need reality to feel and appear different than it is. Need, need, need... The o stands for oppose. We oppose reality through denial, fighting, or escaping when we feel the moment isn't supporting our needs. This creates a separate sense of self or nature in our head that can't be integrated into our spiritual essence because it doesn't resonate the same nature of yes within our heart or soul, which opposes and needs nothing. Needing and opposing: NO is the unconscious pattern we learn from the outer world and eventually we become a vibrational match through perceiving reality in the same unconscious way. Thereby, we keep recreating the misperception of reality from one generation to the next.

As stated in the quote at the beginning of this chapter by Gandhi, our foundation to how we perceive reality is based upon our beliefs. Our beliefs become our thoughts. If we are taught to believe in the evidence of wrong, bad, evil, and darkness that we see and feel from our outer world, we maintain a false sense of Truth through the knowledge of right and wrong. We function from a belief system of two opposing forces in the world and we become needy and live in opposition. These beliefs oppose each other and create thoughts that oppose each other, which we maintain and store in the rational mind. The mind is not in one location, just like the air isn't found in one location. The mind permeates every cell in our body. Our bodies become the first place that war, conflict, dis-ease, struggle, division, and separation is experienced. Pain, resistance, and fear become our underlying experience of reality. The creation of this unconscious war within our rational mind is projected into our experiences and relationships to the outer world. Opposing thoughts produce our opposing reactions. Sometimes we behave in volatile ways because we perceive a threat to our survival due to all feelings and appearances that are unfamiliar to our false sense of reality. When life appears the way we want it to, or in a familiar way, we react in good ways. But when life appears unfamiliar, we react in abusive ways toward ourselves, others, or the world. Our opposing reactions produce opposing habits. We have healthy and unhealthy habits. We have good habits and bad habits. We have habits we show to the world, and habits we hide from the world. Our opposing habits produce opposing values that we pass down to future generations. Our opposing values produce a destiny of highs and lows, good and bad, right and wrong, what I want, and what I don't want.

An entire head-centered false reality is built upon a false belief in wrong, bad, and evil. This false sense of reality distracts our awareness away from sensing into the Truth of our being that lies underneath. The heart-centered me that expresses the voice of my soul is waiting patiently to be acknowledged by faith. But we have to stop eating from the tree of knowledge of good and evil that has grown in our head or rational mind. We have to go through a process of unraveling this false sense of self in our head that is needy and opposes reality. The heart-centered habit is a tool that can unravel the chaos, war, and conflict in our head, so we can remember our authentic sense of the Truth within us; the Truth that needs and opposes nothing, learning how to align with our true nature of Pure LOVE and eat only from the Tree of Life!

As humans we really believe we have to teach right and wrong to our children. What if babies are born remembering their true authentic nature of goodness or pure love? What if they could grow perceiving the magic and miracles that life actually is right now? What if the only law they lived by was Goodness and Pure Love? Have you ever watched a baby when they learn to walk? This happens between nine months and eighteen months. They look at every object with a fearless wonder. Everything is so magical and interesting through their eyes. Is this the childlike mind we have all forgotten because we have unconsciously programmed a virtual reality that believes in the knowledge of right and wrong; a nature of division and conflict? How different could our communication be when we are no longer sharing our files on our knowledge of right and wrong, aka: fears, anxieties, worries, and doubts?

The news on television is a reflection of the noise in our own heads. Consuming the evidence of evil, wrong, and darkness that we see and feel from the exterior world is the root to our suffering, stress, and limitations. Beyond constantly thinking about how reality is evil, bad, and wrong exists an abundance of Life and Love that we could be sharing with one another. Magic, miracles, healing, and God is within you! The answers you seek are within you! Return home to your heart within, where the tree of life exists, which desires to grow and bear fruit of goodness, purity, peace, and abundance through you as you! But first the tree of knowledge of good and evil has to be loved to death!

"This uncomfortable experience is a gift."
You are welcome here.
You are enough!
How may I serve you?

Rational Mind

Most toddlers go through a stage of asking "why" about everything. We are introduced to a world that doesn't make sense to our true nature of goodness. We sense fear from our environment and feel as if we are missing something. So we want to understand, why is this world so different than the one I sense within me? Depending on our environment, we all receive different answers to our questions of why? These answers become the knowledge of right and wrong that we store in our rational minds. We are taught to believe in wrong because there is so much evidence of darkness in the world. Our intentions are innocent because as adults we want to protect our children and future generations. The rational mind is like the surface of mind. The rational mind becomes cluttered with information that we attach awareness to as the "truth." This clouds or blurs our perception from perceiving the world as a manifestation of the authentic nature of goodness and purity. Instead, the rational mind perceives the world as a manifestation of good and evil, good-natured and ill-natured. Sure, we can find a lot of evidence from our environment that evil exists. But remember evil only exists in our world because we believed there is a nature of goodness (knowledge of good) and a nature of evil (knowledge of evil). No matter how much we want to change our world to becoming a better place, we will never achieve such a lofty dream when the majority of humans perceive reality from the rational mind that thinks and places reality into categories of good and evil. It is like trying to remove weeds from your garden. If you do not dig out the root, they will grow back and multiply. The only way to heal the world of suffering is to go within toward your core and perceive divinity in all forms, thereby merging with all of existence, which collapses the divided sense of self in your rational mind that feels separate from God, Divinity, Abundance, Life, and Goodness...

The need to understand God, reality, self, and Truth has caused us to misuse the rational mind, which has become a storage container of accumulated knowledge (understanding of right and wrong). This is pure insanity. How can the rational mind contain the vast infinite Truth? Our true nature cannot be put in a box. Words, beliefs, language, descriptions, stories, thoughts, and feelings can point awareness to sensing the Truth of our being. But they are not the whole Truth in and of themselves. The rational mind has been misguided. It has to remember its true role. The heart-centered habit guides the rational mind to release all of its stored knowledge and understanding about reality, so that it may remember that it is free and connected to the vast infinite source of Truth, which is like an infinite well of wisdom. Wisdom arises from within, and pours through the rational mind when it is free of stored understanding and knowledge. Then the rational mind can surrender its need to protect our identity because the identity has been set free. Our identity was made up of past knowledge and understanding in wrong, evil, and darkness, along with memories of past hurts, pains, and wounds. We have become a victim to our own stored knowledge and memories of evil, darkness, and wrong.

Who we are in this moment is brand new. But when the rational mind is used to storing our past experiences and repeatedly confirming to us that this is who we are, we forget that we are an infinite being that needs and opposes nothing. When the rational mind is free from holding on to the past it aligns with the present moment. However, the past is our identity that we believe is the truth of our being. Therefore, we have to remember our childlike mind that is fearless, and the sense of pure love that we remember from within our heart. This is why we have to be born again by beginning a new habit, a heart-centered habit! Then the Divine wisdom of our true nature expresses and moves the entire mind and body in a harmonious symbiotic relationship without a sense of need or opposition.

"This painful experience is a gift."
You are welcome here.
You are enough!
How may I serve you?

<u>Personal Will</u>

Believing in the knowledge of right and wrong that we unconsciously stored in our rational minds as the Truth becomes our personal will. Depending on when, where, how, and what type of environment you were raised in, your personal will may be similar to particular individuals that were born during the same time, same family, same location, same culture, same religion, same lifestyle, same economic status, same knowledge of right and wrong. However, no two personal wills are exactly the same. This is because our experiences of our environment are unique to us. When we live from our personal will we perceive opposition because some personal wills are similar to ours and some are very different. This creates the settings of what is familiar and what is unfamiliar in our subconscious mind. The relationships that we have similar personal wills with are individuals we call our friends. "I like them." "They know me." "I resonate with them," only because they are familiar. The relationships we have diffcrent personal wills with are individuals that get on our nerves. "I can't stand them!" "They frustrate me!" only because they are unfamiliar.

Our enemies are individuals with an opposing personal will than our own. It is impossible for all humans to live in harmony, equanimity, and peace in the world when we live by our personal wills. Our personal will puts demands upon our relationships, circumstances, experiences, and the world to make us happy. Our personal will says, 'When my life looks like this, I will be happy. When my life does not look like this, I will be unhappy. When my needs are not being met, I will go to war with reality and everything and everyone that feels and appears to be unfamiliar to my false sense of reality.' Our personal will believes that happiness is dependent upon the exterior world to be a certain way. When the exterior world appears as a manifestation or reflection of what I believe to be good, true, familiar, and right; then I will be happy.

We have a knowledge of right and wrong for everything. There is a right and wrong in the way marriage should be. There is a right and wrong in the way friendship should be. There are shoulds and shouldn'ts on everything. Even a should and shouldn't on how to use a tube of toothpaste, hang and fold clothes, ways to communicate, ways to be (a mother, father, child, sister, brother, worker, student, provider, housewife...) How in the world can any relationship be in harmony with so many different should and shouldn'ts? We will never find someone with the same exact personal will of should and shouldn'ts or familiarity as our own! Usually when we marry someone, we think now this person shares the same values (personal will) as I do. Until we live with them for a while. Then we notice the differences in our personal wills and our partner has tendencies that can drive us crazy from the perception of personal will.

The head-centered habit lives as a needy personal will that opposes reality in some way. The personal will creates all of our fears, anxieties, insecurities, and limitations. The heart-centered habit guides the personal will to align with the Divine will of goodness, oneness, and pure love. Are you ready to empty your rational mind of familiarity, so it may surrender to the unfamiliarity of Divine will, which is your soul's destiny? Is your rational mind willing to remember by faith to only eat from the tree of life, which is the intuitive guidance arising from within your own heart? Faith is required because you will not see evidence of the tree of life in the world quite yet. This is because the majority of humanity still eats from the tree of knowledge of good and evil.

Many spiritual teachers and masters went through times of fasting to realign with their spiritual nature. Many followers of specific religions may think that spiritual teachers were fasting food, but they were actually fasting their beliefs in wrong. For instance, Jesus fasted and went to the desert where he was tempted by the devil; the voice in the mind that perceives darkness, wrong, evil, and bad. The devil is the idea that there is a force that is separate from and opposes the nature of God. Jesus was tempted by this idea in evil and chose to align with what his heart sensed as the Truth instead of what he felt and saw from the world as being true.

For the next 21 days, you are being called to fast your beliefs in wrong, evil, and bad. Trust me, over the next 21 days, the voice of wrong in your head will be activated simply by reading this book. If you truly desire to be free and fulfilled, then love the parts of yourself that have been hurt, abused, and neglected. We have all experienced some form of abuse, neglect, rejection, humiliation, embarrassment, judgment, or abandonment in this world. We think these are the parts of ourselves that block us from experiencing freedom, peace, and fulfillment. The truth is, these aspects do not block or stand in your way to be free. These aspects are the doorways to freedom and fulfillment. As you welcome, acknowledge, embrace, love, honor, and thank these aspects as being a part of Life, God, or Divinity, you will experience more wholeness, wellbeing, and healing, thereby becoming an integrated being of Divine Light and love. The heart-centered habit will guide your awareness to fast in believing in wrong, evil, or darkness, so that your perception may align with your true authentic Divine nature of pure goodness and love, which has no opposite.

Imagine that your head is like a garden and your heart is like a garden too. Imagine that every experience that arises within you, whether positive or negative, right or wrong, good or bad, comfortable or uncomfortable, wanted or unwanted, convenient or inconvenient, is a seed. If we label the seed based upon the way it feels or appears then it gets planted in the garden of our head. If the experience is uncomfortable, unfamiliar, negative, unwanted, or inconvenient, then we label the seed as bad. This "bad" seed takes root in the mind and grows weeds that seek to choke out the seeds labeled as good, which are the wanted, positive, comfortable, familiar, and convenient experiences. The garden of our mind becomes entangled with weeds that are overtaking the plants trying to bear fruit. This is a representation of the chaos in our own heads. The voices of fear, victimhood, self-righteousness, entitlement, and neediness are the inner experiences of this good plant versus bad weed battlefield in the head.

The heart is a different kind of garden. The heart receives every experience as a good seed and plants it into the soil of pure love, where it grows, blossoms, and bears fruit of harmony, joy, peace, fulfillment, and freedom. The choice is yours. You can remain stagnant and continue to co-create a battlefield of weeds and plants in the mind through perceiving experiences as right or wrong, or you can co-create a beautiful garden of Life in the mind through perceiving all experiences as goodness and pure life regardless of the way it feels and appears. What will you choose?

"This unfamiliar experience is a gift."
You are welcome here.
You are enough!
How may I serve you?

Reflection

What if you are the ONLY one perceiving reality the way you do?
What if you acknowledged that the way you see reality is perfect for you and no one else?
What would your experience be if you no longer expected others to perceive Truth the way that you do?

Reprogramming the subconscious mind

Say the following out loud:

Dear Rational Mind/Personal Will,

Thank you for trying your best to protect me for all these years. Thank you for trying your best to make me feel safe. Thank you for trying your best to define who/what I am so I could remain in the comfortable, familiar, and wanted habits of "me." I acknowledge all of your effort and hard work. I am giving you an early retirement. Now it is your turn to relax and enjoy reality. I receive you just as you arc. (Breathe in, "I receive you as life," and breathe out, "You are free to be.") "I choose to be the space for you to say whatever you need to say. I choose to be your friend, ally, and loving partner. I love you, I love you, I love you, I love you!" Thank you for helping me to remember my authentic voice of pure love and goodness!

Yours truly,

Your soul-mate

"Be still and know that fear, anxiety, insecurity, and vulnerability is God, a part of your true authentic nature."

Practicing the heart-centered habit: (Example)

Have you ever felt fearful, anxious, unsafe, or vulnerable?

Welcome these experiences as a part of consciousness (You):

H- Honesty

"I fully feel the parts of me that have felt fearful, anxious, insecure, and vulnerable."

A-Acknowledge, allow, ask

"I acknowledge that it is safe and okay to feel this limited experience. I embrace these feelings fully as they are because I know they are here to show me the way into my heart. As I embrace these feelings fully, I ask them to bring with them all of the past meanings, interpretations, beliefs, and judgments that I thought were true, but are not valid in this present moment, so that I may receive them as a gift, guide, and opening toward the infinite perception in my heart. I acknowledge their Divine role in helping me expand awareness into the depths of infinite knowing."

Allow the uncomfortable experience to have a voice. Do not believe what it is saying, but instead be a loving presence that offers a deeper level of safety, comfort, and acknowledgment than the experience has ever received from you before, thereby being the practice of detachment, allowance, pure love, and space.

Ask: "Divine heart, I accept that I don't know how to harmonize with my beliefs in wrong. Therefore, I ask that you guide me to harmonize with the experience of fear, anxiety, insecurity, and vulnerability. Welcome, embrace, honor, and validate these experiences for me, through me, as I am now, healing the inner division within me, so my perception can expand and align with the flow of infinite information." And so it is (Amen).

B- Breathe

Breathe in these feelings (*"I receive you as life"*), and breathe out *("You are free to be")*. Be one with the breath. *"The breath restores me."*

I-I love you!

Place your hands over your heart. Say, *"I love you! All is an expression of one life. I validate this limited experience within me. It is an experience from my past that was not validated by my relationships to the world. Therefore, I choose to be the presence of love that provides this experience the resonation of love that it has never received. May I be all the affirmation that this limited experience needs to remember that it is an infinite expression of divinity, so it may fully awaken from the illusion of limitation. I love you!"*

"I am abundant, wise, infinite, and free!"

T- Thank you

Thank the experience for helping you remember that you are an ever-expanding and unique expression of the Truth. Thank the circumstance, story, or relationship that triggered these feelings in your body, so your entire being can awaken to your innocent nature of authentic freedom that can enjoy all experiences.

> *"Thank you for helping me to align and attune with my heart's ever-expanding unique expression of infinite wisdom and pure love! Thank you for helping me to remember the power of life that I am!"*

Intention: *(say aloud)*

"Today, I choose to merge with all knowledge of wrong, bad, and evil, thereby awakening out of sin or misperception, which allows my rational mind and personal will to align with the authentic Divine nature of pure love!"

Affirmation: *(say aloud)*

Say aloud throughout today:

"All beliefs are infinite because I am infinite!"

DAY 3

Tree of Life

"The point is not to separate the opposites and make "positive progress," but rather to unify and harmonize the opposites, both positive and negative, by discovering a ground which transcends and encompasses them both. And that ground, as we will soon see, is unity consciousness itself."
-Ken Wilber

Mirror Work

Say Aloud: (looking into your eyes in a mirror):
Good morning, infinite one. You are safe to feel. I always want to know how you are feeling. You are the soul-mate I have been looking for my entire life. You matter, and you are enough. You are worthy of being seen and heard. I see you and I am here to listen to you. There is a good reason you are here; you are Divine perfection! Today, I join you in celebrating your ever-expanding unique expression. I am open to receiving new information and new ways of being by choosing to receive all uncomfortable, unfamiliar, painful, inconvenient, and unwanted experiences as a Divine gift from you, my infinite heart. I love all of you! I really love all of you. (your name), I really love all of you. (Feel free to write your own love statement).

On my fortieth birthday, Dr. Wayne Dyer passed away. He touched so many lives in the seventy-five years he was alive. I read many of his books, which inspired me to open up to the Divine wisdom within me. He was the first person who introduced me to the

81

common thread of Truth that all religions speak about. The common thread that is invisible, intangible, and formless, which can be sensed from within us beyond the thinking rational mind. We are Divine love, and that is infinite, therefore it can be expressed in an infinite number of ways. All knowledge, appearances, experiences, thoughts, and emotions are expressions of our true authentic nature of Divine love. However, we have grown in a world where positive and negative experiences seem to exist. We have all experienced negative or limited experiences in our relationship to the world. We didn't know that it wasn't necessary to identify with these limited experiences, so by default we followed in the footsteps of the humans in our immediate environment. We don't know to do any better until we stumble across the lives of humans who resonated a different way to be in the world. When we learn about these enlightened beings who lived in a heart-centered way, we begin to remember why we were born. The truth is, each one of us was born to affirm and validate all negative and limited experiences. Therefore, we become the very presence of infinite love as we receive, welcome, embrace, acknowledge, allow, love, and thank every limited thought, feeling, emotion, belief, perspective, idea, and experience throughout all of existence.

We can choose to stop identifying with the exterior world and become heart-centered, allowing the heart to claim the truth that everything is a symbol of divinity. The first step to becoming heart-centered is welcoming the dark side of your reality into your experience and claiming it as the one light of divinity. Only a fearless, wise, and heart-centered being can live by such faith. This doesn't mean we deny what we feel. Instead, we become honest about what we feel and claim all of our experiences of inner division as pure life. When everything we have denied, repressed, and judged as wrong, uncomfortable, bad, or evil within ourselves is guided into the Heaven in our heart, only life or Divine Love will remain. I am sure you are wondering that if we allow all of our beliefs in wrong to dissolve then how will we know what the right thing to do is? We will know by following the intuitive flow within us, which exudes a feeling of lightness and freedom. The way the Divine flows through my heart may guide me to express, create, and live differently than the way the Divine guides you through your heart. Therefore, we cannot judge one another by the way we appear. When we choose to be heart-centered, we are aligning our entire being, mind and body, with our authentic nature of pure love, pure life, goodness, and abundance. When we perceive ourselves in the light of our heart's awareness of abundant life then we will perceive the same life throughout our entire reality.

When life was guiding me to become heart-centered, life was not showing up the way I thought it would after sixteen years of seeking Truth. I realized that I could not get my ducks in a row before doing the work of the heart-centered habit. Intuition was guiding me into the realization that all of the limited experiences in my reality were past experiences of limitation that I had identified with, and now they were all here to be welcomed, received, and honored with the presence of love they had never received from my relationships to the world. It was time for me to stop searching, fixing, and trying to change, so I could begin to resonate the infinite love within my heart. It was time to welcome these limited experiences and offer them affirmations of love. I chose to stop identifying with them and become the voice that reminded them of their true infinite nature. Taking the time to slow down and embrace all the struggles in my reality was the most important work I have ever embarked upon in this lifetime. These struggles were screaming for my attention. I embraced them all with the heart-centered habit and my inner environment began to shift from fear to love.

As I began to awaken out of the illusion of right and wrong, I began to perceive many of the stories I researched in the Bible through a new light of awareness. In the Bible, it says that God placed a flashing sword at the entrance of the tree of life. Nobody could approach the tree of life without passing through the flashing sword. The sword was used as a symbol of spirit throughout the Bible. Spirit is the formless essence of pure Love that has no opposite. To eat from the tree of life, I had to bring the two sides of the knowledge of good and evil, right and wrong, good and bad, or positive and negative into one perspective of life. It took pure faith for me to align my voice with the spiritual essence of pure love that I sensed from within my heart, so that my mind could eat from the tree of life in the midst of chaos and struggle. Eating from the tree of life meant perceiving reality only from the heart-centered me, which senses only goodness, life, and divinity; instead of eating from the tree of knowledge of good and evil, which labeled and identified with every experience as positive or negative and right or wrong.

By my faith I began to claim that all my struggles were goodness. This doesn't mean that I sat on the couch with a magic wand, zapping all my struggles, and changed them into goodness. I still lived out my roles as mother, teacher, and housewife. I still woke up early in the morning to write, workout, and meditate. Then teach school, fold laundry, clean the house, clean dishes, cook meals, grocery shop, do yard work, parent children, chauffer children, budget bills, and so on. The heart-centered habit helped me to welcome, honor, and receive every circumstance, feeling, emotion, thought, and experience that I had ever considered to be wrong or bad, as pure goodness right in the middle of my normal every day routine.

The heart-centered habit is an exercise of pure faith, which allows every experience to speak its Truth. Of course, there were parts of me that hated the struggles and limitations I was going through. The heart-centered habit allowed these frustrated aspects of myself to feel exactly what was felt without judgment. Nobody can receive your true feelings about reality. However, your heart can and will. The heart-centered me is the only one that can receive all of your limited, unwanted, painful, frustrating, confusing, and uncomfortable experiences, and perceive them as Divine life. The whole world around you may be living by the head-centered me, and by faith you are called to pick up your sword of the spirit and claim all parts of reality as goodness and pure life! We can't wait for the world to become heart-centered first. You might be the first in your marriage, family, community, and other relationships to be faithful. This is your time! This is our time to be the faithful firsts that bring Heaven to Earth! By faith the heavenly love of our soul will flood the atmosphere of our mind before making contact with our bodies and then the world. Healing our world happens from the inside-out. Our being is the first place healing occurs.

"This unwanted experience is a gift."
You are welcome here.
You are enough!
How may I serve you?

"We are not our bodies, our possessions, or our careers, who we are is Divine Love and that is INFINITE."- Dr. Wayne Dyer

<u>Authentic Nature</u>

When I studied the book of Genesis, I found it interesting that God created all of existence and claimed it as "good." So where did evil, wrong, limited, or bad come from if everything was created good? If the source of all creation is good, and goodness is all that has ever existed, where is the source of evil? Well the rational mind has come up with an infinite number of answers to this question. The truth is, I don't know the answer. My whole life I searched for a solid standard of right and wrong and I never found a standard that was universal in every single life situation. There was always an exception to the rule in particular life situations. Therefore, I can only speak of my own direct experience.

When I identify with any experience that I feel from my external environment, I feel limited. When I plug my awareness into what I am experiencing from my relationships to the physical world, I feel a reality of right and wrong, positive and negative, or good and bad. If I use this external information as the source of who or what I am, a divided sense of self is formed in my head. I become a positive and negative identity. The positive "me" is always fighting with the negative "me," and vice versa. War, conflict, and dis-ease is happening within me between these two opposing realities. Identification with my external circumstances creates a false solid sense of self in my head that becomes a standard I use to judge the world around me. This is the head-centered me, which causes an inner experience of restlessness or suffering.

However, when I sense into the depth of my being, I can sense an unlimited source of wisdom, energy, life, love, and freedom. When I sense reality from within my heart beyond the surface of identification with my environment, I discover an authentic nature that resonates an infinite energy of goodness that has no opposite. God told Adam and Eve that if they ate from the tree of knowledge of good and evil they would die. When I identify with my environment or my relationships to this physical world I feel like I have been cut off from the inner source of infinite life that I sense from the depth of my being. The only way I could experience a sense of internal freedom was to merge these two opposing realities that I sensed from my physical connection to the physical world. I became a vessel that merged these two realities of right and wrong into one reality that has no opposite.

First, I began to welcome all past experiences that were judged as wrong, and by faith I became the voice of affirmation that reminded the "wrong" experience of its true infinite nature of pure love or pure life. The first step to being authentic requires a faith into the unknown. It is by your faith that you will be healed!

In the book of Revelations it says the tree of life is in the paradise of God. We have to remember how to use the flashing sword that is placed at the entrance to paradise, which is within our heart. Paradise represents a sense of place where there is no wrong, evil, bad, fear, or negativity. Paradise is a sense of place where there is only peace, love, life, abundance, freedom, fulfillment, and relaxation. We have been misusing the flashing sword by using it to slice reality into two opposing forces called good and evil. We have subconsciously placed our faith in the good and evil that we feel and see in the world. Instead of using the sword of the spirit to create division, we can use it to honor and respect all experiences into the knighthood of the Kingdom of Heaven. The sword of the spirit can be used to touch the shoulder of "good" and the shoulder of "wrong," bringing them together into a perfect union of one life. We are the power that has come into human form to honor every experience and welcome it into the heart of Heaven, where life with no opposite exists. This is our true authentic spiritual nature. We must go within, to sense our authentic nature and through the heart-centered habit reclaim every piece of ourselves that is lost in the rational mind's superficial knowledge of right and wrong. This is how we can remember to eat only from the tree of life, which fuels our mind and body with pure love, wisdom, peace, and eternal knowing.

"This uncomfortable experience is a gift."
You are welcome here.
You are enough!
How may I serve you?

Intuitive Mind

"The intuitive mind is a sacred gift and the rational mind is a faithful servant. We have created a society that honors the servant and has forgotten the gift."

–Albert Einstein

Our true spiritual nature doesn't have one name, form, or way it can be described. We have given it many names throughout history. The tree of life, spirit, God, Buddha nature, pure consciousness, Christ consciousness, chi, prana, life essence, Universe, universal consciousness, unified field of existence, pure unconditional love, agape, intuitive mind, heart-centered consciousness, and so on. We have created a society that believes in the name, labels, ways, conditions, beliefs, words, and stories that are rooted in our external environment. What if every name, label, appearance, emotion, feeling, thought, idea, and experience was pointing to the same infinite life that we are, which cannot be contained by one particular label, name, way, or definition? Our rational mind grows attached to the familiar ways that our external relationships define reality.

Imagine what would happen if you lived in every part of the world and allowed your rational mind the opportunity to observe the millions of different ways that life can be expressed, without viewing any one of them as the only one right way. Imagine the freedom you could experience through the eyes of so many different perspectives. This is the way your intuitive mind perceives reality, through an infinite lens. As a society we have all forgotten the gift of the intuitive mind by focusing more on the ways, names, and labels that the rational mind has believed to be the one right way to express reality. The rational mind fears expanding its perception of God, reality, or self because it will no longer fit in with its like-minded environment.

We all have an inner teacher that will guide our awareness into infinite realms of Divine wisdom. The Bible calls this inner guide the Holy Spirit. I call it the voice of your inner knowing or heart. It doesn't matter what name we give this inner sense that is calling awareness home. It doesn't matter the way we try to explain or describe it. What does matter is that you wake up to your connection to its infinite view of reality, because until you do, you will suffer. Within you lies an infinite perception of reality that perceives only life, love, God, divinity, right, and goodness throughout all experiences of reality. This perception comes from your true authentic nature that is a pure perception of reality, which is untainted by the mind. You can realize this now or when you physically die. This intuition is available to you right now. You can remember the intuitive mind by focusing on breathing in reality, or you can forget the intuitive mind by focusing on what you think about reality. The choice is yours.

Our external environment is evolving toward a tipping point in human consciousness. As diversity increases in our families, communities, schools, cities, states, and nations; our sense of reality becomes challenged. The head-centered habit perceives two options. One, it can fight diversity and defend its borders of belief. Two, it can escape through addictive habits to cover up the inner suffering it experiences because it is attached to old stagnant beliefs. Either choice will perpetuate division, separation, conflict, war, and addiction.

The heart-centered habit has one choice always, and that choice is love. This loving choice perceives diversity as a gift of expansion. You can allow your heart and mind to open and receive new realizations of your infinite nature of oneness. You can participate in the evolution and expansion of human consciousness, or you can try to hide, kick, scream, and fight against the flow of life. You can struggle to hold on to the past, or you can align with the present moment and receive the diversity or unique expressions of life that are surfacing from within every being on Earth.

The intuitive mind is our inner sense of the formless Truth that we are and as we welcome, embrace, and honor all of the diverse ways as being a part of our infinite nature, our head awakens and remembers the Truth: "I am infinite!" The heart-centered habit is a way to sense into the intuition that we are all one life essence that is pure goodness, which appears and expresses itself through infinite, unique, and diverse ways. You can be the first one to be heart-centered because the world may not change as fast you can change your perception of it. You are the only one that can resolve the belief that you are only right when someone else is wrong. You are the only one that can shift awareness toward sensing into the Truth, which is that we are all right, good, pure, and innocent. If there are 7.3 billion humans on this planet, then there are 7.3 billion unique right ways to express the formless Truth that we are. You are right for you and others are right for them. This is true freedom. The transformation from inner suffering to inner freedom can happen within you first, which changes the landscape of your inner life. Instead of feeling divided, chaotic, stressed, and diseased on the inside, you will feel clarity, peace, stillness, harmony, balance, and infinite life. Instead of looking to your environment, family, government, career, business, commerce to change your perceptions of reality for you, you can surrender the struggle and align with diversity and go with the flow.

There is an entire tree of knowledge of good and evil that is ready to be uprooted in your head or rational mind. Receiving the diverse, wrong, inconvenient, uncomfortable, unwanted, and painful ways as a gift helps to loosen these roots of wrong from your perception. The heart-centered habit is a path that can rewind time back to the very source of time itself, which is infinite, meaning it can be used to remove every root of knowledge of good and evil back into the formless space of creation, the heart, as if it never existed. Back to a time in your childhood where you still felt the essence of your abundant true nature. Back before you began to build a tree of knowledge that blocked your intuitive sense of the Truth. Back before you began forgetting your true nature of oneness, unity, abundant love, and abundant life. Now is the only time to remember, wake up, repent, and be enlightened.

"This painful experience is a gift."
You are welcome here.
You are enough!
How may I serve you?

Divine Will

Humanity has believed for so long that the personal will was the one in control of a person's destiny. However, there exists a will that is infinitely greater than your personal will, which is not based upon your personal knowledge or understanding of reality. I call this greater will, Divine will. It is a will that is responsible for the growth, expansion, and evolution of existence for all of eternity. Therefore, Divine will existed before you were physically born, and it will continue to exist when you physically die. Divine will has its own timing and momentum. When your choices are not aligned with Divine will, you function from a will that chooses to hold onto an experience from the past. Divine will continues to flow at its own rate and speed without any hindrances from the past. On the other hand, your personal will becomes a heavy weight that can hold you back from the infinite life that is occurring in the present moment. Therefore, you can remain stagnant and feel like you are being left in the dust. The good news is, you can choose to align with Divine will at any moment. The way to align is to release your borders of belief that are keeping you stuck in the past. The heart-centered habit guides your personal will to surrender its outdated beliefs in right and wrong, by claiming all you have considered to be wrong as Divine goodness.

Divine will is all-inclusive. Every expression, appearance, and experience is included in Divine will. However, your personal will can exclude some appearances, expressions, and experiences by labeling them as not okay, not good, or not right. Divine will is guiding your perception of reality to expand until you perceive all of life as one Divine and diverse view of Heaven. When you surrender your personal will, which thinks it knows what Truth is and what Truth is not, Divine will moves through you as you from a perspective of infinite life, love, and freedom and your life begins to flow with joy and ease. However, when you first embark upon the heart-centered journey by going within to sense the Truth of your being, you may bounce back and forth from your personal will to Divine will. This is the process of self-awareness, which is an awareness of what is going on within you below the surface. Self-awareness is necessary to create a new habit or a new way to respond to all thoughts, emotions, and relationships to the world. The heart-centered habit will train your subconscious mind to perceive all of reality as pure goodness, regardless of the way reality appears and feels.

This 22-day journey of remembrance is a period of Divine integration. The personal will is integrating into the expanded and infinite view of Divine will. During integration you become aware of what you sense is wrong, bad, or evil. Embracing and merging with all of the knowledge of wrong continues until the sense that something is wrong has dissipated. Therefore, continue being heart-centered until every root of the tree of knowledge of good and evil has been consumed in the fire of unity consciousness. Life is the healing hand that uses your relationships to the physical world to trigger all beliefs in wrong only so that you may become aware of the disharmony within you. As you merge with the disharmony within you, whether it feels like fear, anger, stress, struggle, lack, frustration, limitation, confusion, or hatred, your subconscious mind begins to integrate a new way to relate to these unwanted experiences. What your rational mind labeled as wrong or evil begins to shift into a perception of life, love, or divinity. The rational mind will awaken to the Truth that there is no wrong, no opposing force to the one essence of pure life when you choose to perceive wrong in a new light. When your perception shifts from perceiving wrong to perceiving only life, oneness with all life blooms spontaneously in your experience of reality.

The intuitive mind is another way of expressing reality through your internal sense of what lies below the surface of reality. As you remember your true infinite nature, intuition or information from within bubbles up to the surface. Perceiving limited experiences through the lens of this deeper reality allows awareness to remain heart-centered as the limited experiences fades away. Divine will cannot flow freely through you as you until the personal will has

93

collapsed back into its true infinite nature. Life flows in a continual harmonious flow. Anything within us that is not in harmony with the Divine will of unity consciousness will continually be brought into our experiences, so it may be reconciled and return to a harmonious state of balance. Therefore, be excited when life pushes your buttons because awakening, enlightenment, and the Kingdom of Heaven is at hand, my friend!

Divine will functions from the intuitive mind that brings information into the body from the formless space that is within you. Personal will functions from the rational mind that absorbs information from what it sees and feels from outside itself. Once the personal will has been acknowledged piece by piece and loved unconditionally, the division between the outer world and the inner world collapse. This is because what was dividing the space was your personal will or knowledge of good and evil. When the veil of your personal will is removed, the inner and outer world is experienced as one essence appearing in a diversity of life forms. The light that is shining through you is the same light shining through all. You don't have to get distracted by the stories, personal wills, or projections that still exist in the rational minds of other people to be able to feel the light that is shining through them. If you do, then you are recreating another distraction from sensing into Divine will. Remain steadfast, faithful, and continue to be the heart-centered habit, and the Truth shall set you free!

"This unfamiliar experience is a gift."
You are welcome here.
You are enough!
How may I serve you?

Reflection

What if uncomfortable, inconvenient, painful, and unwanted experiences were not showing up to prove your beliefs in wrong? Instead, what if they were showing up to be received as life, part of your infinite nature?

Reprogramming the Subconscious Mind

"Be still and know that the parts of you that have felt rejected, abandoned, and isolated is God, a part of your true authentic nature."

Practicing the heart-centered habit: (Example)

Have you ever felt rejected, abandoned, or isolated?

Welcome these experiences as a part of consciousness (You):

H- Honesty

"I fully feel the parts of me that have felt rejected, abandoned, and isolated."

A-Acknowledge, allow, ask

"I acknowledge that it is safe and okay to feel this limited experience. I embrace these feelings fully as they are because I know they are here to show me the way into my heart. As I embrace these feelings fully, I ask them to bring with them all of the past meanings, interpretations, beliefs, and judgments that I thought were true, but are not valid in this present moment, so that I may receive them as a gift, guide, and opening toward the infinite perception in my heart. I acknowledge their Divine role in

helping me expand awareness into the depths of infinite knowing."

Allow the uncomfortable experience to have a voice. Do not believe what it is saying, but instead be a loving presence that offers a deeper level of safety, comfort, and acknowledgment than the experience has ever received from you before, thereby being the practice of detachment, allowance, pure love, and space.

Ask: "Divine heart, I accept that I don't know how to receive uncomfortable, unwanted, inconvenient, or unfamiliar experiences as life. Therefore, I ask that you receive rejection, abandonment, and isolation as life for me. Welcome, embrace, honor, and validate these experiences for me, through me, as I am now, healing the inner division within me, so my perception can expand and align with the flow of infinite information." And so it is (Amen).

B- Breathe

Breathe in these feelings (*"I receive you as life"*) breathe out (*"You are free to be"*). Be one with the breath. *"The breath rejuvenates me."*

I-I love you!

Place your hands over your heart. Say, *"I love you! All is an expression of one Life. I validate this limited experience within me. It is an experience from my past that was not validated by my relationships to the world. Therefore, I choose to be the presence of love that provides this experience the resonation of love that it has never received. May I be all the affirmation that this limited experience needs to remember that it is an infinite expression of divinity, so that it may fully awaken from the illusion of limitation. I love you!"*

"I am abundant, wise, infinite, and free!"

T- Thank you

Thank the experience for helping you remember that you are an ever-expanding unique expression of the Truth. Thank the circumstance, story, or relationship that triggered these feelings in your body, so your entire being can awaken to your innocent nature of authentic freedom that can enjoy all experiences.

> *"Thank you for helping me to align and attune with my heart's ever-expanding unique expression of infinite wisdom and pure love. Thank you for helping me to remember the power of life that I am!"*

Intention: *(say aloud)*

"Today, I choose to eat from the Tree of Life. Thereby, remembering my authentic Divine nature, which allows me to function from intuition and surrender to Divine will."

Affirmation: *(say aloud)*

Say aloud throughout today:

> *"All ideas are sacred because I am sacred!"*

Day 4

Awakening

"Wisdom is knowing I am no-thing, love is knowing I am everything, and between the two my life moves."
-Nisargadatta Maharaj

Mirror Work

Say Aloud: (looking into your eyes in a mirror):
Good morning, infinite one. You are safe to feel. I always want to know how you are feeling. You are the soul-mate that I have been looking for my entire life. You matter and you are enough. You are worthy of being seen and heard. I see you and I am here to listen to you. There is a good reason you are here; you are Divine perfection. Today, I join you in celebrating your ever-expanding unique expression. I am open to receiving new information and new ways of being by choosing to receive all uncomfortable, unfamiliar, painful, inconvenient, and unwanted experiences as a Divine gift from you, my infinite heart. I love all of you! I really love all of you. (your name), I really love all of you. (Feel free to write your own love statement).

My first awakening experience was when I learned about the life of Jesus. I felt like I knew him intimately. I had finally found someone that resonated what I felt in my heart. He was the first of many who inspired me to live in the fulfillment of heart-centered consciousness. Thereafter, I found many other heart-centered beings throughout history, and that were living in the present world who lived from heart-centered consciousness.

Awakening to my true nature became my passion as I discovered there were others who lived fearlessly. At the same time, life experiences had ushered me into a tight space, where I could no longer live from the outside-in. I got to a place where I couldn't live the same way anymore because it caused me so much suffering, pain, and limitation. I found myself stuck in circumstances that I could no longer change. Finally I had nowhere to go, apart from inside, where intuition grew and formed a voice to rescue the disgraced parts of myself that were left lingering in the rational mind. Intuition had been there throughout my life but I was too distracted by the world around me to notice it on the inside. Finally after forty years of awakening experiences to my true nature, my spiritual nature and my physical nature were starting to no longer feel separate. They were merging together and integrating into one whole being that breathes, moves, and speaks in unison.

In my experience, the heart-centered habit guided my rational mind to awaken from all the accumulated knowledge about Truth, which created many branches of thinking or stories about right and wrong. I woke up from who I thought I was, which were just labels and judgments that my rational mind absorbed like a sponge through my relationships to the outer world. The memory of the head-centered me began to fade as I embraced every emotion that I had judged as wrong. My rational mind began to relax because it no longer needed to stay on high alert to protect me from wrong, bad, or evil forces. Whether somebody treated me unkindly or mean, I received it as life and loved them with my entire being. My rational mind no longer needed to judge every experience as being right or wrong, or good or bad. Instead it was allowed to remain open, awake, and relax into the flow of life and pure love.

I realized that my head had woken up out of the play of thinking myself into existence. My rational mind remembered its true nature that has only one name, label, or definition: pure love. It is just pure, real, infinite, spacious, and empty beingness. It no longer needed to fill itself with the information or knowledge that the exterior world was projecting as their personal Truth. It was free to love, free to be regardless of it being well-received or rejected by the world. It remembered to stop looking for the Truth in what it has experienced from the world. It remembered to focus on feeling and breathing everything in first, then receiving intuition in what the Truth is from within, then resting in the intuitive sense of the Truth. I realized that every moment was a moment of awakening!

"This unwanted experience is a gift."
You are welcome here.
You are enough!
How may I serve you?

Power of the Inner Yes

We learned from our environment what was okay or safe and what was not. What was deemed as okay and safe became our familiar setting. We learned all the ways we should be to fit into the standards of success in our society. This set us up to deny and repress certain experiences of reality that appear and feel unfamiliar. All of the unfamiliar ways we are perceived as by others is our true unique nature. What our rational mind considers to be uncomfortable or unwanted due to our past conditioning becomes the way we filter reality, which means we learn to filter out our true unique expression of life. Some aspects of reality are allowed in while others are not. Unconsciously, we deny our true self. All experiences of no that we haven't taken into our heart and transformed into a yes become dense repressed emotions, which resonate no. When we say no to an experience we suffer because our mind becomes narrow, which closes it off to sensing and receiving the pure infinite nature of love that we truly are. The head-centered me says, "I need this experience to appear and feel different than it is. Therefore, I oppose it and do not receive it as the goodness I am." This is how we create insecurities within ourselves. We either fight or deny the experience, which never leaves us because it is an inner experience of division between our head and heart. Until the experience is perceived through the heart, it will be viewed as an enemy, which victimizes us repeatedly. The enemy that we sense is the love we truly are!

One way to integrate the awakening of heart-centered consciousness is to say an inner yes to all experiences. Experience is happening within us. If we feel pain or anger, it is only because it was already within us to begin with. Our relationships can trigger these repressed emotions that we fight or deny within ourselves. Therefore, our relationships are not to blame. Instead, our relationships are used to bring everything into the light, so we may become one with it by saying yes and changing the quality of our relationship with the experiences we continually cast out of Heaven. Yes anger, you are welcome here. Anger, you are enough for me. How may I serve you? All experiences are waiting to be welcomed, honored, validated, and received as a part of life. All experiences want to be seen and heard. Therefore, be the space to let them speak and feel them fully. This is how we can serve all of our experiences and awaken to our true infinite nature of pure love.

"This uncomfortable experience is a gift."
You are welcome here.
You are enough!
How may I serve you?

This doesn't mean saying yes to everything that the world asks of us. I am not talking about being a 'yes' man or woman like the character Jim Carrey played in the movie, Yes Man. He said yes to everything that was asked by the world around him. I am referring to an internal 'yes' to receiving and allowing the moment to be exactly as it is, especially what is arising within us. It means welcoming every experience as a Divine gift because it is enough as it is and that we are here to serve, honor, and respect it as a beautiful part of life. We no longer perceive separation. Instead, nothing but Holy matrimony with all of life.

The inner yes feels like a crucifixion to the ego or head-centered me. Jesus said, "Whoever wants to be a disciple must deny themselves and take up their cross daily and follow me." Jesus did not run from sin, misperception, evil, or wrong. He walked straight toward suffering, pain, and limitation. Even the Apostle Paul spoke about having a thorn in his side that he asked God to remove, but God never removed it and Paul learned to embrace the pain of that thorn. What is the cross that you are presently here to say an inner yes to and welcome into the loving embrace of your heart-centered nature? What is the annoying, uncomfortable, unwanted, painful, or inconvenient thorn in your side? What part(s) of your life feels painful, limited, unwanted, negative, inconvenient, or uncomfortable? Maybe your health is failing or you have a dis-ease in your body? Maybe you are in conflict in a relationship? Maybe you are in debt up to your ears and you don't know how you will financially survive? Maybe you are miserable in your job? Maybe you are longing for a lover? Maybe you lost your job? Maybe you are being wrongly accused for something you didn't do? Maybe you have lost a loved one who you needed? Maybe nothing in your life is going the way you want? Maybe you are alone, lost, frustrated, and confused? Maybe you long connection with other people, but feel like you don't fit in this world? Maybe you are battling an addiction that you just can't kick?

Whatever unwanted, inconvenient, painful, uncomfortable, and unfamiliar experiences you are experiencing in your life, you have a choice. You can be head-centered toward these uncomfortable experiences, which means you will struggle to fight, change, or escape them. Or you can be heart-centered and choose to realize the greater aspect of yourself, which is Divine, and welcome, embrace, love, and deeply breathe them into your entire being. If you choose to be head-centered you will continue to suffer. However, if you choose to be heart-centered, you will experience a peace and freedom that has been within you all along. The latter choice gives you the opportunity to experience a more fulfilling path because you will awaken more into the realization of your infinite self. Choosing to be the heart-centered habit allows awareness to harmonize with all of life, thereby healing all misperceptions in the mind, which are based upon beliefs in wrong, evil, and bad. This is how we can bring our authentic heavenly vibration of pure love and manifest it on Earth. In order to heal the Earth of war, conflict, separation, division, and limitation, we have to heal the root, which is the misperceptions of wrong, evil, and bad within our own personal experiences of reality.

The inner "yes" begins the integration of the heart-centered habit, which is a path that guides every no experience into heart-centered consciousness. Once we say an inner yes to an unwanted, uncomfortable, unfamiliar, or inconvenient experience, we can receive the experience through being honest. Confess exactly what we feel. Acknowledging the uncomfortable experience as a gift, transforms the no experience into a yes experience because we are opening our mind to allow the experience to flow through the heart; instead of needing it to appear different, creating superficial reasons as to "why" it has appeared, and opposing it through denial or blame. The head-centered me is the gatekeeper to the heart. Therefore, it is in charge of letting experiences in or choosing to fight or flee the experience. The fight or flee option is the result of the head saying no to an experience, which makes us suffer. Letting the experience in is the inner yes experience. Reminding the head-centered me that it is good and okay to let all experiences in, regardless of the way they feel or appear, is necessary because the world teaches us the fight or flee option. When the head chooses to say an inner yes, our heart-centered nature receives all experiences exactly as they are and tunes them into their true Divine nature of goodness. We experience this within our being as relaxation, spaciousness, peace, joy, freedom, fulfillment, abundance, patience, self-control, pure love, faith, gentleness, and goodness. This is how we can choose our quality of experience. If we choose to fight or flee an experience by saying no to it, then we suffer. If we choose to say an inner yes to all experiences, our heart transforms the quality of the experience into a frequency of abundant energy. The choice is up to you. What will you choose?

The heart-centered habit allows us to change our relationship with reality into a relationship that resonates one of an ally, best friend, and loving parent. When we choose to breathe in the experience of our suffering, instead of thinking about how we wish the experience was different, we allow the experience to be free. And then, it no longer places needs or demands on reality to appear and feel a certain way. Saying 'I love you' toward the experience is a celebration of welcoming home every expression of limitation and separation into Heaven, which was once sensed in our body as not a part of the one true nature of goodness. Gratitude is the sense of our rational minds opening and receiving clarity, peace, and relaxation. The inner yes is the first shift in awareness that guides all experiences to being received through the heart-centered habit, allowing the rational mind to relax, so every experience may be welcomed into the heart. The more we practice the inner yes toward everything that arises within us, the more we will program our subconscious mind to receiving every experience as a gift of Divine life. Our subconscious mind will remember to relax by saying an inner yes to all experiences, and then a sense of safety will return to our experience of reality. Our nervous system, which was once over-stimulated, will return to harmony, balance, and peace.

We may say no to something that is asked of us, but inwardly the rational mind says yes to the experience of disappointment, displeasure, and rejection that our no may have triggered as a response from others. When our authentic nature of Truth within our heart guides our decisions through an intuitive knowing, our rational minds can be prepared to allow and accept any type of reaction from our relationships to the world. When we say an inner yes to all experiences of emotions, thoughts, ideas, images, and memories that are happening within us, and respond as the heart-centered habit, we will return to the innocence of our authentic voice. Now is the time to say yes to your authentic voice of pure Divine love!

"This uncomfortable experience is a gift."
You are welcome here.
You are enough!
How may I serve you?

This Moment is a Gift

This moment is a precious gift because it offers everything you need to remember, repent, and awaken. Repentance means to turn your awareness 180 degrees. The ego is the head-centered me that directs awareness outward. EGO stands for Energy (awareness) Going Out. Therefore, repentance means to be heart-centered or direct awareness inward until your awareness stays seated in the heart and no longer drifts out away from its connection to Divine wisdom. Everything that is arising within you in the moment is a gift of enlightenment. You were born to be the angel of light that perceives all inner experiences as the light you are. The way you choose to perceive what you are experiencing within you becomes the quality of your experience with it. You chose to come here to move toward that which humans have considered negative, dark, painful, and unwanted throughout history. You chose to bring the light of consciousness into human consciousness, which heals all perceptions of evil and transmutes them into the higher vibration of Divine light. This is how we become vessels of bringing the light or abundant energy of Heaven to Earth. All of existence has been waiting to be seen, welcomed, embraced, and loved as the light of divinity.

The beliefs in wrong, negative thoughts, stories of victimhood, uncomfortable emotions, and circumstances of suffering are lingering in your experience waiting for you to open them because they are gifts of life returning to your sense of self, which expands your perception of reality. This expansion of your perception shifts your self-awareness from one of believing that you are a limited separate being into one of knowing that you are an infinite being of divinity, one with all of existence.

First, we have to be willing to acknowledge the presence of negativity, evil, wrong, and bad within our experience of reality. This requires us to stop looking at our circumstances and feel inside to see what inner experiences have been triggered by the stories of blame in our head. The limited feelings, stories, ideas, thoughts, memories, and emotions you discover are the gifts that life is offering you. These gifts give you an opportunity to remember the heart-centered me and awaken out of the head-centered me. This allows us to step into more empowerment by becoming the exercise, practice, or habit of Divine power, which receives everything as a gift. The heart-centered habit opens these gifts by removing the wrapping or label of "no" "wrong" "bad" or "unwanted." Once these gifts are fully opened we discover lost treasure; a quality of freedom and fulfillment that we remember from our childhood or innocence. These qualities include peace, pure love, lightness, abundant energy, joy, laughter, stillness, patience, child-like mind, simplicity, harmony, fearlessness, inner strength, Truth and well-being. Our body and mind fills with more light as we open each gift. Every experience is a gift of enlightenment, empowerment, and spiritual remembrance.

The relationships that trigger uncomfortable emotions within us are gifts too. Indirectly they are way showers. They show us what has yet to be resolved within us, and what ways of being we have unconsciously labeled as wrong, bad, or evil. They also show us what we continually say "no" to receiving as a part of divinity. Our so-called "enemies" are a gift because they show us all of our unconscious ways that are waiting to be clothed in consciousness or pure love. Everything is here to help us awaken and become the pure consciousness of spirit as a unique physical form, expression, or way of being.

Allow the people who bug you the most to be the gift they were sent in your life to be. Allow them to show you what part of the dream of separation you are ready to awaken from by receiving them as an expression of pure love and giving them your presence of goodness. It is easy to be good to others when they are good to you. However, what an exciting opportunity to offer your goodness towards someone who has forgotten their pure loving nature. Recently, my son was blaming me for something he felt wrong about. I could tell he was waiting for me to fight back. Instead, I looked at him and said, "You are right, I have failed you!" I wasn't identifying with doing something wrong by saying this. Rather, I was willing to surrender to his ideas in that moment, so he could remember his natural state of surrender. He was lost in a tug of war in his head and I chose not to add any extra resistance to the stories of right and wrong in his head. I am willing to be judged as wrong, bad, and evil because I know that underneath these perceptions is a heart of innocence. He was caught so off guard that he immediately sank right back into his heart and gave me a huge hug. Gratitude is the acknowledgement that every moment is a gift that is here for you, not against you. This was an opportunity to respond in a heart-centered way, which immediately guided my son back into his heart. It was as much a gift for me as it was for my son. Everything that we perceive as an attack is an opportunity to shine brighter than ever. This is how we awaken from the old habit of believing in darkness and into the presence of Divine Light that we truly are!

> *"This painful experience is a gift."*
> You are welcome here.
> You are enough!
> How may I serve you?

All is One

The systems in our society have taught us to imagine a sense of self in our heads, but this is false because it is based upon all of the shoulds and shouldn'ts we have accumulated from society, which don't resonate with what we feel is true in our heart. This false sense of self or ego perceives itself as separate from everything because it feels separate from its Divine heart-centered nature, which opposes nothing. The head-centered sense believes it is separate from aspects of reality but one with other aspects of reality. This sense of separation does not resonate the truth of reality because all of reality is connected by a unified field of energy. On the other hand, our heart- centered nature resonates the Truth because it senses unity with everything.

This sense of inner opposition between our head and heart creates a sense that we are missing something, which we call fear. This fear feels like a void in our life, so we hoard experiences, emotions, thoughts, beliefs, and emotions that make us feel semi-connected to one another. We fill the inner sense of void with food, relationships, money, possessions, success, achievements, knowledge, and this void creates a sense of neediness. We need to feel connected to something or someone. It is a semi-connection because we are connecting with our like thoughts about reality, but we are not connecting with one another through our heart, which is the direct connection to everything. This semi-connection is based upon being like-minded, having similar experiences and values. Creating communities, groups, and friendships that were based upon having like-minds was much easier before the advancements in technology that have been invented over the past few decades. Presently, diversity is sensed everywhere. Our diverse ways of being are seen on reality television shows, the news, social media, the internet, in our neighborhoods, schools, businesses, and families. We no longer live in an age where diversity is able to be pushed aside. Diversification is a gift to our society. The more diversified we become as a society, the more opportunities we have to awaken out of our accumulated knowledge of right and wrong (like-mindedness). This is because we can see that everybody has their own right and wrong, which is rooted in their past experiences. Experiencing such diversity can awaken the rational mind out of its daydream of believing our knowledge about Truth. If Truth is one body of knowledge, then how can there be so many different truths? Because Truth is what we are and what we are is beyond concepts and thoughts about "who" we are. Truth is our formless nature, and that can only be sensed beyond the appearances of mind.

Most people are experiencing an earthquake to their false foundation of self, which is being shaken by diversity. This is an amazing opportunity for all of us to become heart-centered, which is our eternal connection to oneness. When we receive the gifts of the self that are held hostage by our rational minds, we experience that everything is one. All emotions are the light of divinity. All thoughts are the light of divinity. All circumstances are the light of divinity. Imagine lying on a hilltop far away from the city lights at night and the sky is clear. As you gaze into the sky, you feel in awe of the expanse of the night sky that is filled with trillions of stars. You think, "Wow, what a heavenly view!" This is similar to what the view of heart-centered consciousness feels like when thoughts, emotions, feelings, ideas, and beliefs appear in the mind. All thoughts, experiences, and feelings are the light of divinity, a heavenly view of expressions.

If you find yourself being extremely judgmental toward someone in your family, an event in the news, a person on a reality show, a circumstance that won't go away, then this is your opportunity to bring all those judgments, negative emotions, and painful feelings into the heart-centered habit. The heart-centered habit feels like nothingness on the inside, but it feels like everything when looking into the world. Now is your opportunity to wake up to the wisdom that all is one by being the inner "yes' to all experiences by receiving them as a gift.

"This unfamiliar experience is a gift."
You are welcome here.
You are enough!
How may I serve you?

Reflection

What if everything you considered to be against you was for your benefit? What if every unwanted change was a catalyst to expand your perception of reality into the remembrance of your true infinite nature?

Reprogramming the Subconscious Mind

"Be still and know that judgment, criticism, and skepticism is God, a part of your true authentic nature."

Practicing the heart-centered habit: (Example)

Have you ever felt judgmental, critical, or skeptical?

Welcome these experiences as a part of consciousness (You):

H- Honesty

"I fully feel the parts of me that have felt judgmental, critical, and skeptical."

A-Acknowledge, allow, ask

"I acknowledge that it is safe and okay to feel this limited experience. I embrace these feelings fully as they are because I know they are here to show me the way into my heart. As I embrace these feelings fully, I ask them to bring with them all of the past meanings, interpretations, beliefs, and judgments that I thought were true, but are not valid in this present moment, so that I may receive them as a gift, guide, and opening toward the infinite perception in my heart. I acknowledge their Divine role in helping me expand awareness into the depths of infinite knowing."

Allow the uncomfortable experience to have a voice. Do not believe what it is saying, but instead be a loving presence that offers a deeper level of safety, comfort, and acknowledgment than the experience has ever received from you before. In this way, you will practice detachment, allowance, pure love, and space.

Ask: "Divine heart, I accept that I don't know how to awaken from the illusion of wrong. Therefore, I ask that you wake me up out of the illusion that perceives through the limited lens of judgment, criticism, and skepticism. Welcome, embrace, honor, and validate these experiences for me, through me, as I am now, healing the inner division within me, so my perception can expand and align with the flow of infinite information." And so it is (Amen).

B- Breathe

Breathe in these feelings (*"I receive you as life"*) breathe out (*"You are free to be"*). Be one with the breath. *"The breath is spirit in action."*

I-I love you!

Place your hands over your heart. Say, *"I love you! All is an expression of one life. I validate this limited experience within me. It is an experience from my past that was not validated by my relationships to the world. Therefore, I choose to be the presence of love that provides this experience the resonation of love it has never received. May I be all the affirmation this limited experience needs to remember that it is an infinite expression of divinity, so it may fully awaken from the illusion of limitation. I love you!"*

"I am abundant, wise, infinite, and free!"

T- Thank you

Thank the experience for helping you remember that you are an ever-expanding unique expression of the Truth. Thank the circumstance, story, or relationship that triggered these feelings in your body, so your entire being could awaken to your innocent nature of authentic freedom that can enjoy all experiences.

> *"Thank you for helping me to align and attune with my heart's ever-expanding unique expression of infinite wisdom and pure love! Thank you for helping me to remember the power of life that I am!"*

Intention: *(say aloud)*

"Today, I choose to awaken from being head-centered by saying an inner yes to all experiences, receiving every moment as a gift and remembering that all is one essence appearing as many."

Affirmation: *(say aloud)*

Say aloud throughout today:

"The mind is free because I am free!"

Day 5

Breath of Life

"When you move slower than the world, and breathe more deeply than the world, you awaken a consciousness beyond any world."   - -Matt Kahn

Mirror Work

Say Aloud: (looking into your eyes in a mirror):
Good morning, infinite one. You are safe to feel. I always want to know how you are feeling. You are the soul-mate that I have been looking for my entire life. You matter and you are enough. You are worthy of being seen and heard. I see you and I am here to listen to you. There is a good reason you are here; you are Divine perfection. Today, I join you in celebrating your ever-expanding unique expression. I am open to receiving new information and new ways of being by choosing to receive all uncomfortable, unfamiliar, painful, inconvenient, and unwanted experiences as a Divine gift from you, my infinite heart. I love all of you! I really love all of you. (your name), I really love all of you. (Feel free to write your own love statement).

The word Spirit comes from the Greek word "pneuma," which means breath. When I discovered this meaning for breath, I began to relate to the breath in a brand new way. I wondered what controls my breath because I do not have to think about breathing in order to breathe. It happens naturally and effortlessly, like the waves of the ocean or the planets spinning in the Universe. I realized that when I focused awareness on

115

the natural ebb and flow of the breath, I was not lost in the stories in my head. In those moments when I would feel limited, I began to focus on the breath, which became a direct awareness into the deeper awareness of spirit.

The breath became my best friend that accompanied me into uncomfortable feelings. Instead of ignoring or running away from my feelings, I focused on the breath, which guided me into a full experience of everything I was used to denying. Therefore, I began to focus on breathing instead of thinking during moments of suffering to see what I felt. For instance, when I experienced an uncomfortable, inconvenient, or unwanted event I would immediately feel a tightness in my body. My rational mind felt confused because it did not have an explanation for this uncomfortable circumstance. I realized the rational mind has been conditioned to be extremely uncomfortable with confusion or "I don't know why" due to the pressures of a society that functions on the need to know, understand, and manufacture answers. Confusion is a death threat to the rational mind because in the past it was punished for not knowing the answer. Therefore, in moments of confusion it works in high drive to analyze the situation and create correlations to "why" I was experiencing this unwanted situation, manufacturing answers, stories, and judgments that cloud my perception of reality. Instead of thinking about the circumstance, I chose to focus on my breath. I took long, deep conscious breaths and imagined myself becoming one with my breath. I allowed the breath to guide my awareness into the restricted feelings, emotions, thoughts, and parts of my body. Instead of repressing this restricted sense of limitation in my inner experience, I followed the breath that entered straight into the center of them. As I practiced focusing on my breath during moments when I felt tense, I experienced a relaxation that was not dependent upon my circumstances. This was an amazing discovery!

The breath loves to enter tight spaces and expand it with more life. The breath is a simple way to connect with our authentic spiritual nature. Follow the breath and your awareness will be guided on a journey of healing, expansion, and freedom. During moments of suffering, you too can discover this new way of being; breathing, which guides awareness into a stillness that is way beyond the chaos of thinking. Serenity and peace are always one conscious breath away, regardless of your circumstances. I thought discovering inner peace was way more difficult than conscious breathing. The way was right under my nose (literally) the whole time.

I began to realize that my soul or essence is the breath, and the breath is harmonious and balanced. It breathes in and receives everything in the same way as it graciously lets go of every experience it receives and sets it free. The breath cleanses the body and mind, and brings healing into areas that feel closed and tight. I realized that when I became one with the breath I welcomed all experiences into my core without the need to attach to it or identify with it. The breath is a perfect example of how our soul enjoys playing with all experiences.

I also realized that when I reacted to reality by thinking about it, I breathed in shallow patterns. I realized that we label these shallow breathing patterns as anger, rage, frustration, and hatred because shallow breathing gives our body a limited sensation. These emotions are symptoms to not breathing in a natural slow and deep pattern. When we breathe shallowly our body receives a signal that life (air) is being restricted or limited in some way, which makes it feel like it is approaching death. Therefore, these "negative emotions" are sirens trying to signal us to breathe deeper and slower.

When we become aware of being in the middle of reacting to reality in a head-centered, over-thinking, over-analyzing way, we can shift awareness from thinking to breathing. This will open all restricted or "negative" feelings into a more relaxed state of being. All emotions, feelings, and thoughts are made up of the breath. It is as if they are the liquid form of the formless breath. Just like water can evaporate into thin air, emotions, thoughts, and feelings can also evaporate into their natural essence of the breath.

We unconsciously learn our breathing patterns from our environment, family, culture, and relationships to the world. We learned to breathe shallowly during certain types of experiences, which become labeled as wrong or bad. However, maybe the circumstance or experience isn't wrong or bad. Maybe we simply *feel* wrong or bad because we are breathing shallowly? Our subconscious mind controls our breathing. When we are not breathing deeply we are not in the present moment. Instead we are in our head and thinking about the experience, so we don't have to fully feel the experience. However, we can reprogram the subconscious mind to breathe deeply in every moment of reality and receive the life of every moment regardless of the way it is appearing, remaining present within every experience and feeling it exactly as it is. We don't have to hold our breath anymore. We can be the heart-centered habit that meets every moment with open arms, and receives it fully as it is, releasing it back into the world. What could you experience if you breathed deeply through every uncomfortable, unwanted, unfamiliar, painful, or inconvenient experience? Experiment for yourself and find out.

"The voice of your soul is breath."

-Yogi Bhajan

"This unwanted experience is a gift."
You are welcome here.
You are enough!
How may I serve you?

The Middle Way

There is a middle path which is spoken about in many spiritual traditions. In Buddhism it is called the Middle Way, which points to a way of being that transcends and reconciles the extremes of opposing views. Aristotle called this way the "golden mean,"- "every virtue is a mean between two extremes, each of which is a vice." The middle way is great way in *the Tao Te Ching*. The *Tao Te Ching* is a collection of 81 verses authored by the Chinese prophet Lao-tzu. The words Tao Te Ching translate to "living and applying the Great Way." Every verse points to this natural way of being.

25th Verse

There is something formlessly created
Born before heaven and earth
So silent! So ethereal!
Independent and changeless
Circulating and ceaseless
It can be regarded as the mother of the world

I do not know its name
Identifying it, I call it "Tao" (The Great Way)
Forced to describe it, I call it great
Great means passing
Passing means receding
Receding means returning
Therefore the Tao is Great
Heaven is great
Earth is great

The sovereign is also great
There are four greats in the universe
And the sovereign occupies one of them
Humans follow the laws of Earth
Earth follows the laws of Heaven
Heaven follows the laws of Tao
Tao follows the laws of nature

The middle way is a path of awakening to the laws of nature or Divine will. Awakening to our true authentic formless nature is a path, habit, or natural way of being. This path is also spoken about in Christianity.

Jesus described the path as a narrow path. "You can enter God's kingdom only through the narrow gate. For wide is the gate and broad is the road that leads to destruction and many enter through it. But small is the gate and narrow the road that leads to life, and only a few find it." Matthew 7:13-14.

Why is the gate narrow to enter the kingdom of heaven that is within you? Because it is easier for a camel to pass through the eye of a needle, than for a person full of knowledge to enter the Kingdom of Heaven. Your knowledge of good and evil will not guide you into the Kingdom of Heaven or heart-centered consciousness. Instead, as we have experienced as a society, this head-centered way of being guides us into destruction because our knowledge of good and evil does not follow the laws of Heaven or nature. There is only one law and that law is life or pure love. All is life. All is Divine. When you realize that you are the love and life that you have been seeking for in the world, you will have made a 180-degree turn and entered through the eye of the needle. You can't take your knowledge of God, self, reality, or conditional love with you. You can't enter into the realization of your authentic heavenly nature with a single possession or relationship. You can only enter alone. It's just the head-centered me and the heart-centered me. You can only enter as the essence of life and love that you truly are. This law of Pure Love is the Great way, middle path, and narrow path that leads to the Kingdom of Heaven, freedom, fulfillment, joy, peace, harmony, balance, and pure love. This middle path is the holy marriage between your head and your heart.

The wide path is the path of head-centered consciousness, which relies upon our personal knowledge of good and evil. The majority of humanity has been taught to walk the wide path of accumulating and comparing personal knowledge. Thoughts are like a coin. They have two sides; heads and tales. A positive thought has an equal negative thought attached to it. We believe we are the positive and negative thoughts that linger in our heads. We have all been conditioned to think, think, think, think, and as a result we place so much value on thinking. We live in a way where we believe that thinking is the greatest quality we have as a human being. However, focusing too much on what we think about has caused war, conflict, suffering, and struggle because we believe in our dualistic thoughts. We learn to identify with a particular set of thoughts, which excludes the vastness of what we really are!

Thoughts allow us to play out a life where weexperience unity through the appearances of separation, division, duality, polarity, and opposition. Thoughts are creations of God; they are not the voice of God. God is formless, so if God speaks it is through the formless breath. Every word, thought, action, body, and appearance is formed by the breath and collapses back into the breath. The acknowledgement that you don't know why you think what you think, or feel what you feel, or know anything at all, allows awareness to sink out of the head and into the breath, which flows through your entire being. The breath becomes the doorway to being the middle way, narrow path, golden mean, present moment, path of neutrality, singularity, and heart-centered habit. Few find this way of being because we search for it through the perception of the rational mind "thinking." The truth of our being is formless and the rational mind can only sense forms, concepts, knowledge, and appearances. Therefore, it always misinterprets the truth of our being as something concrete, solid, and known. The truth of our being is so vast and infinite it cannot fit into any one container of knowledge, belief, thought, or perception. Inner knowing infinitely flows from the truth of our being. It is fluid and flows in and out of different containers. Therefore, when we attach to the knowing and store it as knowledge in our rational minds, we impede the flow or infinite expression of the truth. The breath reminds us to fill our being with intuitive knowings of the truth and then let them go. As we take the narrow path and choose to breathe in the moment, instead of thinking about the moment, we connect to the intuitive flow of existence. Thinking creates two paths or extremes: right path and wrong path. Breathing is the one path between the two extremes. Breathing is the middle way; a natural way of being that allows life to remain free.

"Fear is excitement without breath."
-Robert Heller

"This uncomfortable experience is a gift."
You are welcome here.
You are enough!
How may I serve you?

Release Control

Many spiritual traditions point to the natural way of being; a way that remains in a constant state of surrender, detachment, allowance, acceptance, and faith. The human species has unconsciously manufactured an unnatural way of being, which causes suffering, conflict, division, and limitation. It is unnatural because we are taught to push and pull at reality, instead of receiving and accepting it as a part of eternal life just the way it is. We believe we are the ones in control of judging the way reality should be. Therefore, at a young age we forget our true formless spiritual nature, which merges and is in a harmonious flow with reality. Our intuitive mind isn't against any part of reality. Rather than our rational mind being in alignment with the intuitive mind, it feels separate from reality, thereby cutting itself off from the natural consciousness that sustains the entire Universe. Unconsciously we cut our awareness off from the pure consciousness that flows through all of existence. We breathe in a shallow way because we think we need to control reality, and if it doesn't appear the way we think it should our breathing becomes compromised and limited, allowing the rational mind to control our breathing and dictate what we can receive and what we cannot receive. Our patterns of breathing and receiving become hindered and unnatural.

We believe that the accumulated knowledge of good and evil is the truth to our being. This knowledge that we have accumulated from our environment clutters the rational mind and fills our head with incessant noise. Divine wisdom or infinite knowing is within us, but we can't sense this deeper knowing over the noise in our head. Therefore, we repeat the same information of good and evil over and over again. Our life becomes static and we repeat the same challenges throughout our entire life. Sin or the misperception of reality is an unconscious way of being, where we restrict our breathing and feel limited. The rational mind can release control by letting go of old outworn beliefs or knowledge of right and wrong by breathing deeply. By aligning with the breath, the breath does the releasing for us. Any part of our self that needs healed or unraveled, the breath will automatically and miraculously do it for us. We simply have to remember to align awareness with the breath, instead of thinking. The only remembrance necessary is to be with the breath, which awakens consciousness out of all limited forms.

We do not have to hold onto knowledge and live a shallow life; we can let it flow in and out without grasping it as the one way of truth. We breathe shallow because we think we must hold onto certain knowledge. This attachment restricts our natural breathing, which limits our sense of our abundant nature. We don't have to remember any knowledge, as the breath has access to the library of infinite wisdom, which exists at the core of our being. The breath will access all wisdom in the moment we need it. We no longer need to store knowledge in the rational mind. The rational mind needs to be free to align with the free spacious nature of the breath. Therefore, allow the breath to release all stored knowledge. The breath is our bridge between Heaven and Earth. Allow it to function in a heavenly way here on Earth through you as you!

There is a pure consciousness that controls nature and the wellbeing of existence that is far beyond our knowledge of right and wrong. The rational mind must undergo a season of remembering its direct connection to Divine consciousness by aligning with simplicity; the breath. It has forgotten. Infinite knowing within our heart awaits beyond the limited knowledge that is contained in our head. We simply have to release this limited knowledge to the breath and receive access to an infinite knowing of Divine wisdom. Divine wisdom is a like a never-ending river that carries you through life with ease and joy. The heart-centered habit is a way or practice that awakens the rational mind out of the unconscious dream, and remember, it is not separate, but rather a part of the magical splendor of life. Just breathe!

"This painful experience is a gift."
You are welcome here.
You are enough!
How may I serve you?

Human Being

"I am the way, the truth, and the light."

– Jesus

The unconscious way of living is a belief that separates our physical nature from our spiritual nature. Hence, our foundational of belief perceives our spiritual nature as good or right and our physical nature as bad or wrong. Our physical nature is a creation of our spiritual essence. Therefore, it is one, not separate. It is this unconscious belief that our physical bodies are separate from our spiritual essence that is the root of all human suffering.

Growing up in the Christian church, I was taught that Jesus was the way, the Truth, and the light. I was taught to take what was written in the Bible as literal in meaning. Therefore, I used to believe that Jesus was literally saying that He was the only way to salvation. Christian evangelism is rooted in this literal belief. Evangelists go out into the world preaching to the masses to believe in the life of Jesus and that He died for their sins and they would be saved. I know this because I was one of them. I evangelized for a few years before I realized Jesus was pointing to a way of being. This way of being can be exemplified but not taught. That is why He said that we are ever hearing but never perceiving.

When I attended the Christian church, I did not perceive what He was saying when He said, "I am the way, the Truth, and the light." However, when I began to study the Bible for myself and open my mind to other spiritual teachings, I awoke out of the modern day Christian belief that God is separate from humanity. I realized that Jesus was saying that the "I am" is the way of our spiritual nature. I realized the bridge to our spiritual beingness is present in every experience of the human condition. Sadness is the way, the Truth, and the light. Anger is the way, the Truth, and the light. Depression is the way, the Truth, and the light. There is not a single human experience that isn't the way, the Truth, and the light because at the core of every experience is the unified field of existence. What is the unified field of existence? It is a field of formless infinite energy that connects all of existence and is the source, which creates all of existence. Humanity is connected by the breath, which is an invisible formless energy that supplies life here on Earth. Therefore, the breath is an example of a unified field that connects all of humanity, nature, and life on Earth.

Every aspect of your physical nature is connected to your spiritual nature. It has never been separate. We have just held onto a belief that it was separate. Our experience is dictated by the way we perceive. If we perceive reality through a lens of separation, then we experience separation. Therefore, we judged everything as a part of our spiritual nature (good, right, true) or not a part of our spiritual nature (bad, wrong, false), which created a separation of knowledge in the mind. Yes, Jesus was pointing to our spiritual nature. But he was not the only physical expression that points to God. Jesus was not saying he is the only way or expression of God. Rather he was saying that all "I am's are expressions or ways of God. All the I am's that you are and have been. All the I am's that others are and have been. Everything in nature points to our spiritual nature. Every emotion points to our spiritual nature. Every thought points to our spiritual nature. Every physical expression points to our spiritual nature. You can trace all ideas, expressions, appearances, emotions, feelings, and perceptions back to its source, which is *I am no-thing or formless* and *I am everything or form.*

The physical nature of our beingness is unique and there will never be another unique expression of God or Spirit like it. However, our spiritual nature is the same one infinite nature that exists in all physical entities and is the essence that connects all of existence. There are over seven billion people on this planet. Therefore, there are seven billion unique expressions of spirit or God. The rational mind has to release its belief that there is a right expression of spirit and a wrong expression of spirit. Or there is a right way to be and a wrong way to be. This is impossible because there is an infinite number of ways for spirit to express itself as a physical form. If the breath is our true spiritual essence, as Jesus said it was, then what in our world does not contain breath? Our words are formed from breath. Thoughts are formed from breath. Emotions are formed by the breath. Bodies exist by the breath. Nature exists from the breath. Let it go, stop thinking you know the one right way, and breathe in the one way that is all ways! What is right for you is right for only you; that is how special and uniquely made you are.

Today, we have an opportunity to create a new culture for future generations, one that allows the integration of our human and spiritual nature, as one embodied nature of innocence! When we remember our Divine voice of love and begin loving every aspect of our human journey, we will be set free from the paradigm of breathing shallow and creating the experience of fear, limitation, scarcity, lack, division, and separation. Now is the time for our human nature to breathe with our spiritual nature and breathe as one! Now is the time to be an awakened and enlightened human being here on Earth!

"This unfamiliar experience is a gift."
You are welcome here.
You are enough!
How may I serve you?

Reflection

How different would the quality of your relationships be if you focused on breathing in every word that was spoken to you, instead of judging every word as right or wrong?
How different would the quality of your experience with reality be if you breathed in every experience instead of judging it as right or wrong?

Reprogramming the Subconscious Mind

"Be still and know that heartbreak and depression is God, a part of your true authentic nature."

Practicing the heart-centered habit: (Example)

Have you ever felt heartbroken or depressed?

Welcome these experiences as a part of consciousness (You):

H- Honesty

"I fully feel the parts of me that have felt heartbroken and depressed."

A-Acknowledge, allow, ask

"I acknowledge that it is safe and okay to feel this limited experience. I embrace these feelings fully as they are

because I know they are here to show me the way into my heart. As I embrace these feelings fully, I ask them to bring with them all of the past meanings, interpretations, beliefs, and judgments that I thought were true, but are not valid in this present moment, so that I may receive them as a gift, guide, and opening toward the infinite perception in my heart. I acknowledge their Divine role in helping me expand awareness into the depths of infinite knowing."

Allow the uncomfortable experience to have a voice. Do not believe what it is saying, but instead be a loving presence that offers a deeper level of safety, comfort, and acknowledgment than the experience has ever received from you before, therefore being the practice of detachment, allowance, pure love, and space.

Ask: "Divine heart, I accept that I don't know how to receive painful experiences as a gift. Therefore, I ask that you receive heartbreak and depression as a Divine gift for me. Welcome, embrace, honor, and validate these experiences for me, through me, as I am now, hence healing the inner division within me, so that my perception can expand and align with the flow of infinite information." And so it is. (Amen)

B- Breathe

Breathe in these feelings (*"I receive you as life"*), and breathe out (*"You are free to be"*). Be one with the breath. *"The breath is the Kingdom of Heaven."*

I-I love you!

Place your hands over your heart. Say, *"I love you! All is an expression of one life. I validate this limited experience within me. It is an experience from my past that was not validated by my relationships to the world. Therefore, I choose to be the presence of love that provides this experience the resonation of love that it has never received. May I be all the affirmation that this limited experience needs to remember that it is an infinite expression of divinity, so that it may fully awaken from the illusion of limitation. I love you!"*

"I am abundant, wise, infinite, and free!"

T- Thank you

Thank the experience for helping you remember that you are an ever-expanding unique expression of the Truth. Thank the circumstance, story, or relationship that triggered these feelings in your body, so your entire being could awaken to your innocent nature of authentic freedom that can enjoy all experiences.

> *"Thank you for helping me to align and attune with my heart's ever-expanding unique expression of infinite wisdom and pure love! Thank you for helping me to remember the power of life that I am!"*

Intention: *(say aloud)*

"Today, I choose to breathe deeply throughout every experience, so that I may discover the middle path that guides awareness inward, thereby releasing control over reality and being the embodiment of Divine perfection in spirit, mind, and body."

Affirmation: *(say aloud)*

Say aloud throughout today:

"All of life is abundant because I am abundant!"

Day 6

Authentic Freedom

"Go back to center! If you can find tools to help you go back to center, go back to singularity, go back to that point, that connection with the world."
–Nassim Haramein

Mirror Work

Say Aloud: (looking into your eyes in a mirror):
Good morning, infinite one. You are safe to feel. I always want to know how you are feeling. You are the soul-mate that I have been looking for my entire life. You matter and you are enough! You are worthy of being seen and heard. I see you and I am here to listen to you. There is a good reason you are here; you are Divine perfection! Today, I join you in celebrating your ever-expanding unique expression. I am open to receiving new information and new ways of being by choosing to receive all uncomfortable, unfamiliar, painful, inconvenient, and unwanted experiences as a Divine gift from you, my infinite heart. I love all of you! I really love all of you. (your name), I really love all of you. (Feel free to write your own love statement).

Science and spirituality were once viewed as opposing perspectives of reality. These two views seemed to prove existence through polarizing perspectives. Science was out to prove that we were physical in nature. Spirituality was out to prove that we were spiritual in nature. Today, scientific research is showing evidence that our physical nature and spiritual nature

131

are actually one. Therefore, the two opposing fields of thought are merging into one field. This is an exciting time to be alive, where everything is waking up to the authentic freedom of unity consciousness. Unity consciousness is a full awareness that all experiences of energy, whether spiritual, mental, or physical, are interconnected through a multidimensional relationship.

In 2008, I watched a documentary that showcased research from a fascinating quantum physicist whose name is Nassim Haramein. He spoke about the research on subatomic particles, that proves at the center of atoms is a black hole, which is infinitely dense meaning it is infinitely full of energy, information, or potential. This space of infinite energy at the core of every atom in our bodies comprises 99.999 percent of the atom. This means we are actually 99.999 percent space and only .001 percent physical matter. I guess Jesus was right when he said, "The Kingdom of Heaven is within you." Haramein's research indicates that this 99.999 percent space of infinite energy is a unified field that connects all of existence. We are connected within this space of infinite energy. We are actually 99.999 percent the same energy and only .001 percent unique or different. After I watched the documentary about Haramein's discoveries I was astounded to say the least. As a society we have focused more on the .001 percent of reality than the 99.999 percent of reality. This was a huge game changer for me. We have scientific evidence that proves we are all one!

Science, religions, nature, emotions, thoughts, and the rest of existence is trying to point us inward toward our one infinite nature. For sixteen years I tried to stop judging, analyzing, interpreting, pushing, pulling, and so on, but it never stopped. Rather, it got worse. Until the season it overwhelmed me and I was too exhausted to try stopping it. So I merged, experienced, and embraced it all as the one reality of pure life through being the heart-centered habit. Spontaneously, the heart-centered habit became a new response to everything that arose in the moment. Freedom is our true nature. Therefore, it is already what we are! We are infinite free beings. The heart-centered habit is a useful tool to unravel all of the unresolved experiences, emotions, beliefs, and knowledge that captivates our awareness from perceiving our true free nature.

Our heart nature is connected to this unified field of infinite energy, which is our spiritual nature. We have conditioned our head to connect or attach to the information from our environment. These conditions clog the connection between the head and the heart, clouding our rational mind's perception from sensing into our infinite nature. However, once we let go of our attachments to how we think we should act, speak, or be based upon our personal knowledge of right and wrong, the connection between the head and heart become opened and united once again, returning back into our authentic self, which resists no experience, feeling, knowing, expression, or way of being. When you become fully aware of the greater self that you are, which isn't separate from any part of existence, you will perceive reality through the greater reality or 99.999 percent of reality.

Being heart-centered means being willing to experience all possibilities of good and bad; right and wrong; should and shouldn't; wanted and unwanted; comfortable and uncomfortable; good and evil; convenient and inconvenient; happiness and pain; abundance and lack; limited and unlimited. How can we sense our infinite soul when experiencing circumstances that appear dreadful, painful, limited, stressful, and unwanted? Your rational mind or head will not understand how because its understanding is based upon what it sees, hears, and feels from its environment. However, your heart always knows the

Truth of your being, which is not based upon your circumstances. Trusting in what your heart knows is the only way to experience authentic freedom. It is an experience of freedom from the inside out that floods the rational mind with a peace that surpasses its understanding. Your heart-centered nature perceives reality through the 99.999 percent of reality. Allow your heart, which perceives only goodness and love, guide the way you perceive everything that your environment believes is wrong, bad, or evil. Perceiving reality through the lens of Truth will set you free. The Truth is, there is no part of reality that is not a part of the greater you. This includes all of the parts of reality where your head says, "I am not that," or "I would never do that," or I do not like ..."

"This unwanted experience is a gift."
You are welcome here.
You are enough!
How may I serve you?

Singularity

Scientific research confirms Nassim Haramein's proposition of a fractal and holographic Universe. Haramein proposes that the Universe is made up of scalar dimension of the sphere in all sizes at all scales of the Universe; from infinitely large to infinitely small, which are embedded within one another. For instance, we live in a vast Universe made up of an unknown amount of stars. Those stars are made up of galaxies, including The Milky Way, which is the galaxy we live in. The Milky Way galaxy is made up of many solar systems, including the one we live in. Our solar system is made up of eight or nine planets, including Earth. Earth has over seven billion humans living on it, and you are one of them. Your body is made up of organs and tissue. Those organs and tissues are made up of trillions of cells. Cells are made up of a lot of subatomic particles. At the center of atoms is a black hole of infinite energy, which is connected to the same black hole at the center of our galaxy and connected to the same black hole at the center of our Universe. All of existence from infinite large scales to infinite small scales are connected and kept in balance by the infinite energy of the black hole or unified field that exists at the center. Nassim Haramein calls this center within all systems of existence, singularity. Science is proving that God or the unified field of infinite energy is omniscient, omnipresent, and within us; just like the spiritual teachers throughout history spoke about.

Basically reality is a bunch of spheres, some which conglomerate to form other objects from stars, to galaxies, to trees, to you, and I. Nassim Haramein and Elizabeth Rauscher scientifically verified that there is a relationship between objects at all scales in the Universe. Therefore, the Universe does have a Scaling Law for Organized Matter. This research brings about three conclusions **One: There is an underlying order in the Universe.** There is a direct relationship between all objects; macro-cosmic and micro-cosmic. **Two: There is a fundamental principle of division.** The Universe divides itself in a fractal nature or similar pattern and creates a resonant structure or pattern on all scales. We can see this fractal nature at the point of human conception. **Three: All objects on all scales of the Universe are black holes.** Black holes are not gobble monsters as we once thought. We thought that black holes consumed objects and anything that fell into a black hole was never to be seen again. There used to be a lot of fear about black holes. We thought that the one at the center of our galaxy would eventually consume all the planets, stars, and moons that surrounded it. Well, now we see clearly that black holes are the containers of the entire scale. Therefore, our galaxy is a black hole and the 99.999 percent space of infinite energy that is spinning at its core is maintaining the equilibrium and supporting all objects contained within it. All the objects were created from the division of the infinite space and are connected through their core of singularity or the unified field. Black holes keep all objects within it in a perfect relationship of order, balance, and harmony for them to coexist as a whole. Our body is a black hole. The force of the spin of the black hole provides the perfect gravitational pull for all atoms, cells, tissues, and organs to remain as a unified body. This new scientific evidence provides our minds the proof it always needed to believe that we are all connected.

If we could zoom our perception in closer toward the point of singularity and look out from there at our body, it would look like the Universe does to us when we receive satellite images from space. We would be able to see all of the infinitely small scales that make up larger scales. Our atoms would look like stardust, our cells would look like trillions of stars, our organs would look like planets, and our bodies would look like a galaxy, along with over seven billion (other bodies) galaxies within this one Universe (Earth). We are so much more than we think!

Life is infinitely vast, but we can only perceive the wonder and amazement of reality when we sense reality from the space (99.999 percent of reality). Instead of the way we have all been born into perceiving, which perceives reality from the matter (surface .001 percent of reality). This is the misperception of reality or sin we are born into believing is the Truth. The whole of humanity is waking up from perceiving reality from the .001 percent of reality to the realization of the 99.999 percent of reality. Once we awaken to the Truth of reality, we can reconnect in a new relationship at the surface of reality; a relationship that is rooted in equanimity, love, unity, and reverence for all of life!

"This uncomfortable experience is a gift."
You are welcome here.
You are enough!
How may I serve you?

The Space Program

The old paradigm or perception of dimension in geometry is no longer valid. It was believed that Dimension 0 is a point in space-time with no volume, therefore it doesn't exist. Dimension 1 is a line with length but no width, which doesn't exist. Dimension 2 is a plane with length and width, but doesn't exist. Dimension 3 has length, width, and height, and can enclose space, thus it exists. How can a point, line, and plane that do not exist form something that does exist? This is the old paradigm that focuses on existence being only the .001 percent of reality, the appearance within the space of infinite energy. This is what physics and our understanding of the Universe has been based upon up until now. In the past, scientists were interested in studying the .001 percent of reality because it was believed it was the true nature of reality. Now that we know better, which is that Dimension 0 does exist and makes up the greater portion of reality, shouldn't scientists and physicists be studying and researching Dimension 0, which is what all of existence is made of?

Nassim Haramein was one quantum physicist who questioned this paradigm when he was in elementary school. This question led him into studying the 99.999 percent space more than the .001 percent matter. There are still many quantum physicists that continue to study physical matter by colliding particles in machines that cost billions of dollars. Just like many humans still function from the paradigm of deducing knowledge based upon what they see and feel from their relationships to the physical world. When we focus awareness on the .001 percent of reality, we perceive the collisions of our thoughts and emotions as separate forces that are not in a harmonious relationship with each other. What if we could be like Nassim and focus awareness on the space that the emotions and thoughts are contained within? What if we could use tools to shift our perspective from the outside-in; .001 percent surface reality, to the inside-out; 99.999 percent of infinite reality? This would require each individual to let go of the old paradigm of perceiving through the limited understanding at the surface (knowledge of right and wrong) and sense into the 99.999 percent space that exists in and between all appearances and experiences of reality, which can be directly sensed from the point of singularity within you; your heart.

It is time to embark on setting up a new program in human consciousness. I call it the space program. Our awareness has an opportunity to go within and explore the amazing Universe from the inside-out. Our rational mind focuses outward. Our intuitive mind focuses inward. So why don't we use the natural flow of each sensory function of mind to be human. We can gather information through intuition from within the infinite space of Divine wisdom, the unified field where the origin of creation emanates from into three dimensional forms. Then express that intuitive information through the rational mind to communicate and express reality at the surface. This is the natural way of living the true nature of reality; from the inside-out. This is true repentance. Turning awareness into sensing the truth of present moment reality, then embodying that presence of Truth, and being an expression of that Truth. Lastly, letting the expression of that Truth go out to support, nurture, encourage, and inspire to manifest a world that reflects pure indiscriminate love. Therefore, no longer needing to maintain, contain, or manage information within our brains. Instead, just total freedom to be heart-centered, innocent, and infinite beings.

"This painful experience is a gift."
You are welcome here.
You are enough!
How may I serve you?

The Vast Unknown

We have lived as the head-centered me that needs to know, understand, and comprehend the Truth of reality, so that we can enforce laws and rules to help protect and keep humanity safe. This desire keeps our attention focused on consumption, creating a false sense that we are in charge of feeding ourselves information and knowledge. As we are discovering through the current information age, information is not stagnant. Information changes and flows like the rest of nature. Therefore, we cannot rely upon information that is passed down to us from the experiences of the past.

There is a more simple way to live. We can relax, enjoy, embrace, and fully experience each moment as it is. Intuitive knowing arises from the vast unknown space that makes up 99.999 percent of our being. It is always readily available. We just have to surrender our knowledge and remain open to the unknown. The vast unknown is infinitely full of information, potential, and energy. The premise of the Holographic Unified Field Theory research is that space is not empty, it is infinitely full. It is full of an energy that, through a specific set of fractal geometry, creates atomic structures that are themselves made of 99.999 percent space.(*The Laughing Coach Newsletter, 2000*) Since this is what we are mostly made of, we can easily live as the unknown. The unknown makes itself known through us and as us. Our thoughts, words, emotions, and actions can become motivated by this inner power of infinite wisdom when we fully release all stored information of the past from our rational minds, removing the clouds in our head that block the intuitive information of Divine Light that is streaming through our mind and body's connection to the unified field, which is the heart.

The heart-centered habit can guide awareness into the remembrance of intuition. When we embrace every experience of reality as pure life, all that will remain is intuition. Being intuitive and settling into the unknown may feel strange at first because we have been accustomed to dwelling in the knowns of the head-centered me. When we first turn awareness inward toward our inner life, we see thoughts and emotions that have been stuck dwelling inside, which blocks our heart's intuitive knowing. Usually our first reaction is to avoid them and try to maneuver around them. But this is impossible because they dwell in between our head and our heart. We have to go through each one and they will not let us in if we try to bulldoze through them like a linebacker. They will only open their doors if we embrace them with love.

Imagine that you are this infinite soul, which is an energy field of every experience that has ever happened, ever will happen, and is happening now throughout the Universe. Your soul came into the body to experience these in a physical reality. You forgot that you came to experience infinite experiences in this one lifetime and went with the rest of humanity believing that you needed to pick and choose what experiences you wanted to have and what experiences you did not want to have. Then your life bounces back and forth between experiencing what you want and what you don't want. All the while your soul feels imprisoned by this reality because it came to experience everything. Then one day you wake up and remember that you are infinite, so you begin to merge with whatever experience arises within you. Each time you do this, even with experiences that you used to label as unwanted, uncomfortable, painful, and inconvenient; all experiences become one experience of freedom and joy. Now you are perceiving experience from the inside out, no longer perceiving from the outside-in. No longer feeling separate from anything. Nothing to fear anymore. Nothing to fix or change anymore. Nothing to escape anymore. Now you are free! Now you dwell in the vast unknown!

The heart-centered habit is a practice that guides awareness home into the vast unknown. All of the thoughts, memories, and emotions that were once exiled from our loving attention, receive acknowledgement and love. In return they gift us with a deeper sense of oneness as we journey home to the pure vast unknown space of unity consciousness. Authentic freedom is our true nature that all of existence shares, breathes, and expresses. A freedom that perceives no opposition. A freedom that perceives one reality of pure life and Love expressing itself in an infinite display of magic and wonder. May you remember our one true spiritual nature through being the heart-centered habit!

Thank you Nassim Haramein!

"This unfamiliar experience is a gift."
You are welcome here.
You are enough!
How may I serve you?

Reflection

What if wisdom spontaneously occurred within the moment that you need to know, without you needing to look to the past?

Are you willing to acquaint yourself in present moment awareness, which feels unknown, new, and fresh?

Reprogramming the Subconscious Mind

"Be still and know that feeling bored, stuck, and impatient is God, a part of your true authentic nature."

Practicing the heart-centered habit: (Example)

Have you ever felt bored, stuck, or impatient?

Welcome these experiences as a part of consciousness (You):

H- Honesty

"I fully feel the parts of me that have felt bored, stuck, and impatient."

A-Acknowledge, allow, ask

"I acknowledge that it is safe and okay to feel this limited experience. I embrace these feelings fully as they are because I know they are here to show me the way into my heart. As I embrace these feelings fully, I ask them to bring with them all of the past meanings, interpretations, beliefs, and judgments that I thought were true, but are not valid in this present moment, so that I may receive them as a gift, guide, and opening toward the infinite perception in my heart. I acknowledge their Divine role in helping me expand awareness into the depths of infinite knowing."

Allow the uncomfortable experience to have a voice. Do not believe what it is saying, but instead be a loving presence that offers a deeper level of safety, comfort, and acknowledgment than the experience has ever received from you before, thereby being the practice of detachment, allowance, pure love, and space.

Ask: "Divine heart, I accept that I don't know how to perceive reality from the 99.999 percent unified field of infinite information. Therefore, I ask that you perceive the experiences of boredom, stuckness, and impatience through the lens of the infinite field of wisdom for me. Welcome, embrace, honor, and validate these experiences for me, through me, as I am now, healing the inner division within me, so that my perception can expand and align with the flow of infinite information." And so it is. (Amen).

B- Breathe

Breathe in these feelings ("*I receive you as life*"), and breathe out (*"You are free to be"*). Be one with the breath. *"The breath is my healer."*

I-I love you!

Place your hands over your heart. Say, "*I love you! All is an expression of one life. I validate this limited experience within me. It is an experience from my past that was not validated by my relationships to the world. Therefore, I choose to be the presence of love that provides this experience the resonation of love that it has never received. May I be all the affirmation that this limited experience needs to remember that it is an infinite expression of divinity, so that it may fully awaken from the illusion of limitation. I love you!"*

"I am abundant, wise, infinite, and free!"

T- Thank you

Thank the experience for helping you remember that you are an ever-expanding unique expression of the Truth. Thank the circumstance, story, or relationship that triggered these feelings in your body, so your entire being could awaken to your innocent nature of authentic freedom that can enjoy all experiences.

> *"Thank you for helping me to align and attune with my heart's ever-expanding unique expression of infinite wisdom and pure love! Thank you for helping me to remember the power of life that I am!"*

Intention: *(say aloud)*

"Today, I choose to align with the authentic free nature that emanates from the unified field of singularity, which exists within the unknown spacious core of all experiences of reality, which is discovered through the heart of all matter, including me."

Affirmation: *(say aloud)*

Say aloud throughout today:

"All feelings are pure goodness because I am pure goodness!"

Day 7

Remembrance is Now

"The present moment is filled with joy and happiness. If you are attentive, you will see it."

–Thich Nhat Hanh

Mirror Work

Say Aloud: (looking into your eyes in a mirror):
Good morning, infinite one. You are safe to feel. I always want to know how you are feeling. You are the soul-mate that I have been looking for my entire life. You matter and you are enough. You are worthy of being seen and heard. I see you and I am here to listen to you. There is a good reason you are here; you are Divine perfection. Today, I join you in celebrating your ever-expanding unique expression. I am open to receiving new information and new ways of being by choosing to receive all uncomfortable, unfamiliar, painful, inconvenient, and unwanted experiences as a Divine gift from you, my infinite heart. I love all of you! I really love all of you. (your name), I really love all of you. (Feel free to write your own love statement).

I used to believe that joy, happiness, and fulfillment was a destination. I believed I had to work at it by doing the right thing, getting what I wanted, making others happy, and being the good girl. The head-centered me was always judging every moment and imagining a goal in the future that would bring me some kind of fulfillment. The problem was, I could never reach the goal of experiencing fulfillment because it lingered somewhere out there in front of me. As soon as

I seemed to achieve what I thought I wanted, my mind was on to the next achievement in the future. My rational mind was never interested in enjoying and savoring each moment exactly as it was. It was in a constant state of wanting, wanting, wanting, constantly thinking that when I got all that I wanted I would be satisfied, but instead it only fueled more wanting. When things didn't go the way the head-centered me had planned on its "what I want" list, it would shut down and become depressed. It even had thoughts of wanting to die. It felt like it had failed at creating happiness, joy, and fulfillment.

In moments of deep despair I began to investigate this experience by asking myself "what is this really?" Intuitive insights began to surface because my rational mind had given up trying to fix, change, or escape reality. My experience of depression, failure, despair, frustration, and confusion were moments when my awareness sank in away from the surface of reality. My rational mind thought these experiences meant something was wrong. I thought, "Well if all that exists is Divine, goodness, and pure life, then these experiences are good and right." What if, instead of something being wrong, something right is happening?

I realized that the sense of depression was actually awareness returning to the present moment, which felt uncomfortable to the rational mind. The present moment felt like a death to the rational mind's imagined "wanting." When the rational mind wasn't in a state of wanting, it felt empty because it wasn't imagining anything. This emptiness has been labeled as depression, despair, confusion, frustration, anxiety, and void. In Truth, it is just the present moment that is void or empty of imagined ideas, thoughts, and feelings of wanting.

I realized the only way I could help my rational mind relax into the present moment was to honor the experience of depression, anxiety, emptiness, boredom, sadness, frustration, and confusion. I realized the present moment that feels empty is my true nature of authentic love. I just had to have the faith to choose to perceive these experiences through an expanded view of reality; my heart's view. Every moment has become an opportunity for my rational mind to remember its true nature of love and fulfillment that is always right here and right now within me!

"This unwanted experience is a gift."
You are welcome here.
You are enough!
How may I serve you?

Love is All That Remains

Every time we face difficulty in our lives, we are faced with a precious moment to discover what remains. When life circumstances strip you of what you thought you wanted – or how you thought life should be – or what you planned life to look like, all that remains is love. When people you love move away or die, all that remains is love. When your marriage ends in divorce, all that remains is love. When you feel betrayed or abandoned in a relationship, all that remains is love. When you have been abandoned, neglected, rejected, or abused, all that remains is love. When you have been wrongly accused or blamed for something you didn't do, all that remains is love. When you have been cheated, used, or robbed, all that remains is love. When you have been misunderstood, judged, or criticized, all that remains is love.

Everything you do in this life is motivated by a need for love. Everything that happens to you is motivated to help you remember that you are the love you are seeking from the world. When you don't receive the honor, recognition, acceptance, and love from your

147

relationships to this world it is only because you are being reminded that you are the only one who can give yourself the love you think you need. Therefore, when you are not honored by the world, honor yourself. When you are not accepted by the world, accept yourself. When you are not loved by the world, love yourself. When you are not recognized by the world, recognize yourself. This is the path of self-realization, self-empowerment, or spiritual remembrance.

You are made up of 99.999 percent pure infinite love, power, and wisdom. You are deity, which means you lack nothing. You have everything you need within you. You are the power, Truth, and wisdom of God. When life circumstances seem to be against you, be the one that is for you! Whether life gives you what you want or not, love remains. Remembrance is always now! When you can perceive this, you will be filled with joy and fulfillment, which has nothing to do with the way this moment appears. If guilt or shame arises in your experience you can celebrate them as they are and they will return to the source of love from which they were created. Remember that love is on the other side of every dark feeling, thought, emotion, and experience. Love is the light at the end of every dark tunnel. As you remember that the darkness you experience is reminding you of the light you truly are, the dark tunnel disappears. Remembrance of the pure love that you are is now, not somewhere in the future or when you physically die!

"This uncomfortable experience is a gift."
You are welcome here.
You are enough!
How may I serve you?

148

Symbols of Love

You learn at a young age how to define love. Love is defined by your relationships to this physical world. We are taught a conditional love that says love is this and love is not that. The way we define, express, and label love is a conditional love. It is a love based on the conditions of your surroundings. It is a familiar love. When life is going your way, you feel loved. When life is not going your way, you feel unloved or unsupported. The truth is, everything is a symbol of pure love. Everything that you have labeled as wrong, evil, bad, unwanted, uncomfortable, unfamiliar, and unsafe is as much a symbol of Divine love as everything you have labeled as right, good, wanted, comfortable, familiar, and safe.

It is easy to offer yourself love when things are going smooth. But when life takes a turn in a direction that is difficult, you withhold love from yourself because you think you did something wrong. You think you are being punished, and in the past you were only punished when you did something wrong. This is only happening to allow pure Divine love to awaken within you. True love is infinite and it lays dormant until you invite it in by offering yourself love, acknowledgement, encouragement, and kindness. This requires courage and faith because you don't see others living this way in the world. You and only you can embody pure unconditional Divine love. Nobody can fill you with love from the outside-in. Relationships that appear to fill you with love, will eventually fail in their attempt to meet your demands. You are the ONE that has been hired for the job to love you!

Even guilt and shame are symbols of pure love that we have denied and imagined to be great demons. They are angels here to be seen for what they really represent, the one God almighty! Faith is required to claim everything in existence as a symbol of pure love because your rational mind can still find evidence of that which appears and feels like the opposite of pure love. The only way to transform our outer world is to transform our inner world of perception. If we continue to believe in love, and an opposite force of love, then we will continue to experience a reality that reflects good and evil. If we choose to be the fearless faithful ones that allow our inner perceptions of reality to merge into one pure love, we are being the vessels of change, healing, and peace, instead of waiting for some outside power, force, or being to change the world for us. We can stand in the perception of Divine light and perceive everything as a symbol of pure love. The way we perceive determines the quality of our experience. The quality of our experience affects the quality of our relationships to the physical world. This is how we can be the change we wish to see in the world.

"This painful experience is a gift."
You are welcome here.
You are enough!
How may I serve you?

Love Stories

Every moment is a love story between the one that exists in all, and the you that feels separate from the one. The one essence is here meeting all aspects of itself. The one pure love that you are is here to marry every experience that arises in the moment that feels separate. The present moment is a Divine marriage between Source and its creations. It is amazing that you get the opportunity to experience both, the savior and the sinner. You are the savior that is here to love the sinner, which is you too. Every moment you choose to love what you used to hate, you embody pure love and awareness awakens out of the head and into heart-centered consciousness. Every moment you choose to encourage yourself when you feel discouraged, you embody pure love and awaken out of suffering. Every moment you choose to be kind to yourself when you are in the midst of judging yourself, you embody pure love and awaken from the perception of limitation. Every moment you choose to inspire yourself in the midst of depression, you embody more of your authentic nature and awaken from separation. Every moment you choose to compliment yourself in the midst of criticizing yourself, you embody Divine wisdom and awaken from hell. Every moment you choose to relax in the midst of chaotic thinking, you embody more present moment awareness and awaken from stress. Every moment offers you an opportunity to write your own love story with whatever is happening in the moment. When you love every piece, part, and aspect of yourself, you will naturally accept, love, encourage, and inspire the world around you.

Guilt and shame are lonely wanderers waiting for you to embrace them and love them just as they are! The heart-centered habit guides perception to see all experiences from the inside-out. The inside out view is a perception that sees everything as appearing from pure formless love or one Divine essence. Guilt and shame are repressed energies from moments in your past when you perceived yourself from the outside-in, believing that they were against you. When we perceive from the head-centered me or outside-in we see everything as either for us or against us. Being heart-centered opens our perception to seeing the love story or union between our formless spiritual and physical human nature. The guilt and shame you feel or have felt in the past are repressed spiritual energies that only emerge up to the surface of your experience to be seen as a part of the truth of your eternal presence. Your heart can become the safe place for all repressed energies to emerge, so they can be acknowledged, embraced, and loved. Then you will perceive them from your eternal soul of Divine love.

"This unfamiliar experience is a gift."
You are welcome here.
You are enough!
How may I serve you?

Reflection

What if the only power in all of existence is pure love and our minds have been programmed to express that love in a conditional way? What would happen if we allowed the love we feel within our being to flow through us without set parameters, conditions, or filters? Maybe we would feel freer and more fulfilled?

Reprogramming the Subconscious Mind

"Be still and know guilt and shame is God, a part of your true authentic nature."

Practicing the heart-centered habit: (Example)

Have you ever felt guilty or ashamed?

Welcome these experiences as a part of consciousness (You):

H- HONESTY

"I fully feel the parts of me that have felt guilt and shame."

A-ACKNOWLEDGE, ALLOW, ASK

"I acknowledge that it is safe and okay to feel this limited experience. I embrace these feelings fully as they are because I know they are here to show me the way into my heart. As I embrace these feelings fully, I ask them to bring with them all of the past meanings, interpretations, beliefs, and judgments that I thought were true, but are not valid in this present moment, so that I may receive them as a gift, guide, and opening toward the infinite perception in my heart. I acknowledge their Divine role in helping me expand awareness into the depths of infinite knowing."

Allow the uncomfortable experience to have a voice. Do not believe what it is saying, but instead be a loving presence that offers a deeper level of safety, comfort, and acknowledgment than the experience has ever received from you before, thereby being the practice of detachment, allowance, pure love, and space.

Ask: "Divine heart, I accept that I don't know how to perceive every experience as a symbol of Divine love. Therefore, I ask that you perceive guilt and shame as symbols of Divine love for me. Welcome, embrace, honor, and validate these experiences for me, through me, as I am now, healing the inner division within me, so that my perception can expand and align with the flow of infinite information." And so it is (Amen).

B- BREATHE

Breathe in these feelings (*"I receive you as life"*) breathe out (*"You are free to be"*). Be one with the breath: *"I am the breath."*

153

I-I LOVE YOU

Place your hands over your heart. Say, *"I love you! All is an expression of one life. I validate this limited experience within me. It is an experience from my past that was not validated by my relationships to the world. Therefore, I choose to be the presence of love that provides this experience the resonation of love that it has never received. May I be all the affirmation that this limited experience needs to remember that it is an infinite expression of divinity, so that it may fully awaken from the illusion of limitation. I love you!"*

"I am abundant, wise, infinite, and free!"

T- THANK YOU

Thank the experience for helping you remember that you are an ever-expanding unique expression of the Truth. Thank the circumstance, story, or relationship that triggered these feelings in your body, so your entire being could awaken to your innocent nature of authentic freedom that can enjoy all experiences.

> *"Thank you for helping me to align and attune with my heart's ever-expanding unique expression of infinite wisdom and pure love! Thank you for helping me to remember the power of life that I am!"*

Intention: *(say aloud)*

"Today, I choose to remember the presence of eternal love by acknowledging the love story between the physical form and spiritual essence of all. I choose to embrace every experience as a symbol of pure love"

Affirmation: *(say aloud)*

Say aloud throughout today:

"All thoughts are pure love because I am pure love!"

Day 8

Delete the files of "me"

"When I let go of what I am, I become what I might be."

- Lao Tzu

Mirror Work

Say Aloud: (looking into your eyes in a mirror)
Good morning, infinite one. You are safe to feel. I always want to know how you are feeling. You are the soul-mate that I have been looking for my entire life. You matter and you are enough. You are worthy of being seen and heard. I see you and I am here to listen to you. There is a good reason you are here; you are Divine perfection. Today, I join you in celebrating your ever-expanding unique expression. I am open to receiving new information and new ways of being by choosing to receive all uncomfortable, unfamiliar, painful, inconvenient, and unwanted experiences as a Divine gift from you, my infinite heart. I love all of you! I really love all of you. (your name), I really love all of you. (Feel free to write your own love statement).

The head-centered me or ego was a way of being that I learned to be from my physical environment. Awareness or consciousness became lost in a way of judgment. Judgment isn't bad or wrong and is as okay as acceptance, but judgment always led to an inner sense of limitation. Judgment says, "This experience is not okay." Then the rational mind fights to make things okay by creating a way out through "fight" or "flight." I learned to fight certain experiences and to repress (flight) or escape other experiences. Awareness was limited to experience only certain aspects of reality or life.

The head-centered me was a social chameleon because it was focused on fitting into the world. Therefore, it had to learn to adapt to the particular judgments that were present in my relationships. Each relationship posed different judgments, so I subconsciously became a master people-pleaser in an effort to avoid judgment. I used empathic abilities to sense other people's judgments and stored them as a file in my rational mind. My rational mind kept a record on knowing how to respond in all of my relationships in a way that would create a sense of comfort within the relationship. As I got older I enjoyed being by myself more than around other people because I was getting too exhausted with making other people's experience of me pleasant.

In my heart, I always loved new experiences and didn't believe that I was only one way or one file of "me" that I had stored in my rational mind. But I was too afraid to be the infinite "me" because I feared being judged as weird and being rejected. Creating files of "me" was a subconscious habit and in no way was I trying to be fake. I had no solid sense of who or what I was. Therefore, in an effort to fit into this world, I matched other people's judgments.

After many years of desiring to fit in with my environment, I realized I was never going to feel like I fit in. There wasn't a single judgment that felt like the truth of my being. I began to question this desire to fit in and realized there was an intention that dwelled deeper within me, in my core, my heart. It was an intention to be AUTHENTIC! I was taught that being real involved fitting in and finding your place in the world. This way did not guide me to being authentic or real. I didn't know what it would feel, look, or be like to be authentic. I began to focus more time on being authentic and real than focusing on fitting in and pleasing others. I went through a period of transformation where I didn't want to fit in with the world anymore. Therefore, I stopped getting involved in relationships outside of my home. Of course, I continued my relationship with my husband and children. During this period of solitude, I began to delete the files of judgments that I had accumulated throughout all of my experiences. I wasn't getting rid of these files of judgment. Instead, I was deleting them from my rational mind, so that their programs would no longer run and override my authentic experience of reality. It was like deleting a file from my computer that I no longer needed. The file still exists in hyperspace, but it isn't using up my computer's memory. I no longer needed these files of judgment because they were using up memory that I could use to remember my authentic nature. I desired to be authentic in all of my relationships to this physical world. Finally, my desire for authenticity was greater than my desire to fit into the world.

Over time I realized that being authentic meant being heart-centered. Being heart-centered is very different than being head-centered. Heart- centered functions from a deep spaciousness of unformed potential or energy. Head-centered functions from preconceived judgments. My rational mind had to remember to keep space or memory available for intuition to flow freely from my authentic self, which feels like no-self at all. Therefore, its function shifted from accumulating judgments to remaining free and open. I didn't delete the files of judgment through "fight" or "flight." Instead, I deleted them by acknowledging every inner experience of thoughts, emotions, feelings, ideas, moods, and images as totally okay, instead of filtering them through judgments of past experiences. Judgment has two sides, like a coin. One side is positive and the other side is negative. Acknowledging both perspectives of positive and negative judgments is equally okay and acceptable to be experienced deletes the judgment. As I sat with my emotional self and brought both sides into oneness, I felt more empty and spacious. My rational mind was waking up to its natural habit of allowance, which no longer saved new data, information, or judgments from my relationships.

As I stepped back out into the world I continued to feel other peoples' judgments. Finally I had become the safety and loving assurance that my rational mind needed, reminding it that all is okay. People aren't judging me; they are showing me how they judge. Therefore, I acknowledged the way they judge as totally okay. Now I didn't have to change myself to fit in with their judgments because judgment was no longer perceived as wrong.

The heart-centered habit became a practice for my rational mind to remember its authentic nature of stillness, so that it could allow the pure love of the heart to flow through freely. The heart-centered me guided the rational mind to perceive disturbance, discomfort, inconvenience, unwanted change, judgment, and limitation as okay, without concentrating on it, identifying with it, and storing it in memory. As I result I remained open, relaxed, still, and spacious in the risings and fallings of all experiences.

"This unwanted experience is a gift."
You are welcome here.
You are enough!
How may I serve you?

Attachment

"A thought is harmless unless we believe it. It's not our thoughts, but our attachment to our thoughts that causes suffering."

– Byron Katie

We weren't taught by a society that acceptance, love, and freedom dwells within us. Instead, we were taught that we have to earn acceptance, love, and freedom. The truth is, we were already born fulfilled. We have all become a bit lost in believing that fulfillment is something we have to attain or earn from our physical relationships. This belief guides our rational mind to seek fulfillment from the world and strive to attain what it thinks will make it feel fulfilled. The way the rational mind tries to accomplish fulfillment is through attachment.

The head-centered me is a conglomeration of thoughts, feelings, beliefs, judgments, and perceptions that it attaches to and embodies. This gives the rational mind a false sense of fulfillment. It is filled with judgments, stories, and thoughts about reality, but nonetheless it is not truly fulfilled. Attachment determines our preferences that get stored in our memory as what I like, want, or need to be happy, creating an energetic flipside that opposes this attachment; what I fear, don't like, want, or causes unhappiness. This way of being projects happiness as a state that is outside of us. We have to experience a particular circumstance or set of thoughts to feel good or be happy, creating an unnatural role for the rational mind. Now it is in control of our happiness and has to work itself into a frenzy to create happy thoughts,

160

circumstances, situations, feelings, and experiences. It seeks out relationships that will maintain our preferences. Those that don't meet its demands or preferences become the enemy. Attachment manufactures a false sense of control and separation.

The rational mind is not in control of all of life. It is a piece of consciousness controlled by a higher consciousness that is ever-present, infinite, and all encompassing. Intuition is our inner sense of this higher consciousness that is omniscient and omnipresent. Omnipresent and omniscient means it is in every point in space all at the same time. Pure or higher consciousness is our authentic nature that is like the ocean. The ocean is one vast body of water. The wave does not control the ocean. The ocean controls and supports the wave. The rational mind is like a single wave of consciousness in the vast ocean of pure consciousness. Another way to describe the rational mind is through the example of how pure light creates a diverse rainbow of colors. The pure light is like pure consciousness that emanates from within all of existence. The pure light of consciousness streams through multidimensional layers of energy, creating unique variations of consciousness; the rational mind, being one variation of consciousness, which has its own unique way of being. Just like the pure light that comes from the sun and when refracted in a raindrop creates a unique variation of color called a rainbow, the rational mind is also like one color of the rainbow. Imagine a rainbow that has an infinite variation of color. Every rational mind is like one color of this infinite rainbow. The intuitive mind is the one light that creates the infinite rainbow or different frequencies of the one light.

The head-centered habit believes it is just the one color of the rainbow because it has forgotten its roots or connection to the pure light of consciousness. When the head-centered me forgets its origin it judges all the other colors that don't appear to be similar. Thereby the head-centered me or rational mind is unable to acknowledge that all personalities, egos, and rationales emanate from the same source of light. On one hand, the heart-centered habit perceives that it is all one light shining in and through infinite layers creating a magical display of color. The heart-centered habit guides the head-centered me to remember its true origin of being the one pure light of the entire rainbow of existence.

Remaining detached allows the rational mind to remember it is a part of the vast, pure, or higher body of consciousness. Therefore, it remembers to remain in a state of surrender awaiting intuitive movement from within. The rational mind can remember that it is connected with all other rational minds through the vast pure consciousness that resides from within all of existence. Therefore, it doesn't have to accumulate and identify with certain information, data, or judgments to make itself known and seek out other rational minds or waves of consciousness that move with the same judgments.

When each rational mind or wave of consciousness looks outward, it sees a different landscape. The head-centered me is focused outward into perceiving reality by what it sees and feels from the outside-in. However, when each rational mind looks within it sees the same vast, infinite, and empty space of infinite energy. Therefore, the heart-centered habit guides the head-centered me to look within and perceive reality from its source, origin, or essence of oneness. For instance, the waves in Hawaii see a different landscape than the waves crashing on the beaches of Australia. But when these waves look back into the ocean, they see the same vast ocean. The waves never lose their connection to the one massive body of water that connects all the land masses in the world. Just like the waves of the ocean, the many bodies that reside on Earth don't have to feel isolated and separate because we are all connected to the one pure consciousness that connects the whole world and even larger cosmos.

Perceiving reality through the information from the physical landscape of our external reality creates a partial perspective that feels separate from all the other partial perspectives. Attaching to this landscape or partial perspective creates judgments that are filed away and stored in memory as "Truth." When the rational mind is focused outward it is creating a separate sense of reality. It has many options and will move toward whatever options feel familiar. These options become our particular way of being that creates a sense of separate self in the mind. These partial perspectives become the head-centered me's that feel lost and disconnected from the whole of existence.

Through being the heart-centered habit we sense reality through intuition, which gathers information from the vast formless space within our heart. This heart-centered awareness opens the head-centered me to sensing the connection between all partial perspectives because awareness is guided to follow the head-centered partial perspective inward toward its roots. There at the root, awareness can discover that all partial perspectives are created from the same source. Here in the heart we sense the oneness or pure consciousness that make up all partial perspectives, appearances of "Truth," and unique landscapes. When the rational mind turns inward to sense reality it senses the one essence or the one reality that already exists. This one reality is infinite. Therefore, we do not need to attach to information from our environment, store judgments, and create a separate reality. Each rational mind can feel the one essence that already exists within and express it in a new unique way in every moment. This is authentic freedom; the freedom to express the essence of Truth without restrictions, misperceptions, or judgments from the head. The heart is free to be. No more conflict or war between the heart's expression of Truth and the head's judgment of right and wrong.

We have believed that being detached from any particular perspective makes us immature, weak, and foolish. This is because the perspective which is most popular is strengthened by the number of people that believe in it as truth. Therefore, if we have our own unique perspective of the Truth, it is viewed as weak because there is only one that perceives Truth in that way. This is the reason Jesus was crucified. He expressed the Truth in a unique way that did not reflect the same exact expression of the masses in religion. Value and worth in our society was and still is dependent upon how much our expression reflects the truth of the majority. Therefore, someone who didn't fill their head with the most popular expression of Truth was judged as worthless or blasphemous. However, Jesus' expression was of great value because he allowed infinite knowing to flow through him because his head was spacious and free of the mass knowledge of the Truth. Jesus was judged as weak and foolish because he spoke as the very essence of God, not the majority knowledge of God. This is why he pointed to himself as the way. When we express the Truth that we are as a unique expression of the one essence of Truth, we become the direct path to the Truth too!

You are the way, Truth, and Light and so am I!

"This uncomfortable experience is a gift."
You are welcome here.
You are enough!
How may I serve you?

Emptiness

The rational mind has been programmed to store information from our environment and store it as a belief system of right and wrong. This unnatural role for the rational mind creates a distraction that awareness gets lost in, which creates a sense of separation from our authentic nature of oneness. When we bring both sides of our personal belief systems into unity by declaring both perspectives as equally good to be experienced, the rational mind becomes empty. Our willingness to experience both sides of what we used to label as right and wrong, empties our rational mind of stored knowledge. The trick is to remember not to fill it up again by attaching to new information and creating new belief systems of right and wrong. Being the heart-centered habit opens the rational mind and allows it to become a portal that receives all experiences just as they are, and breathes them into our entire being. As our heart receives the experience, it releases intuition to guide the rational mind's expression and movement. Intuition has free access to utilize the entire brain; both the left logical side, and the right creative side to form new ways of expressing our infinite authentic essence of divinity.

As we practice being the heart-centered habit, our rational mind can feel uncomfortable with this new sense of emptiness because it has been accustomed to the feeling of being full of stored information and beliefs from our external environment. It has been a long time since it functioned from the authentic intuitive heart. The rational mind had been conditioned by our environment to fill the void or emptiness and stay full of laws, rules, standards, conditioned ways, and beliefs in right and wrong! Our family, education, government, church, and relationships taught us to be full of the knowledge of a personal self. This is similar to how your stomach feels when you reduce the amount of food you eat in a day. If you have eaten and filled your stomach full to a certain capacity all of your life, then you reduce the amount of food to half that capacity, your stomach aches and feels empty or hungry. It can even feel painful. But what we have labeled as empty, painful, fearful, or aching is actually a natural state of spaciousness.

Our true nature is the void or that sense that something is missing – that something is the real authentic formless you! You are that sense of void! Therefore, don't fill it up or cover it up! Let it shine! Until you are willing to merge and embrace the sense that something is missing, you will continue to perceive that something is really missing. This is our perception of our true nature from the outside-in and you will go out into the world and find something to fill the void that can never be filled. It cannot be filled because it is not truly empty. Instead, it is infinitely full of energy, potential, information, love, and life. We have been taught to perceive emptiness, void, or the sense that something is missing as bad, wrong, weird, awkward, scary, and unsafe. This is a huge misperception because that empty feeling is all good! The one place we would never look for our true self, God, Truth, or Soul is in the emptiness. But that is exactly where you will discover your true essence!

We will need to remind our subconscious mind that this emptiness or spaciousness is the new normal because it allows the body to feel the whole essence of its true spiritual nature. Compassion and kindness can be our new way of being as we practice being heart-centered toward every aspect of our being and every aspect of life, allowing our rational mind to remain empty, so it may be of service toward every experience in existence. We serve each experience by welcoming it in, giving it the space to be acknowledged, and receiving it as a beautiful aspect of our one Divine nature.

We have labeled this emptiness as many things. Emptiness has been labeled as pain, lack, limitation, stress, suffering, unworthiness, evil, bad, wrong, uncomfortable, unwanted, inconvenient, enemy, "not enough," stupid, lazy, boredom, and so on. Emptiness is the new genius. Being the heart-centered habit allows our perception to see that the emptiness we have been so afraid of is actually the door to realizing the Truth of our being!

"This painful experience is a gift."
You are welcome here.
You are enough!
How may I serve you?

Clarity

Once the clouds of judgment have passed away, and our rational mind remains spacious and free, our entire being perceives with an intense clarity. All dimensions of consciousness from our subatomic particles to our molecules to our cells to our organs to our body to our relationships to the physical world and cosmos, line up perfectly to the unified field that exists at the core of all dimensions. Pure consciousness from the space or spiritual essence becomes the living water that flows from within, through, and as "I am." We can sense that all is one Divine essence appearing and disappearing within the space of itself. Clarity allows us to sense our authentic essence that is one with all of life. We feel like the only identity we are is "I am," which is pure Love. Pure love appears as a flower, tree, cloud, body, cell, animal, mind, food, water, emotion, feeling, thought, idea, and the all that exists. The mind becomes crystal clear. When the mind is clear, awareness is free to sense divinity in and through everyone and everything. The body tunes into the clarity of your soul. Harmony, equanimity, and balance are sensed and experienced from the inside out. An astounding peace covers you like a warm blanket. There is an inner knowing that all is well and is always okay. There is nothing wrong. There is no evil. There is nothing chasing you. There is nothing against you. You are free to live, love, and dance!

When the rational mind becomes heart-centered it becomes a beautiful crystal that appears unique, but transmits the one light of pure consciousness. The rational mind recognizes everything as a beautiful symbol of the one essence that it has discovered itself to be. The words that flow through its unique expression of the one true nature are like healing powers that fulfill the prayers of rational minds that have forgotten their origin of Truth. Our entire being becomes a vessel that serves every experience of reality and the world at large. We were born to serve the physical Universe and all of existence. But first we had to remind our rational mind that it was created to serve the heart.

The heart-centered habit reminds the rational mind of its Divine purpose of surrender and service to the Divine heart of pure love. As the rational mind remembers its Divine purpose it receives clarity and is glorified by the Divine wisdom that flows through it as it. Divine wisdom flows into our relationships to the physical world to serve, support, and validate its authentic nature of divinity.

"This unfamiliar experience is a gift."
You are welcome here.
You are enough!
How may I serve you?

Reflection

What if the feeling of emptiness within you that you have been hiding from the world or distracting yourself from by being a busy body, is a part of the Truth, freedom, and fulfillment that you truly desire?

What if every feeling you fear or feel separate from is the doorway to feeling one with God because God is everything?

Reprogramming the Subconscious Mind

"Be still and know that feelings of limitation, unworthiness, and void is God, a part of your true authentic nature."

Practicing the heart-centered habit: (Example)

Have you ever felt "not enough," limited, and unworthy? Or a void in your life like something was missing?

Welcome these experiences as a part of consciousness (You):

H- HONESTY

"I fully feel the parts of me that have felt "not enough," limited, and worthless." "I fully feel into the sense of void in my life, like something is missing."

A-ACKNOWLEDGE, ALLOW, ASK

"I acknowledge that it is safe and okay to feel this limited experience. I embrace these feelings fully just as they are because I know they are here to show me the way into my heart. As I embrace these feelings fully, I ask them to bring with them all of the past meanings, interpretations, beliefs, and judgments that I thought were true, but are not valid in this present moment, so that I may receive them as a gift, guide, and opening toward the infinite perception in my heart. I acknowledge their Divine role in helping me expand awareness into the depths of infinite knowing."

Allow the uncomfortable experience to have a voice. Do not believe what it is saying, but instead be a loving presence that offers a deeper level of safety, comfort, and acknowledgment than the experience has ever received from you before, thereby being the practice of detachment, allowance, pure love, and space.

Ask: "Divine heart, I accept that I don't know how to say an inner "yes" to experiencing the vast unknown within me. Therefore, I ask that you say an inner "yes" to experiencing emptiness, worthlessness, and limitation for me. Welcome, embrace, honor, and validate these experiences for me, through me, as I am now, healing the inner division within me, so that my perception can expand and align with the flow of infinite information." And so it is (Amen).

B- BREATHE

Breathe in these feelings (*"I receive you as life"*) breathe out (*"You are free to be"*). Be one with the breath: *"The breath is my best friend."*

I-I LOVE YOU

Place your hands over your heart. Say, *"I love you! All is an expression of one life. I validate this limited experience within me. It is an experience from my past that was not validated by my relationships to the world. Therefore, I choose to be the presence of love that provides this experience the resonation of love that it has never received. May I be all the affirmation that this limited experience needs to remember that it is an infinite expression of divinity, so that it may fully awaken from the illusion of limitation. I love you!"*

"I am abundant, wise, infinite, and free!"

T- THANK YOU

Thank the experience for helping you remember that you are an ever-expanding unique expression of the Truth. Thank the circumstance, story, or relationship that triggered these feelings in your body, so your entire being could awaken to your innocent nature of authentic freedom that can enjoy all experiences.

> *"Thank you for helping me to align and attune with my heart's ever-expanding unique expression of infinite wisdom and pure love! Thank you for helping me to remember the power of life that I am!"*

Intention: *(say aloud)*

"Today, I choose to allow the stored files of "me" in my head to be deleted by detaching from all knowledge and understanding, merging with emptiness and relaxing into the infinite mind of clarity, which functions spontaneously as Divine wisdom in the present moment."

Affirmation: *(say aloud)*

Say aloud throughout today:

"All words are pure life because I am pure life!"

Day 9

Transmutation

"Since everything is already the Supreme Buddha (God) nature, where are you going to find it?"

–Adyashanti

Mirror Work

Say Aloud: (looking into your eyes in a mirror)
Good morning, infinite one. You are safe to feel. I always want to know how you are feeling. You are the soul-mate that I have been looking for my entire life. You matter and you are enough. You are worthy of being seen and heard. I see you and I am here to listen to you. There is a good reason you are here; you are Divine perfection. Today, I join you in celebrating your ever-expanding unique expression. I am open to receiving new information and new ways of being by choosing to receive all uncomfortable, unfamiliar, painful, inconvenient, and unwanted experiences as a Divine gift from you, my infinite heart. I love all of you! I really love all of you. (your name), I really love all of you. (Feel free to write your own love statement).

The power inherent in the pure consciousness that is ever-present throughout all of existence is similar to transmutation. Transmutation is the transformation of one form into another. Awakening out of the head-centered me is like a process of transmutation. Pure awareness is the expansion of perceiving all experiences of existence as the life and love that I am. Therefore, it is a perception that includes all experiences; no experience is excluded from being received as the love that I am. Pure awareness is able to transform all perceptions of right and wrong into one perception of pure life, pure love, or one essence. It is the very power that perceives only itself throughout all appearances and forms of existence. I experienced this power within me as awareness awoke out of judgment by being the heart-centered habit. I began to write about what I felt on the inside. I allowed all judgments, emotions, feelings, and beliefs to have a voice. I even asked them what they wanted to say and I allowed them to use my hand to express what they were forbidden to express. I wrote for an entire weekend, and by the end of the weekend, I was shocked as to what I experienced within: emptiness.

All diverse forms; thoughts, beliefs, emotions, feelings, appearances, people, things, and everything else seemed to melt into oneness. I could still see how all appeared different, but I experienced all experiences as the same life or love that I am within my heart. First my inner experience of reality melted into one reality. Then I began to notice that when my children and husband become angry, frustrated, or sad, I experienced it as life too. Experiences that used to bother the head-centered me didn't bother me anymore. The head-centered me that was comprised of judgments transmuted into the heart-centered me, which sensed harmony with all of reality. When pure consciousness is experienced from within, all forms are experienced through an infinite depth of perception. Everything is in a constant state of transformation and pure consciousness is the fuel for its expansion. Being the heart-centered habit provided my being the awareness to rest in the river of life or the pure consciousness of existence.

"This unwanted experience is a gift."
You are welcome here.
You are enough!
How may I serve you?

Labels and Names

"The Tao (God) that can be spoken is not the eternal Tao (God). The name that can be named is not the eternal name."

-Tao Te Ching ch.1

If everything is the nature of God, then why do cultures fight over the different names of God? God is not an object, label, name, or form. God is the spiritual essence, pure conscious-awareness, or formless infinite energy that exists at the core of all matter. God is the infinite potential that is 99.999 percent of the make-up of all forms, matter, or appearances. When we identify with our authentic nature of God or divinity, we don't have to believe in the superstitions or meanings of particular names and labels. When Jesus was on the cross, a thief was on a cross next to him. Jesus told the thief that soon he would enter paradise. When we die we return back into a dimension of oneness; a consciousness that isn't rooted in judgment or separation. Jesus said we could enter this dimension, which he called the Kingdom of Heaven, before we physically die. The judgmental mind or head-centered me is rooted in fear. There are parts of our self that we have refused to fully feel. These parts of our self are experiences that we were taught to deny and not embrace as goodness. These experiences were shunned and we labeled them with a name and placed them in the section of our rational mind that perceived similar experiences in the present moment as wrong.

These unpleasant experiences will continue to get triggered within us, until we allow our being to embrace them by feeling them fully. Even though we use names in practicing the heart-centered habit at the end of each day along this 22-day journey, these names do not truly define the experience. They are just repressed energies that we refuse to feel. We must feel to heal. It is easier to feel when we sense that these repressed energies that we call emotions are just aspects of the one self that we have denied. When we bring everything into the light, the light of oneness will shine through us as us.

The rational mind defines and labels every experience as good and bad. It doesn't understand oneness or fearlessness. It literally has to be reprogrammed to being heart-centered. The more it tunes in with the heart-centered habit, the more it remembers the dimension of oneness. Reprogramming the head-centered me to sense information from within instead of without requires faith because in the beginning oneness isn't experienced as the Truth. Instead, sensing the right and wrong meanings of names and labels that it has been programmed to believe still make sense because most of the world still functions from these definitions.

Remembrance of our true authentic nature of oneness requires redefining every label and name as an expression of divinity. Remembrance is experienced when awareness no longer swings to the "right" or to the "wrong." Instead, it rests in the center, in the knowing, in the pure consciousness that all is one. Divinity, God, or Buddha has no opposite. All names and labels point awareness into center; singularity. We just have to allow awareness to drop into the black hole and stop jumping back and forth in polarity or duality.

We have thought that we were responsible to chase after everything that is considered good, right, and true. We have been chasing after our dreams, which are listed on the "good" side. We have created a role for our rational mind that is an impossible feat. The only responsibility we have is to reconcile all rights and wrongs into a unified perception of life, oneness, and love. We don't have to like what we are experiencing to perceive it as a symbol of harmony. Everything is a

175

symbol of harmony or life, thereby releasing the rational mind of its unnatural role to choose whether the experience is good (harmony) or bad (disharmony), so that we may return to our innocent, vulnerable, open nature that perceives harmony and oneness throughout all experiences. This is our authentic nature that is connected throughout all of existence. It is time to surrender to our true nature, which is the director to all of life that has no opposite.

The source of life has no opposite. When we remember to be the heart-centered habit, which loves all parts, aspects, and experiences of reality, we remember that all is one life, creating a harmonious, balanced, and coherent Universe that works together as one.

"This uncomfortable experience is a gift."
You are welcome here.
You are enough!
How may I serve you?

Conscious Evolution

Conscious evolution is an invitation within human consciousness to participate in harmonizing with our authentic nature of pure Love to evolve the human species. We feel this calling deep within our core. There are many people on the planet right now who are searching for enlightenment or spiritual awakening. Right now we are at a place in our evolution where we can be the heart-centered habit and be the love that the world has never seen. A conscious awake being is someone who knows in every moment that they are in harmony with all experiences of reality whether emotional, physical, mental, spiritual, metaphysical, or relational. You are invited to become a conscious heart-centered being and love every piece, part, and experience of yourself more than you ever have before. If you have chosen to take this 22-day journey of remembrance, then you are ready to step into harmony with all of existence.

The words in each chapter of this 22-day journey are guides that point awareness inward to sensing the love which you truly are. These words come from the essence of your soul, which is awaiting your return. The intuition within your heart holds the keys of remembrance to your authentic spiritual nature that opposes nothing. Ask your heart or innocent nature to open the files of remembrance of what life really feels like when there is no belief system held in the rational mind, no sense of opposition, and no sense of division. Allow yourself to go deeper until you remember your innocent, vulnerable, loving nature. Maybe you won't remember it from your childhood in this lifetime, but the remembrance is still there. Come home and remember your mission to be pure love, allowing space for all judgments to express themselves inside yourself. Writing about your judgments or your inner experiences that have not had a voice is very healing. When you can be the vessel that allows everything to have a voice within you, everything returns home to oneness. Continue writing until you feel spacious and still on the inside. This is a necessary step in participating in being heart-centered. Will you accept the invitation to participate in the conscious evolution that is happening within human consciousness or the mind of humanity?

In truth there is no evolution because what we are is already whole and complete. What evolves or changes is actually our perception of reality. Our perception shifts from the outside-in, which perceives everything as separate and divided, into perceiving from the inside-out, which perceives oneness, unity, harmony, beauty, and love. It is like looking back in history and being amazed how people in the world believed the world was flat. Now that we know the world is round, we won't go back to believing that the world is flat. The world didn't evolve from a flat world into a round world. It was round the whole time, but our perception of the world changed. Once we live by our knowing that we are infinite beings that are connected, we won't go back to believing that we are limited beings that are separate.

"This painful experience is a gift."
You are welcome here.
You are enough!
How may I serve you?

States of Matter

Conscious evolution is a process of guiding all outside-in perceptions back toward center or singularity. When we are heart-centered, we are willing to embrace experiences that feel like enemies to what we want. Our heart- centered knowing guides our perception to seeing them as symbols of harmony and we open the door of our heart by loving them as they are. These unwanted experiences, which felt immovable, stable, and impenetrable then feel as if they are melting into a fluid or liquid state. We feel lighter. This is an indication that our perception is shifting from the outside-in to the inside-out. As we continue to love, honor, and thank them for helping us remember our heart-centered perception of divinity, we feel as if they evaporate from a liquid into a gas. Now we feel even lighter. Lightness in our body allows us to know that we are shifting from perceiving reality as the head-centered me to the heart-centered me. The shift in our perception occurs through the light of awareness. As we are willing to look at, embrace, and experience everything we feel in every moment, all solid belief systems of right and wrong return to their formless nature of pure life.

The dense repressed, negative emotions that continually get triggered by inconvenient, painful, uncomfortable, unwanted, and unfamiliar experiences are the solid objects we are here to transmute. We have the ability to align our perception with the power of divinity to transmute these negative emotions. We feel these experiences as negative because they are not in the formless flow of energy or life, which is the beginning and end of their destiny. Instead, they are stuck in the solid state of being because they have become repressed, compressed, and denied as a part of the goodness of life.

The heart-centered habit guides our perception into alignment with our infinite powerful authentic spiritual nature. Be honest with the negative experiences within you. Know that it is okay to feel what you feel, as you haven't done anything wrong. Acknowledge that there is nobody or anything to blame for how you feel. Breathe and be willing to be with what is here. Love the part of you that feels this way. Be thankful for the experience that was an angel in disguise guiding you back to your authentic power of pure love. As these solid experiences transmute into formless gas and disappear from your experience, spacious awareness remains. We fill the space in our heads and bodies with love. This love ripples out into our relationships to the physical world. The invitation to participate in being heart-centered gets sent out to everyone and everything you come across.

The human species is in the midst of the transformation that many spiritual teachers prophesied about in history. What an exciting time to be here with you! Thank you for participating in humanity's conscious evolution, where we will take a quantum leap into authenticity, harmony, and peace.

"This unfamiliar experience is a gift."
You are welcome here.
You are enough!
How may I serve you?

179

Reflection

Are you willing to participate in transmuting all solid beliefs of right and wrong into the formless essence of pure life? Are you willing to perceive through the heart of the matter?

Reprogramming the Subconscious Mind

"Be still and know that anger and rage is God, a part of your true authentic nature."

Practicing the heart-centered habit: (Example)

Have you ever felt anger or rage?

Welcome these experiences as a part of consciousness (You):

H- HONESTY

"I fully feel the parts of me that have felt angry and furious."

A-ACKNOWLEDGE, ALLOW, ASK

"I acknowledge that it is safe and okay to feel this limited experience. I embrace these feelings fully just as they are because I know they are here to show me the way into my heart. As I embrace these feelings fully, I ask them to bring with them all of the past meanings, interpretations, beliefs, and judgments that I thought were true, but are not valid in this present moment, so that I may receive them as a gift, guide, and opening toward the infinite perception in my heart. I acknowledge their Divine role in

helping me expand awareness into the depths of infinite knowing.”

Allow the uncomfortable experience to have a voice. Do not believe what it is saying, but instead be a loving presence that offers a deeper level of safety, comfort, and acknowledgment than the experience has ever received from you before, being the practice of detachment, allowance, pure love, and space.

Ask: “Divine heart, I accept that I don’t know how to transmute solid beliefs and experiences back into unity consciousness. Therefore, I ask that you transmute anger and rage back into the pure state of oneness or pure love for me. Welcome, embrace, honor, and validate these experiences for me, through me, as I am now, healing the inner division within me, so that my perception can expand and align with the flow of infinite information.” *And so it is (Amen).*

B- BREATHE

Breathe in these feelings (*“I receive you as life”*) and breathe out (*“You are free to be”*). Be one with the breath: *“The breath is God.”*

I-I LOVE YOU

Place your hands over your heart and say, *“I love you! All is an expression of one life. I validate this limited experience within me. It is an experience from my past that was not validated by my relationships to the world. Therefore, I choose to be the presence of love that provides this experience the resonation of love it has never received. May I be all the affirmation that this limited experience needs to remember that it is an infinite expression of divinity so that it may fully awaken from the illusion of limitation. I love you!”*

181

"I am abundant, wise, infinite, and free!"

T- THANK YOU

Thank the experience for helping you remember that you are an ever-expanding unique expression of the Truth. Thank the circumstance, story, or relationship that triggered these feelings in your body, so your entire being could awaken to your innocent nature of authentic freedom that can enjoy all experiences.

> *"Thank you for helping me to align and attune with my heart's ever-expanding unique expression of infinite wisdom and pure love! Thank you for helping me to remember the power of life that I am!"*

Intention: *(say aloud)*

"Today, I choose to allow the head-centered "me" to transmute into the heart-centered "me" by acknowledging that all labels and names point to the essence of Divine oneness. I choose to participate in the conscious evolution of all states of matter, therefore perceiving through the heart of the matter."

Affirmation: *(say aloud)*

Say aloud throughout today:

"All beings are authentic because I am authentic!"

Day 10

Surrender

"Peace comes from within. Do not seek it without."

-Buddhism

Say Aloud: (looking into your eyes in a mirror)
Good morning, infinite one. You are safe to feel. I always want to know how you are feeling. You are the soul-mate that I have been looking for my entire life. You matter and you are enough. You are worthy of being seen and heard. I see you and I am here to listen to you. There is a good reason you are here; you are Divine perfection. Today, I join you in celebrating your ever-expanding unique expression. I am open to receiving new information and new ways of being by choosing to receive all uncomfortable, unfamiliar, painful, inconvenient, and unwanted experiences as a Divine gift from you, my infinite heart. I love all of you! I really love all of you. (your name), I really love all of you. (Feel free to write your own love statement).

Throughout my whole life I never felt like I had my own experience. I was always running away from feeling everybody else's experience of reality. I realized that experience is comprised of what thoughts, beliefs, judgments, and emotions we attach to within our rational mind. We are actually having a mental experience about reality instead of receiving and merging with reality itself. The mental delusion that we subconsciously create within our rational mind functions by trying to control reality through manipulation, expectation, comparison, and judgment to get what we think we want. This mental delusion began to unravel in my rational mind as I remembered my authentic nature of no experience or peace.

I can remember being a child and not having a single thought about reality. I was in a state of full surrender to the moment. I felt one with everything that arose. I merged with everything. Then once I entered school I began attaching to other peoples' experiences about reality. Their thoughts became my thoughts. Their experience became my experience. Over time I got lost and partially forgot my authentic nature of peace, which had no experience or attachment to thoughts about reality. I began believing in these thoughts. I noticed that all thoughts about reality point awareness to either accept what is or deny what is being experienced in the moment. Denial toward my inner experiences is what began to create a division between my head and my heart.

When I began waking up out of the attachments to thoughts, beliefs, judgments, and ideas by being the heart-centered habit, which welcomes, merges, and loves everything exactly as it is, I felt like I was being transported back into the innocence, vulnerability, openness, and curiosity that I remember as a child. Underneath the mental delusion exists an ever-present living existence that is pre-thought, pre-form, pre-identity, and pre-feeling. It is a peace that surpasses our rational mind's understanding. I also realized the mental delusion focuses on feeling a certain way. When I stopped expecting life to appear a certain way, I remembered peace. When I stopped expecting to feel a certain way, I remembered peace. When I stopped expecting to think or act a certain way in my relationships, I remembered peace.

As I became the practice of the heart-centered habit, the rational mind's functions of judgment, control, expectation, manipulation, and comparison began to slow way down and eventually disappeared from my experience. The more I focused on the energy I sensed within me, the less I focused on the energy outside of me. Inner freedom began to emerge as I stopped expecting reality to be a certain way by acknowledging every experience as Divine and loving the part of me that lived in the land of expectation. I remembered to fully receive and love the part of "me" that only knew how to survive through expectation.

The head-centered me creates two separate qualities that we are able to experience. One is happiness and the other is suffering. Happiness is the quality of our experience when our expectations are being met by life. Suffering is the quality of our experience when our expectations are not being met. We suffer because we expect life to be different than it is by saying, "I don't want this." "This shouldn't be happening." "This isn't fair." "This is wrong." This is a way of thinking that we tune into because it is a dominant way of thinking in our world. We are all connected by our essence. Therefore, we feel this way of thinking regardless of where we grow up in the world. Like everyone else, I too became lost in this delusional thinking, misperception, or sin. The denial of receiving certain experiences because they do not fit into our head's expectations misaligns us with the perception of our heart. Our heart receives everything as life. Our heart perceives the light of divinity in all experiences.

The good news is that life continuously brings us opportunities of insight to realize or remember our authentic nature of peace. The shift from delusional thinking to authentic peace has been occurring for a long time. The tipping point is fast approaching, where more people will be in a total state of surrender. Living from the heart-centered habit allows our rational mind to surrender all of its content of delusional thinking. Tuning into the authentic peace that we are is key to our spiritual remembrance. The heart-centered habit is a tuning fork that engages all of life and returns everything back into the full expression of peace. A peace that isn't thought into existence. A peace that isn't physically manifested. A peace that isn't felt through emotion. Instead, a peace that existed before the mind, body, and all other forms of reality. Every moment is an invitation to surrender to the peace that is always present.

"This unwanted experience is a gift."
You are welcome here.
You are enough!
How may I serve you?

Atonement

"No problem can be solved from the same level of consciousness that created it."

–Albert Einstein

Atonement means to be at one with everything. Every moment is an opportunity for us to make atonement with it. We were born to become one with all of life. Our life purpose is to become one with existence. When we say, "no" to any part of life, we are saying, "I am fearful," and, "I don't want to know this part of myself." Then we become imprisoned by what we are saying "no' to. It sticks to us like glue. If we say "no" to the experience of fear because we are expecting to feel happy all the time, then we become imprisoned by fear. It sticks around in our rational mind and we become imprisoned by fear, skepticism, worry, doubt, and anxiety.

If we continue to relate with the physical world as a head-centered me, which is a divided self that functions on delusional thinking, then we will continue to suffer. We cannot heal human suffering by being the habit of the head-centered me, which is one with some of existence but NOT with the rest of existence. We can participate in being the heart-centered habit to heal our

186

own rational minds, thereby aligning with the healing quality of our one eternal presence. When challenged by a condition we can say "yes" to the condition. So we may know the eternal self more. By saying "yes" to the unwanted condition, we allow it to crucify the consciousness of right and wrong. The path to awakening is through the darkness, unwanted condition, and inconvenient circumstances. The head-centered me that feels separate from God, divinity, love, life, or eternal self will unravel when we love every part of it and surrender to the peace or unity consciousness that has always been here.

Our problems cannot be solved from the head-centered consciousness of separation. This is because our problems are symptoms to believing in separation and division. If we want to solve our problems, then we will need to adopt a new level of consciousness than the one that created them. Heart centered-consciousness or unity consciousness is a consciousness that will dissolve all of our problems, suffering, and pain. The heart-centered habit can guide the head to functioning from heart-centered consciousness, which welcomes, honors, and respects all experiences. Instead of fighting, escaping, or denying experiences through the outdated head-centered consciousness, which has created the symptoms of conflict, division, war, separation, and suffering. The answer to healing our planet has been within us all along.

"This uncomfortable experience is a gift."
You are welcome here.
You are enough!
How may I serve you?

Relaxation

"Nothing can trap you in Life once you see the good of it."

-Guy Finley

Every moment is for our good. Not the good that we think into existence through mental delusion of good and evil. Instead, every moment appears the way it does to remind us of our eternal fearless self. Anything in life that can trap us, is showing us the head-centered me that is based upon delusion. Our authentic eternal self cannot be trapped. Therefore, if we ever feel trapped by a moment, then the head-centered me is being invited to expand and transform into the eternal self by saying "yes" to the unwanted condition. Once we see this intention of good within all unwanted, inconvenient, uncomfortable, and stressful experiences, we remember the eternal self that dwells in our heart that is always authentically free.

The head-centered me, which perceives limitation, lack, and separation is attracting all of our unwanted conditions. What the head-centered me perceives as a trap, the heart-centered me perceives as a spiritual teacher. The trap or spiritual teacher is here to set the head-centered me free. The head- centered me's innate desire is freedom. Authentic freedom is the good that is at hand when we are faced with unwanted, unwelcomed, unpleasant conditions.

When we choose to perceive all unwanted experiences as a gift of goodness our bodies sink into a relaxed state. The key during moments of stress, pain, suffering, strife, conflict, and fear is to relax. Relaxation is the natural symptom to being the habit of the heart-centered me. The heart-centered me needs nothing. Therefore, for the head-centered me to relax it must lay down what it thinks it needs. The head-centered me is manufactured through a foundation of neediness. It needs to know, understand, and find answers to its questions. It needs to fit in with its external environment. It needs approval, acceptance, love, and admiration from its external environment. It needs affirmation and validation from its external environment. It needs to feel happy all the time, denying, repressing, escaping, or fighting any emotion that does not evoke happy feelings. It needs to be comfortable, wanted, and needed by its external environment. It believes it is wrong to waste time, which is impossible to do because time doesn't exist. It believes it is wrong to feel bored because it can only survive through a constant state of distraction.

Needing to stay distracted is a conditional response that the head-centered me functions from because it was taught that it is not okay to feel certain experiences. Therefore, the head-centered me remains over-stimulated by attaching to its external environment.

The heart-centered habit guides the head-centered habit part of me to relax. Honesty induces relaxation, acknowledging that we don't need to create a story of blame for the way we feel and it is okay to feel. Focusing on being the breath with whatever we are feeling in the moment helps to circulate relaxation into every cell of our bodies. Saying, "I Love You" to the part of our self that feels this way sends ripples of relaxation through our heart to the hearts of all. Being thankful for the good that came about due to the unwanted condition integrates this new heart-centered way of being into the subconscious mind.

Then when we experience an unwanted experience, we have a new way of responding to it. The more we relax, the more our subconscious mind programs an internal response of relaxation throughout any chaos in life. Therefore, each moment we are heart-centered, we are downloading new files of relaxation into our human consciousness. May these be the files that new babies download when they are born. May these be the files we swap with people who we interact with in the world. May we all awaken to our authentic natural state of relaxation, instead of the old files of "fight" or "flight," which have dominated human perception with clouds of delusion, imbalance, and disharmony. Stress, overwhelm, and chaos are indicators that life is inviting us to become heart-centered and offer relaxation to the head-centered me through harmony, love, and support.

"This painful experience is a gift."
You are welcome here.
You are enough!
How may I serve you?

189

Gratitude

The head-centered habit believes we are blessed when life is void of unwanted conditions. We are conditioned to only be grateful when life is going the way we have imagined it should go. This doesn't last long before an unwanted condition shows up. Then the head-centered me feels like it is being punished or victimized. The unwanted condition is proof that a part of the self is asleep or unconscious, lost in a delusion of right and wrong, should and shouldn't, good and bad, punishment and reward. The unwanted condition says, "All right, let's get to work on waking up this unconscious part out of delusion and into the authentic reality of life." The unwanted condition is an answer to a prayer. We have been praying for peace, fulfillment, and freedom for ages. Now here it is, our opportunity to uncover everything we have always desired. It is here, right now, only covered up by delusions of separation. We can say, "Yes, thank you for finally coming to wake me up out of this nightmare! I am so grateful to have an opportunity to be heart-centered. I am so grateful to remember the eternal self that is already here! I am so grateful to receive the spiritual gifts of peace, fulfillment, and freedom that are within this unwanted condition."

When we can remember to be grateful for everything we want and don't want; we like and don't like; we expect and don't expect; we judge as right or wrong; acknowledge as good or bad; we will have transcended into a heart- centered being. We don't have to wait for the rest of the world to be grateful. We can be grateful first. We can be grateful right now within whatever circumstances we are faced with right NOW. We don't have to wait for something "good" to happen to be grateful. If only "bad" things are happening in our life, we can be grateful for every single one of them and we will transcend faster than the speed of light. Stop and take a moment to be grateful for every circumstance

190

in your life right now! It takes faith to be grateful for everything that has happened or is happening that you have judged as "bad," "wrong," "shouldn't," or "don't want." It is okay to feel whatever arises as you exercise faith. You can acknowledge not liking what you are experiencing at the same time, acknowledging it as a gift of awakening. Welcome all of your experiences through the heart-centered habit.

Examples:

I am grateful that I have experienced rejection, fear, insecurity, ego, head-centered me, drunkenness, gluttony, manipulation, expectation, anxiety, pain, heartbreak, evil, darkness, hell, anger, rage, coldness, sadness, depression, poverty, bankruptcy, separation, debt, sin, rape, martyrdom, exhaustion, fatigue, disease, vulnerability, judgment, criticism, guilt, shame, boredom, impatience, suffering, striving, struggling, abandonment, stress, chaos, overwhelm, jealousy, envy, lust, wrongness, badness, stubbornness, ignorance, hatred, murder, frustration, confusion, disharmony, grief, closed-mindedness, heathen, unknown, hopelessness, lack of motivation, lack of purpose, doubt, worry, skepticism, distraction, addiction, alcohol, drugs, solitude, loneliness, noise, disturbance, aging, illness, grey hair, balding, wrinkles, sagging skin, poor eyesight, obesity, and emptiness.

I admit that I did not like experiencing these experiences and I love the part of me that felt uncomfortable through each experience. I acknowledge that all of these experiences are gifts of divinity that showed up to remind me of the all-powerful infinite nature that I AM, which does not identify with any particular experience. I am the infinite nature that is all experiences rolled into one. Therefore, what I am changes from one moment to the next. If I choose to linger within these uncomfortable experiences then I choose to forget that I am infinite. I ask that the memories, stagnant beliefs, and identifications with these unwanted experiences pass through me as me, so that I may align once again with the infinite flow of life. I acknowledge that enlightenment is the recognition that all experiences are expressions of the one Divine light, the light I AM.

Wayne Dyer said, "When you change the way you look at things, the things you look at change." What if you looked at all of the above unwanted conditions with gratitude? They may transform into blessings that were disguised as a curse. I am grateful for all generational curses and inner demons because they were my spiritual opportunities to practice being the heart-centered habit, which is my authentic nature of power, light, love, freedom, and fulfillment. We were born to experience love in all of these diverse ways throughout the whole spectrum of good and bad. Faith is the courage to perceive it all as life, love, divinity, and pure Light, even when we don't like what we are experiencing, such as times of adverse, inconvenient, uncomfortable, and unwanted circumstances.

When we are equally willing to be bored as we are to being motivated, the head-centered me relaxes into the heart. When we are equally willing to waste time as we are to getting a ton done in a short amount of time, the head- centered me relaxes into the heart. When we are equally willing to be exhausted as we are to having tons of energy, the head-centered me relaxes into the heart. The heart-centered habit guides the head-centered me to be equally willing to embrace, welcome, and fully feel all experiences regardless of the way it appears or feels. Then the head-centered me will awaken to the infinite flow of life that is in control of every piece, part, and aspect of existence. The head-centered me will realize it hasn't created anything or done anything because all experiences are happening without reason. Therefore, your heart has no reasons for being grateful because gratitude is the heart's natural state of being.

An attitude of gratitude toward all experiences, circumstances, conditions, emotions, actions, and thoughts creates coherency between the intuitive heart and the rational mind. A coherent signal is energy that is naturally together. It is a signal where information or energy is consistent and resonates together. Coherency creates a relaxed response. When the heart and mind are coherent they resonate an inner sense of peace, fulfillment, and freedom. Life flows easily without struggle or difficulty. When the mind and heart are coherent our entire being transcends the limitations and boundaries of the head-centered me or mental delusional self.

When the heart and mind are non-coherent, the head-centered me thinks it is in control. A non-coherent signal is where energy is not consistent, not together naturally. It is an unclear signal with resistance, static, and interference. When we remember to be the heart-centered habit and welcome all unwanted conditions by greeting them with gratitude, we are participating in maintaining a coherent signal of unity, harmony, and peace. Stress, overwhelm, and chaos are indicators that life is inviting us to love the head- centered me and experience more coherence with the true nature of existence through gratitude.

"This unfamiliar experience is a gift."
You are welcome here.
You are enough!
How may I serve you?

193

Reflection

What if you didn't need to feel a certain way other than the way you feel right now? What if you didn't need to think a certain way other than the thoughts that are arising right now? What if you didn't need to act a certain way other than the way you are acting right now? What if you are the only one who has a problem with the way you are? Will you choose atonement or division? The choice is yours in every moment.

Reprogramming the Subconscious Mind

"Be still and know that chaos and conflict is God, a part of your true authentic nature."

Practicing the heart-centered habit: (Example)

Have you ever felt conflicted and chaotic?

Welcome these experiences as a part of consciousness (You):

H- HONESTY

"I fully feel the parts of me that have felt conflict and chaos."

A-ACKNOWLEDGE, ALLOW, ASK

"I acknowledge that it is safe and okay to feel this limited experience. I embrace these feelings fully just as they are because I know they are here to show me the way into my heart. As I embrace these feelings fully, I ask them to bring with them all of the past meanings, interpretations, beliefs, and judgments that I thought were true, but are not valid in this present moment, so that I may receive

them as a gift, guide, and opening toward the infinite perception in my heart. I acknowledge their Divine role in helping me expand awareness into the depths of infinite knowing."

Allow the uncomfortable experience to have a voice. Do not believe what it is saying, but instead be a loving presence that offers a deeper level of safety, comfort, and acknowledgment than the experience has ever received from you before, being the practice of detachment, allowance, pure love, and space.

Ask: "Divine heart, I accept that I don't know how to be grateful for uncomfortable, unwanted, painful, inconvenient, and unfamiliar experiences. Therefore, I ask that you fill my being with gratitude for the experience of conflict and chaos for me. Welcome, embrace, honor, and validate these experiences for me, through me, as I am now, thereby healing the inner division within me, so my perception can expand and align with the flow of infinite information." And so it is (Amen).

B- BREATHE

Breathe in these feelings (*"I receive you as life"*), breathe out (*"You are free to be"*). Be one with the breath: *"The breath is my authentic nature."*

I-I LOVE YOU

Place your hands over your heart. Say, *"I love you! All is an expression of one life. I validate this limited experience within me. It is an experience from my past that was not validated by my relationships to the world. Therefore, I choose to be the presence of love that provides this experience the resonation of love that it has never received. May I be all the affirmation that this limited experience needs to remember that it is an infinite expression of divinity, so that it may fully awaken from the illusion of limitation. I love you!"*

"I am abundant, wise, infinite, and free!"

T- THANK YOU

Thank the experience for helping you to remember that you are an ever-expanding unique expression of the Truth. Thank the circumstance, story, or relationship that triggered these feelings in your body, so your entire being could awaken to your innocent nature of authentic freedom that can enjoy all experiences.

> *"Thank you for helping me to align and attune with my heart's ever-expanding unique expression of infinite wisdom and pure love! Thank you for helping me to remember the power of life that I am!"*

Intention: *(say aloud)*

"Today, I choose to surrender my personal understanding of reality, so that I may atone or become one with all experiences and relax into my authentic nature of gratitude."

Affirmation: *(say aloud)*

Say aloud throughout today:

"My breath is relaxed because I am gratitude!"

Day 11

Give Away Possessions

"Don't look for your dreams to come true; look to become true to your dreams."
– Michael Bernard Beckwith

Say Aloud: (looking into your eyes in a mirror)
Good morning, infinite one. You are safe to feel. I always want to know how you are feeling. You are the soul-mate that I have been looking for my entire life. You matter and you are enough. You are worthy of being seen and heard. I see you and I am here to listen to you. There is a good reason you are here; you are Divine perfection. Today, I join you in celebrating your ever-expanding unique expression. I am open to receiving new information and new ways of being by choosing to receive all uncomfortable, unfamiliar, painful, inconvenient, and unwanted experiences as a Divine gift from you, my infinite heart. I love all of you! I really love all of you. (your name), I really love all of you. (Feel free to write your own love statement).

Life is such a mystery, where we experience being an individual within a web of interconnected and unified energy. We are the .001 percent individualized unique forms appearing within the 99.999 percent unified field of infinite energy. In my experience of being in this world, the mystery of life becomes obscured by an illusion; that happiness is something to pursue. Therefore, we chase after happiness and believe our happiness is somewhere out there within a future goal. We think once we attain that future goal or we possess what we think will make us happy this void within us will feel satisfied. We may also believe it is the world's job to make us happy. In my experience, nothing that I possessed or attained in this world satisfied the inner urge or calling to listen and follow the intuitive guidance of my heart.

This pursuit to find happiness creates a sense of separation between us and our true nature of fulfillment. Why would we settle for happiness when we can remember our infinite nature, which brings infinite fulfillment and freedom? Happiness is just pennies compared to the fulfillment of the realization of our true abundant nature.

Our rational mind settles on the appearances of happiness that it sees in the world. The head-centered me is focused on possessing a life of happiness. Possessing a life of happiness takes God or Divine will out of the driver's seat and puts our rational mind in control. Now we have a separate personal will, which strives to achieve a life of happiness, which is an illusion. It is an illusion because what our rational mind truly desires is the relaxation, peace, freedom, and fulfillment that it receives when it is aligned with the intuition that arises from within the heart, which is Divine will.

When I perceived reality through the head-centered nature, I worked to earn a living, instead of being the living presence of divinity. Money became my God because it dictated to me how much life I possessed by the amount of money I had in my bank account. Rarely did I feel free to do what I loved, which was an ever-expanding expression of the living presence within me. Instead, I struggled to gain more money, so I could live more. Money became my guidance on what to do, which came from a place of trying to create more. I struggled to possess happiness through my personal will. Happiness was a state that would come and go. I couldn't hold onto that happy life. Life had another plan and I suffered terribly until I finally wanted what life wanted, which required faith to choose love in every moment.

When I wanted what I thought I needed to be happy, I was constantly struggling with the moment. I was rarely present with what I felt because I was so focused on what I thought about the moment and how it was not meeting my expectations of happiness. I existed in a mental world of judgment and criticism, always analyzing the moment and comparing it to how I thought it should be. Life within me was calling for my attention through writing, but my rational mind had other plans that constantly distracted me from moments of writing. Writing for me was an expression of tuning in to what I felt underneath this false life I was living to please the world. Writing expressed the Divine wisdom within me that wanted to express itself through my rational mind.

Writing was an act of surrender, where my rational mind stopped projecting an image of a happy life and listened intuitively to the information that was coming through the heart of the matter. The life within me was calling out to my rational mind to listen and express the infinite love it felt from within. Life used writing as a practice of remembrance; reprogramming the rational mind to tune in to the life and love that was present from within and not without, hence unraveling all of the misinterpretations of truth that were held hostage in my rational mind because I thought they were stepping stones to possessing a happy life.

My rational mind was in a momentum of habits, routines, and plans of trying to possess a happy, healthy, and free life. Therefore, it was hard to stop it from its pursuit of happiness. Life had to step in and stop it for me. Life put me in my place to resolve, reconcile, and unravel the head-centered me. Many of my relationships to the physical world began to end and become extremely painful. There was nowhere else to run except to go within and discover the love that I am!

Life was shouting at me through my finances, marriage, career, and roles. All of my relationships to this physical world needed healing. The head-centered me had unraveled to a point that there was no way that I could go back to the old way of trying to fix things from its limited vantage point. I knew the only way my life would heal is by being heart-centered. This book is the reflection of the head-centered me unraveling into the pure love, life, passion, excitement, enthusiasm, and intuition of the heart-centered me. This book reveals the journey of my resurrection. May the writing in this book be a mirror that reveals your authentic heart-centered nature.

The life that we are is always trying to get our attention in every moment. The head-centered nature perceives this life within us as foolishness because it doesn't follow the plan that the rational mind has created in an effort to possess a happy life. The heart-centered nature is the doorway to expressing a life of infinite wisdom. This is our true nature. In my experience, I had to give up all of my possessions to sink into the heart-centered nature of my being. These were not physical possessions. Instead they were the mental ideas, plans, judgments, thoughts, routines, schedules, beliefs, and ways that my rational mind had attached to as my personal will to possess a happy life.

I gave away these possessions in every moment I declared that I wanted the moment to be just as it was, especially when it appeared and felt like everything my rational mind didn't want. When my rational mind's plans were not being played out in the moment, I surrendered its plan by loving the one that needed a plan. Life had provided many opportunities for me to do what it wanted me to do, which was to write. But it wasn't until my rational mind had no other choice but to write that true surrender began. My rational mind experienced that no matter how hard it tried to possess a happy sustained life, it was impossible.

Life is a creative power that creates infinite potential. The rational mind can be used to express this infinite potential when it is in a state of surrender. However, when it gets in the driver's seat it creates a limited reality on its own. The rational mind is not the source of infinite potential. It is a limited creation that can only manifest a limited reality when left to its own devices of judgment, control, manipulation, comparison, and expectation. However, when the rational mind surrenders its plans of possessing a happy life and aligns to the unified field of infinite life within, it can resonate unlimited potential through infinite creative ways.

"This unwanted experience is a gift."
You are welcome here.
You are enough!
How may I serve you?

Relationships

In our pursuit to possess a happy life, we unconsciously project happiness outside of our self. We think it is our role to make other people happy, and in turn we expect them to make us happy. Both individuals have different expectations for happiness in a relationship. Therefore, it is an impossible task to meet other people's expectations without sacrificing your own ideas of happiness. The head-centered me is always keeping record of who is doing more to make the other person happy. If we are doing more than the other then we feel like a victim. This sets the stage for the highs and lows within our relationships. We feel high, happy, and loved when they make us happy or we feel low, depressed, and unloved when they don't make us happy. It is impossible to maintain a steady sense of life, happiness, and love in relationships when we

201

perceive reality in a head-centered me way. This is conditional love, which is dependent upon the other person to meet our expectations and plans for possessing a happy life. The head-centered habit in relationships cultivates a foundation of control, expectation, manipulation, comparison, and judgment.

Being the heart-centered habit allows awareness to sink into the ever-present life that we are and always have been. This life is always here now. It isn't a life that we create, manifest, or possess in the future. What would our relationships be like if both partners gave away their possessive ideas of what they think would make them happy? What if both partners realized the life that they are and no longer demanded life to appear or feel a certain way? What if both partners freely expressed the life they were without judging each other's expression? We are capable of realizing the life we are now by being the heart- centered habit. This will enable us to love everything that arises in the moment.

When the head-centered me gets triggered, the heart-centered habit is the first to love and accept its possessive, controlling, and manipulative nature. The heart-centered habit becomes the first one to love the part of our self that compares, judges, criticizes, complains, and expects the moment to be different than it is. The first relationship we become heart-centered with is our self. When we become the habit that loves the head-centered me that opposes itself, then we will oppose nothing.

When somebody opposes us, it is because they perceive reality from the head-centered me. They actually oppose themselves and withhold love from aspects of them self. They are showing us what they have yet to love within them. Therefore, how other people treat us has nothing to do with us. However, if they oppose us and we oppose them back, then we know they are showing us that our head-centered self needs more love. This is why we can love our enemies. If we view another as our enemy, then we know that we are misperceiving reality through the head-centered me. The head-centered me thinks it knows how to possess a happy life. Therefore, if anyone stands in the way of that plan, then they are an enemy to our pursuit of happiness.

On the other hand, the heart-centered me has no enemies because it opposes nothing. Loving the head-centered me in every uncomfortable relationship that we have will allow the living presence of divinity to abide through us, as us! Frustration and confusion in our relationships are indicators that life is inviting us to become heart-centered. When we become heart-centered, abundant life will shine through us and attract relationships that far exceed our expectations!

We have to be willing to experience both sides of what we think is right and wrong in relationships. When we open our rational minds to be willing to experience what it used to believe it needed to be happy in a relationship, we will no longer have a problem. For instance, can you be as willing for your relationship to stay as it is as you are willing for it to change? Are you willing to add no value to your partner as much as you are willing to add value? Are you willing for your relationship to end as much as you are willing for it to continue? Are you willing to trigger unresolved emotions, experiences, and belief systems in your partner as much as you are willing to not trigger them? Are you willing to be judged as much as you are willing to be accepted? Are you willing to be misunderstood as much as you are willing to be understood? Are you willing to be rejected and abandoned as much as you are willing to be received and validated?

Our problems in our relationships have to do with experiences we said "no" to in past relationships. We thought, "This is not okay." Abuse is a result of not being willing to embrace what we feel, which becomes our stored pain and we cause pain in our future relationships. Even if we are in sexual, physical, emotional, or mental abusive relationships, we have to be honest about what we feel. These feelings become the first ones in line to be embraced and loved. But we have to be willing to experience these uncomfortable feelings, and then our intuitive heart will guide our choices. The heart may guide us to leave right away. But if our heart chooses to stay then maybe it has something to communicate in the relationship, empowering our authentic voice. Then your intuitive heart may guide you to leave the relationship, once it has been fully used to facilitate your return to the loving presence of your soul.

When we live by the head-centered me we function from reasoning. We have reasons why we should stay in relationships and reasons why we should leave. When we live from the heart-centered me we will no longer make choices based on reasoning, but instead from an intuitive heart-centered knowing! When you become willing for both scenarios of right and wrong in your relationship, then you will sense your heart's intuitive knowing. And then everything you choose to say, do, and be will come from the real authentic unconditional you!

You are more than your relationships. Therefore, relationships do not belong to you and do not define you. Let go of the demands you place upon all of your relationships to define, perceive, and judge you in a "good" light. You cannot control the way your relationships perceive you. Therefore, discover the truth of your being, which is not defined by any relationship that you have to this physical world and set your relationships free!

"This uncomfortable experience is a gift."
You are welcome here.
You are enough!
How may I serve you?

Experiences

The head-centered me desires to possess experiences that it imagines will enable it to possess a happy life. We have all imagined how we think life should look and feel for us to be happy. Therefore, we choose to perceive experiences as bad or wrong that appear to oppose our imagined expectations of happy experiences, causing mental suffering. We will continue to suffer as experiences arise that seem to oppose our plans for happiness. We will continue to strive and work ourselves into exhaustion to change these experiences into experiences that fit within our imagined plan of happiness.

When we are children we express our distress through tantrums and fits of anger. But as we become adults, most people suppress the distress and put on a happy face. Then when we are alone the distress becomes a voice of tantrums in our head called depression. Depression is the energy of experiences that we withhold love from. When we deny certain experiences the love that we are, we become lost in the head-centered habit of trying to get our way. We become selfish, arrogant, prideful, rude, and mean. By repressing certain experiences that don't fit within our plan, we feel disconnected from the love or infinite energy that we are. Having faith in our intuitive knowing that love is all that exists, we can embrace every experience as life itself, admiring its unique appearance and feeling. In the meantime, remembering to love the part of the self that is uncomfortable or uneasy about the moment. Every experience is an opportunity to practice being the heart-centered habit. We can give away our possessive ideas about how we think this moment should be to make us happy and be the Love that experiences all of life just as it is.

When we experience unwanted, uncomfortable, or inconvenient experiences, life is inviting us to become more heart-centered. Life is presenting us with an opportunity to love the head-centered habit of fight or flight even more, which allows it to remember its true role of surrender. The first signs that indicate life is inviting us to be the heart-centered habit is we feel confused and frustrated as to why we aren't experiencing what we think will make us happy. Our heart's desire is to experience love beyond measure. When we become the love toward all experiences, life will unfold through miraculous experiences that far exceed what we could have ever imagined because this is the energy flowing through us as us.

You are more than your experiences, so stop grasping hold of your experiences and defining yourself by them. Stop demanding them to meet your needs to feel good about yourself. You do not possess or own your experiences. They are not yours. Let them go and realize your true nature, which is NOT defined by any experience.

"This painful experience is a gift."
You are welcome here.
You are enough!
How may I serve you?

Thoughts

Unwanted, uncomfortable, and inconvenient experiences trigger thoughts we have yet to embrace and love as a part of life. The head-centered me, which is based on opposition, believes that there are happy thoughts and unhappy thoughts. We believe that unhappy thoughts oppose the pursuit of happiness that our rational mind was trying to possess. Thoughts are just thoughts; infinite pathways of Divine expression. Words are just words. They, too, are infinite pathways of Divine expression. Feelings are just feelings. They, too,

206

are infinite pathways of Divine expression. In my experience I never had control over which kind of thoughts appeared in my mind.

What if you aren't in control of your thoughts and feelings? What if the unified field of existence or your heart-centered nature was in control of thoughts, feelings, and words that happened through you as you? What if a thought, feeling, or word could never oppose or hurt you? Instead of fearing certain thoughts, feelings, and words you could embrace every single one as an expression of God. This is the heart-centered perception. Our heart-centered nature fears and opposes nothing! Our authentic nature never takes anything personal from another person, therefore never receiving hurt from another's expression. Until this authentic reality dawns within our inner experience, we can practice loving the head-centered me that takes everything personal, perceives fear and opposition, and is easily offended and victimized.

The heart-centered habit recognizes frustration and confusion as entry points to love the head-centered me even more. Instead of repressing negative thoughts or fighting to change negative thoughts, the heart-centered habit embraces negative thinking with love, not positive thinking. We have all been taught to change negative thinking into positive thinking. However, this is a way that opposes negative thoughts, which makes them more intense by adding fuel to their fire. Love guides perception into a neutral space of peace and relaxation. Love says, "Yes, it's okay to feel that way. You are not wrong! I am here for you, I love you! Thank you for being a beautiful expression of the Divine just as you are!" The heart-centered habit is a way that validates every experience, thought, feeling, word, and relationship as an expression of God or divinity that is here to help us remember our authentic nature of pure love, becoming the way showers that guide the whole nature of existence back into the remembrance of its source of infinite love!

You are more than your thoughts. Therefore, you do not have to define yourself by them. You are not what you think or understand yourself to be. You are always more than the way you express, define, or appear in this world. Stop grasping hold of your thoughts and set them free.

Even as I write this I know I am failing to point to our true infinite nature. As soon as I write something, it vanishes in my mind. I can't grasp hold of the intuitive information that flows through me as I write this book. Every thought, word, and insight is free to be. There is always more to see. Once you think you have the Truth or you understand the Truth or you know the Truth, that is the instant you have forgotten the Truth. The Truth cannot be grasped or possessed because it is infinite!

"This unfamiliar experience is a gift."
You are welcome here.
You are enough!
How may I serve you?

Reflection

Are you willing to allow negative emotions, thoughts, relationships, and ideas to have a voice in your presence without judging it as wrong or identifying with it as being right?

Are you willing to simply listen and offer love to parts of yourself and others that have never been welcomed, embraced, and loved by relationships in the past?

Reprogramming the Subconscious Mind

"Be still and know that confusion and frustration is God, a part of your true authentic nature."

Practicing the heart-centered habit:

Have you ever felt confused or frustrated?

Welcome these experiences as a part of consciousness (You):

H- HONESTY

"I fully feel the parts of me that have felt confusion and frustration."

A-ACKNOWLEDGE, ALLOW, ASK

"I acknowledge that it is safe and okay to feel this limited experience. I embrace these feelings fully just as they are because I know they are here to show me the way into my heart. As I embrace these feelings fully, I ask them to bring with them all of the past meanings, interpretations, beliefs, and judgments that I thought were true, but are not valid in this present moment, so that I may receive them as a gift, guide, and opening toward the infinite perception in my heart. I acknowledge their Divine role in helping me expand awareness into the depths of infinite knowing."

Allow the uncomfortable experience to have a voice. Do not believe what it is saying, but instead be a loving presence that offers a deeper level of safety, comfort, and acknowledgment than the experience has ever received from you before, being the practice of detachment, allowance, pure love, and space.

Ask: *"Divine heart, I accept that I don't know how to let go of past experiences and perceive the newness of this present moment. Therefore, I ask that you release me from the past, so I may perceive the new that is arising through the experience of confusion and frustration. Welcome, embrace, honor, and validate these experiences for me, through me, as I am now, thereby healing the inner division within me, so my perception can expand and align with the flow of infinite information."* And so it is (Amen).

B- BREATHE

Breathe in these feelings (*"I receive you as life"*) breathe out (*"You are free to be"*). Be one with the breath: *"I am reborn in every breath. The breath is my connection to the eternal self."*

I-I LOVE YOU

Place your hands over your heart and say, *"I love you! All is an expression of one life. I validate this limited experience within me. It is an experience from my past that was not validated by my relationships to the world. Therefore, I choose to be the presence of love that provides this experience the resonation of love that it has never received. May I be all the affirmation that this limited experience needs to remember that it is an infinite expression of divinity, so that it may fully awaken from the illusion of limitation. I love you!"*

"I am abundant, wise, infinite, and free!"

T- THANK YOU

Thank the experience for helping you remember that you are an ever-expanding unique expression of the Truth. Thank the circumstance, story, or relationship that triggered these feelings in your body, so your entire being could awaken to your innocent nature of authentic freedom that can enjoy all experiences.

"Thank you for helping me to align and attune with my heart's ever-expanding unique expression of infinite wisdom and pure love! Thank you for helping me to remember the power of life that I am!"

Intention: *(say aloud)*

"Today, I choose to give away my possessive ideas about happiness, so that I may connect to all of my relationships, experiences, and thoughts in a loving heart-centered way that is always fully present now."

Affirmation: *(say aloud)*

Say aloud throughout today:

"My relationships are harmonious because I am harmony!"

Day 12

The Truth Shall Set You Free

"The ache for home lives in all of us, the safe place where we can go as we are and not be questioned."

-Maya Angelou

Say Aloud: (looking into your eyes in a mirror)
Good morning, infinite one. You are safe to feel. I always want to know how you are feeling. You are the soul-mate that I have been looking for my entire life. You matter and you are enough. You are worthy of being seen and heard. I see you and I am here to listen to you. There is a good reason you are here; you are Divine perfection. Today, I join you in celebrating your ever-expanding unique expression. I am open to receiving new information and new ways of being by choosing to receive all uncomfortable, unfamiliar, painful, inconvenient, and unwanted experiences as a Divine gift from you, my infinite heart. I love all of you! I really love all of you. (your name), I really love all of you. (Feel free to write your own love statement).

I grew up in this world never having a solid sense of right and wrong, good or bad, should or shouldn't. But I still believed in the idea that there must be a good way and a bad way because of all of the suffering I had experienced and perceived in this world. I was so afraid to be the pure allowance of love and merge with suffering, separation, judgment, hatred, pain, discontent, and depression. I feared that if I allowed myself to embrace these aspects of life, I would surely die. I remember feeling so disconnected and separate from my husband within our marriage. I thought there must be something wrong with our partnership. Instead of merging and allowing myself to embrace these uncomfortable experiences within marriage, I tried to change our marriage. I did this by trying to change myself and trying to change him, however, this only created a deeper sense of disconnection and separation. It didn't matter how much we communicated or were physically intimate or tried to make each other happy, nothing worked to fix this sense of separation, disconnection, and dissonance.

Finally, I chose to be the heart-centered habit and merge with these experiences within myself. I was honest about what I felt. I acknowledged that I didn't know why I felt this way. It wasn't his fault or my fault. Neither of us had done anything wrong. It wasn't the world or our family conditioning that was to blame. I acknowledged that I had been born to experience separation and disconnection. They weren't experiences that validated my authentic presence, rather they were a part of consciousness; a part of the whole of existence; a part of my authentic self. I had to be completely honest with myself about how I felt on the inside, and acknowledge the separation I felt within my marriage, which had nothing to do with the circumstances in our marriage. My rational mind had always believed the separation was because of something outside of me. In truth, the separation was within me and my marriage was triggering all feelings, emotions, thoughts, beliefs, and experiences that felt separate from the truth that I am. As I began to merge and embrace these experiences through the heart-centered habit, a deep sense of peace and relaxation began to bubble up from inside until it overtook my entire experience of marriage.

The truth is, when you acknowledge, embrace, merge, and love all experiences, they transform from a consciousness of separation into a consciousness of unity, which shift changes our perception of reality. The feelings we once feared and ran away from are now experiences of joy. We are the beings of light here to remind all aspects of darkness that they come from the same Divine light. This shift is happening in human consciousness, where individuals are awakening to the truth of our being, which opposes, hates, resists, chases, and runs away from nothing. We are remembering the truth of what we are, which is all encompassing pure love!

"This unwanted experience is a gift."
You are welcome here.
You are enough!
How may I serve you?

Projection

We have all learned to project a reality that feels separate in our rational mind. This limited reality feels separate from the all-inclusive power and eternal presence of our true nature. Our projected sense of reality is the head- centered me. This head centered "me" exists in the imagination of existence. It is like a movie, play, or drama that runs automatically in our heads. Just like a cross has four points, so does our projected sense of self. Our projected sense of self has four aspects that oppose each other to create an illusion of a self. Our accumulated knowledge of right and wrong create the horizontal thinking about reality. Judgment pushes reality into one side or the other, which keeps it from entering the center, our heart. This creates vertical thinking about a past and a future. Our memory of what we have done right and what we have done wrong from our past projects an imagined life into the future that we chase after and focus on creating. Therefore, the head-centered me operates from the horizontal thinking of how it is doing right and wrong, as well as functioning from the vertical thinking of a past that it is trying to recreate into a better future.

The misperception is that goodness, life, abundance, truth, oneness, unity, divinity, and wellbeing are not here now in the present moment. Heart- centered consciousness is the space where the horizontal right and wrong merge at the center with the vertical past and future merging at the center of the cross. This is the heart space. Here in the heart where all projection meets in the center, there is no division of reality into right and wrong or past and future. There is only what is now with no opposition to any of it. There is only total allowance, acknowledgement, and loving embrace to whatever is arising within the moment. The heart or the space where right, wrong, past, and future meet is the intuitive sense of the Truth we actually are. This is the space of heart-centered consciousness where all awareness that makes up our beliefs in wrong merge with all awareness that makes up our belief in right AND where all awareness that makes up the memories of the past and all awareness that makes up the projections of a future merge and return to their original essence of oneness. If there is only one life experiencing itself in an infinite array of appearances, experiences, and expressions, then whatever wrong you perceive in another is the wrong you perceive in yourself. The mind knows there is only one! Therefore, it is impossible for the mind to perceive wrong in the world without perceiving that wrong within yourself and creating an inner atmosphere that feels wrong, which we experience as fear. Our beliefs in wrong create all of our inner fears.

Jesus' crucifixion reminds us that the pain we feel is due to the way we have been programmed to project a reality that is not rooted in the heart. His hands were nailed to each end of the cross, as well as his feet and a crown of thorns placed on his head. The pain in our reality is the doorway back into the center of heart-centered consciousness. Sin or the misperception (projection) of reality is what causes our pain and

215

suffering. Bringing our pain into the heart-centered habit guides all projections back in toward the Truth, which exists within the heart of the matter, allowing us to perceive from the heart-centered perception of the eternal present moment. The present moment is where past, future, right, and wrong collapse into the space in between or the point where all four crosses merge as one.

"This uncomfortable experience is a gift."
You are welcome here.
You are enough!
How may I serve you?

Heaven is Within You

"God is in you."

–Vedas

Jesus said to follow him, we would have to pick up our cross and crucify the self. If you are experiencing pain in your reality then life is crucifying the projected head-centered self. Life is showing us that we cannot continue living as a false projected self that perceives a divided reality. Life is placing nails into our knowledge of right and wrong, as well as our projections of a better future due to an unwanted past. The diversification of projected realities of right and wrong are now experienced on a daily basis. We can no longer hide in our "like-minded" groups or communities. We will only suffer more and more if we continue living from a projected sense of self in our head. Life is pointing us inward, toward the center. This requires us to walk toward the pain of separation we feel within. Welcome, acknowledge, embrace, breathe, love, and thank the pain. This requires pure surrender to the pain we feel underneath our hopes and dreams, so that we may discover that Heaven is within us, here and now. It isn't just a place we go to when we physically die. It is a place that is within us now, which we can experience as we surrender our projected sense of self (beliefs in right and wrong and beliefs in past and future). Surrender happens when we become heart-centered and merge with everything that is experienced in this very moment.

The crucifixion of our projected self brings all experiences, feelings, emotions, and memories that we have labeled as wrong to the surface. Everything that we have projected as bad, wrong, unwanted, uncomfortable, inconvenient, unwelcome, and shouldn't feel becomes the doorway to heaven. We enter heart-centered consciousness, unity consciousness, heaven, or Divine consciousness by embracing all that we have denied as a part of goodness. We merge with every aspect and remember the unity that exists throughout all experiences. Practice being heart-centered toward all experiences and enter the doorway to the heavenly presence of now!

Say Aloud:

Dear projected reality of right/wrong and past/future,

Today I allow the reality that your perception has created to fall apart into the loving embrace of my heart. I can no longer support your existence by trying to put the pieces of this limited reality back together. However, I welcome you to return into the loving and harmonious nature that you came from. I stand here at the door of Heaven, acknowledging you for all that you are! I lovingly embrace all that you are as you transition from the physical into the spiritual dimension of Heaven. I breathe deeply as I watch you expand into your infinite nature. I love you! Thank you! Welcome home!

Love,

Your angel

"This painful experience is a gift."
You are welcome here.
You are enough!
How may I serve you?

Peace that Surpasses Understanding

We have become accustomed to living from our understanding based upon right/wrong and past/future. This limited understanding about reality created our boundaries of security. When we allow our projected sense of self to merge into oneness, we feel a raw vulnerability, which makes us feel open to attack because we don't have those old boundaries. Now we understand what Jesus and many other spiritual masters felt from the world that has yet to surrender to its authentic way of being. We will be judged as foolish and many will misunderstand or misperceive the Truth of our being. The world may not know us if it lives from a projected reality of right/wrong or past/future. The only thing we can do is be the peace that surpasses understanding. We can choose to perceive the light of being in others even when they cannot because we know they are doing the best they can in this moment. We can choose to love the parts of them that don't understand the Truth. We can be for them the unity consciousness of kindness and love that they have yet to remember. This is a way that we can offer support to a world that is suffering and struggling to remember.

When we feel their experience of separation and disconnection to the source of pure love within them, we can merge with their experience and breathe it into our hearts for them. If we try to understand why our loved ones are struggling to remember, we will momentarily forget our center and merge with their projection. Therefore, do not try to understand another. Instead, be the peace and love that they have forgotten.

Being heart-centered toward other people's experience of reality can help guide them into their center and remember the Truth of their being that opposes nothing. We can remain calm in the face of adversity by choosing to be peace and forgo trying to understand "why." We will continue to experience persecution, opposition, and adversity as long as others are still projecting this reality into human consciousness. Therefore, remain steadfast in your faith of being the heart-centered habit! Remember that all experiences relax into their natural state of peace when they are embraced by love and allowance. Anger relaxes into peace. Hatred relaxes into peace. Pain relaxes into peace. Suffering relaxes into peace. We cannot change the world; we can only be the heart- centered consciousness that is here to awaken in the hearts of all! Let the pure love that you are bloom in human consciousness as you choose to love all human conditions and experiences as they are in the moment!

"This unfamiliar experience is a gift."
You are welcome here.
You are enough!
How may I serve you?

Reflection

Are you ready to allow your right self and your wrong self to merge as one self? Are you ready to allow your past self and your future self to merge as one self? If yes, then pick up your cross and carry it straight to the doorway of your heart.

Reprogramming the Subconscious Mind

"Be still and know that part of you that feels misunderstood and feels like an outcast is God, a part of your true authentic nature."

Practicing the heart-centered habit: (Example)

Have you ever felt like an outsider and misunderstood?

Welcome these experiences as a part of consciousness (You):

H- HONESTY

"I fully feel the parts of me that have felt like an outsider and misunderstood."

A-ACKNOWLEDGE, ALLOW, ASK

"I acknowledge that it is safe and okay to feel this limited experience. I embrace these feelings fully just as they are because I know they are here to show me the way into my heart. As I embrace these feelings fully, I ask them to bring with them all of the past meanings, interpretations, beliefs, and judgments that I thought were true, but are not valid in this present moment, so that I may receive them as a gift, guide, and opening toward the infinite perception in my heart. I acknowledge their Divine role in helping me expand awareness into the depths of infinite knowing."

Allow the uncomfortable experience to have a voice. Do not believe what it is saying, but instead be a loving presence that offers a deeper level of safety, comfort, and acknowledgment than the experience has ever received from you before, thereby being the practice of detachment, allowance, pure love, and space.

Ask: "Divine heart, I accept that I don't know how to perceive through oneness. Therefore, I ask that you merge my past/future self with my right/wrong self into perceiving through the lens of one whole self. Welcome, embrace, honor, and validate these experiences for me, through me, as I am now, healing the inner division within me, so that my perception can expand and align with the flow of infinite information." And so it is (Amen).

B- BREATHE

Breathe in these feelings (*"I receive you as life"*) and breathe out (*"You are free to be"*). Be one with the breath: *"The breath is my guide, teacher, and guru."*

I-I LOVE YOU

Place your hands over your heart. Say, *"I love you! All is an expression of one life. I validate this limited experience within me. It is an experience from my past that was not validated by my relationships to the world. Therefore, I choose to be the presence of love that provides this experience the resonation of love that it has never received. May I be all the affirmation that this limited experience needs to remember that it is an infinite expression of divinity, so that it may fully awaken from the illusion of limitation. I love you!"*

"I am abundant, wise, infinite, and free!"

T- THANK YOU

Thank the experience for helping you remember that you are an ever-expanding unique expression of the Truth. Thank the circumstance, story, or relationship that triggered these feelings in your body, so your entire being could awaken to your innocent nature of authentic freedom that can enjoy all experiences.

"Thank you for helping me to align and attune with my heart's ever-expanding unique expression of infinite wisdom and pure love! Thank you for helping me to remember the power of life that I am!"

Intention: *(say aloud)*

"Today, I choose to be honest and truthful about how I feel with myself, so that I may acknowledge the peace that surpasses my personal understanding (projection), which is discovered within the eternal presence of my heart!"

Affirmation: *(say aloud)*
Say aloud throughout today:

"My desires are innocent because I am innocent!"

Day 13

Refinement

"Being spiritual has nothing to do with what you believe and everything to do with your state of consciousness."

-Eckhart Tolle

Say Aloud: (looking into your eyes in a mirror)

Good morning, infinite one. You are safe to feel. I always want to know how you are feeling. You are the soul-mate that I have been looking for my entire life. You matter and you are enough. You are worthy of being seen and heard. I see you and I am here to listen to you. There is a good reason you are here; you are Divine perfection. Today, I join you in celebrating your ever-expanding unique expression. I am open to receiving new information and new ways of being by choosing to receive all uncomfortable, unfamiliar, painful, inconvenient, and unwanted experiences as a Divine gift from you, my infinite heart. I love all of you! I really love all of you. (your name), I really love all of you. (Feel free to write your own love statement).

Refinement is the process of making something pure. Humanity is undergoing refinement on a massive scale. Our pure spiritual heart-centered nature has intensified to the point where all aspects of the self that have forgotten their authentic pure nature are bubbling to the surface to become purified through the loving presence of existence. The head-centered me is an awareness that thinks it knows the path it should be on to be happy. When we align with the heart-centered habit, we remember that we don't need to know the way our life should feel or look to be happy.

We are in the midst of forgetting where we are going, so that we may align with the one, true, loving, and eternal way that is here now. Many are allowing the Truth to bubble up into our head, which is that we don't know how to make ourselves happy, free, and peaceful. This allowance opens the door within our heart, which allows our infinite nature to fill our head, mind, and body with pure life and love that accepts the moment exactly as it is. Our infinite nature, which opposes nothing, is a state of heart-centered consciousness that works all things together for the good of all. Therefore, it does not have a problem with any part of humanity, the self, reality, life, or God. We don't have to focus on creating a better future. We can be goodness now when we choose to align our personal perceptions in wrong with the Divine perception of perceiving only life, goodness, God, and love!

In my experience of refinement, I went through a very dark period, which was the experience of awareness opening and shedding light on my rational mind's limited understanding of reality. Everything I understood and thought to be true was crumbling and I found myself unable to grasp the Truth. I became acutely aware of my beliefs in right and wrong. All of my relationships to the physical world were reflecting my limiting beliefs. I experienced everything that I believed was wrong, bad, uncomfortable, unwanted, and inconvenient. Not because life or God was punishing me for doing something wrong. Instead, the negative or repressed side of my beliefs in wrong were becoming illuminated, so I could shift awareness from fear to faith. I sank into my mental hell, so I could practice being the light of consciousness that has always been here to welcome, embrace, and love the dark side of "me."

Over a period of about eleven years, I became the love toward all aspects that felt separate from the light of divinity. I became the voice of God or pure love that gently reminded all parts of existence that they too are included and perceived as Divine. Throughout the eleven years, my faith was strengthened in perceiving only divinity regardless of what the moment felt or looked like. Faith is like a muscle... the more you use it, the stronger it becomes. Fear began to dissipate and an innate power of Divine loving authority took over and saved every aspect of existence that humans had kicked out of Heaven throughout human history. Of course they were never really kicked out of Heaven, but the head-centered me bought into a reality of grasping and possessing experiences and certain experiences were reflections of "who" I thought I wanted to be and others were reflections of "who" I thought I did not want to be. Therefore, the experiences I judged as "not me" needed to dwell in a dark place that was separate from goodness.

In my experience Heaven is the authentic nature of all of existence. Hell is a place the head-centered me has manufactured in the mind of human consciousness that only exists by our belief in it. Refinement is the process where we become the consciousness of divinity that enters hell (the human beliefs in darkness, evil, and wrong) and become the purifying agent that returns it to its original state of purity. The heart-centered habit purifies the hell we have manufactured and returns it to its natural state of Heaven. This is how we can bring Heaven to Earth.

"This unwanted experience is a gift."
You are welcome here.
You are enough!
How may I serve you?

Refiner's Fire

The authentic Divine nature of pure love is awakening in the hearts of humanity. This awakening comes like the refiner's fire that purifies precious metals such as gold and silver. What does this fire look like in our reality? The heat gets turned on high intensity where everything in our reality looks and feels like it is going wrong or bad. We may feel like we are being punished for something we have done wrong. We may feel like we can't do anything to fix or change the problems and issues we are experiencing in our life circumstances. No matter how hard we try to change our reality, it will not change for the better. Instead, matters only get worse. If this is occurring, we must remember we have not done anything wrong. If we do believe we have done something wrong then we will remain in the same head-centered consciousness that manufactured the meanings and interpretations that give us a false sense of wrongness.

The truth is, we are in the midst of the refiner's fire. Who is the refiner? Our Divine infinite soul. The Divine consciousness of our soul has increased from within so much that its abundant light (fire) has melted or liquefied every solid belief that is rooted in a view of opposition. The mess and chaos we perceive in our individual lives and in the collective is the remnants or broken pieces of these long held beliefs in separation, division, and judgment. These pieces are waiting to be refined. However, refinement is only possible when we jump on the bridge of faith and choose to align with the intuition that we sense from the consciousness of our soul. Every time we choose to perceive our miserable life circumstances as symbols and reflections of divinity, we align with the nature of existence in refining human consciousness. Every time we choose to perceive only light and divinity within the suffering, pain, and struggle that humanity is facing as a whole, we align with the natural process of refinement that is occurring in human consciousness.

When life appears in a way that is unpleasant, uncomfortable, or unwanted, we can become the heart-centered habit, which refines our experience into a perspective of purity and divinity. We cannot avoid struggle, suffering, and pain. Instead, we can head straight into the center of it all and align with the power that refines and reminds all of existence of its one Divine nature.

"This uncomfortable experience is a gift."
You are welcome here.
You are enough!
How may I serve you?

The Dross

During the process of refinement to metals, a dross emerges at the surface. Dross is the foreign matter, mineral waste, or scum that forms at the surface of molten metal. This dross is discarded because it is no longer needed. In spiritual refinement, the dross is limited behaviors, actions, ways, and beliefs. When the head-centered me becomes refined through being the heart- centered habit, what floats to the surface are habits that no longer align with our authentic nature of purity. These limited habits were symptoms of our belief in wrong, evil, bad, or unwantcd circumstances. These were ways or conditions that have existed in human consciousness for thousands of years. They are based on judgment, control, comparison, expectation, and manipulation.

When the head-centered me goes through the process of loving refinement, it returns to its innocent, vulnerable, and pure nature. The old habits, which limited our perspective of reality begin to fall away. Our addictions, cravings, and neediness normalize into its natural state of wellbeing. Life removes the dross for us and we realize in a spontaneous way that we are not the same as we used to be. We don't sense the mental demands that once motivated our actions. Calmness, serenity, joy, and peace are realized as the ever-present existence, which is always here in every moment. Life balances and harmonizes to reflect our authentic nature of abundance. We can observe how our inner reality is connected to our outer reality as they merge as one experience. Separation, division, fear, struggle, suffering, and pain become distant memories. As we welcome the remembrance of our Divine nature, we lose sight and forget the limited nature that we used to believe was who we were. We feel like we have been born again every day, as we continue to step into the living presence of pure love.

"This inconvenient experience is a gift."
You are welcome here.
You are enough!
How may I serve you?

Infinite Abundance

The process of spiritual refinement opens the head-centered me into the infinite abundance of existence. Abundance is no longer tied to a certain definition or meaning of material possession, consumption, and accumulation. Instead, abundance is sensed through the five physical senses in every moment. We notice the infinite smells, tastes, sights, textures, and sounds that pulsate in every moment. The moment becomes a vibrant dance of infinite abundance that is received as a gift of pure joy. Abundance is no longer dictated by the head-centered me that is attached to a particular outcome, result, or image that it has imagined out in the future, which it feels separate from in the present moment. Instead, abundance is received in whatever arises in the moment.

Our soul breathes the entire experience in as it feels so grateful to exist as a human. Everything is honored and revered as divinity, abundance, and pure life. We remember this perception as a child, where everything felt magical and interesting. Fearlessness and pure love abound for all of existence. Judgment is received as abundance. Negative thoughts are received as abundance. Fear is received as abundance. Frustration is received as abundance. Thoughts are received as abundance. Bills are received as abundance. Suffering is received as abundance. Jealousy and envy are received as abundance. Everything is arising in its natural flow of abundance. Everything that we experience is abundant.

Notice the abundance of thoughts that arise in the mind. Notice the abundance of oxygen for every human to breathe. Notice the abundance in nature of plants, animals, grass, and leaves. Notice the abundance of feelings you experience each day. Notice the abundance of people in the city you live in. Notice the abundance of facebook posts and junk mail. It doesn't matter what it is, everything and every experience appears as a symbol of abundance. Abundance is our authentic nature!

"This unfamiliar experience is a gift."
You are welcome here.
You are enough!
How may I serve you?

Reflection

Have you ever noticed that all of existence, whether you perceive it in a positive or negative way, appears in abundance?

Reprogramming the Subconscious Mind

"Be still and know that jealousy and envy is God, a part of your true authentic nature."

Practicing the heart-centered habit: (Example)

Have you ever felt jealousy and envy?

Welcome these experiences as a part of consciousness (You):

H- HONESTY

"I fully feel the parts of me that have felt jealous and envious."

A-ACKNOWLEDGE, ALLOW, ASK

"I acknowledge that it is safe and okay to feel this limited experience. I embrace these feelings fully just as they are because I know they are here to show me the way into my heart. As I embrace these feelings fully, I ask them to bring with them all of the past meanings, interpretations, beliefs, and judgments that I thought were true, but are not valid in this present moment, so I may receive them as a gift, guide, and opening toward the infinite perception in my heart. I acknowledge their Divine role in helping me to expand awareness into the depths of infinite knowing."

Allow the uncomfortable experience to have a voice. Do not believe what it is saying, but instead be a loving presence that offers a deeper level of safety, comfort, and acknowledgment than the experience has ever received from you before, thereby being the practice of detachment, allowance, pure love, and space.

Ask: "Divine heart, I accept that I don't know how to perceive through a lens of infinite abundance. Therefore, I ask that you perceive infinite abundance through me as me and heal the experience of jealousy and envy. Welcome, embrace, honor, and validate these experiences for me, through me, as I am now, healing the inner division within me, so that my perception can expand and align with the flow of infinite information." And so it is (Amen).

B- BREATHE

Breathe in these feelings (*"I receive you as life"*) and breathe out (*"You are free to be"*). Be one with the breath: *"The breath is my salvation."*

I-I LOVE YOU

Place your hands over your heart. Say, *"I love you! All is an expression of one life. I validate this limited experience within me. It is an experience from my past that was not validated by my relationships to the world. Therefore, I choose to be the presence of love that provides this experience the resonation of love that it has never received. May I be all the affirmation that this limited experience needs to remember that it is an infinite expression of divinity, so that it may fully awaken from the illusion of limitation. I love you!"*

"I am abundant, wise, infinite, and free!"

T- THANK YOU

Thank the experience for helping you remember that you are an ever-expanding unique expression of the Truth. Thank the circumstance, story, or relationship that triggered these feelings in your body, so your entire being could awaken to your innocent nature of authentic freedom that can enjoy all experiences.

> *"Thank you for helping me to align and attune with my heart's ever-expanding unique expression of infinite wisdom and pure love! Thank you for helping me to remember the power of life that I am!"*

Intention: *(say aloud)*

"Today, I choose to allow the eternal light of my soul to refine or make pure my perception of reality and remove the dross (unconscious habits) from my experience so that I may perceive every experience as a symbol of infinite abundance."

Affirmation: *(say aloud)*

Say aloud throughout today:

"My body is healthy because I am perfect health!"

Day 14

The Eye of the Storm

"Serenity isn't the peace away from the storm; it's the peace at the eye of the storm."

– Ed Martin Cruz

Say Aloud: (looking into your eyes in a mirror)
Good morning, infinite one. You are safe to feel. I always want to know how you are feeling. You are the soul-mate that I have been looking for my entire life. You matter and you are enough. You are worthy of being seen and heard. I see you and I am here to listen to you. There is a good reason you are here; you are Divine perfection. Today, I join you in celebrating your ever-expanding unique expression. I am open to receiving new information and new ways of being by choosing to receive all uncomfortable, unfamiliar, painful, inconvenient, and unwanted experiences as a Divine gift from you, my infinite heart. I love all of you! I really love all of you. (your name), I really love all of you.

I have survived many storms in my life. These storms were fears that lurked in the shadows of my experiences. When I began focusing on the spiritual life of all existence, my fears came out of the shadows and into the light of experience. I had an abundance of fears! I first thought I had done something wrong to deserve these tumultuous storms in my life. As I began practicing the heart-centered habit, I realized that these storms were opportunities to enter them and connect to the peace that surpasses my personal, rational, and logical understanding. As I grew into being heart-centered I began to perceive storms as blessings that were here to provide me an opportunity to become the practice of peace. At the center of every storm is a stillness that I could access by focusing on being the breath. The breath would guide awareness away from thinking about what caused the fear to breathing in the fear, so I could experience the fear from the inside-out.

The breath guided me into the eye of the storm (fear) where divinity is perceived as everything and nothing. The eye of the storm feels like no-thingness or emptiness, but the eye of the storm is the center of all of existence. For instance, the center of fear is stillness. The center of anger is stillness. The center of all negative emotions is peace. The center of all "negative" thoughts is purity. The spacious serene center is the core of all forms, including perceptions, beliefs, thoughts, words, emotions, feelings, objects, bodies, everything. The eye of the storm is the heart of the matter. Therefore, no matter what way something appears, at its core we can sense into this peace, purity, freedom, stillness, or no-thingness.

Our breath reminds us that these uncomfortable storms are okay and a part of God or divinity. Therefore, we do not have to view them as something that is separate from us and oppose it. Opposing the storms will only give us a sense of separation from the unconditional loving presence of our soul, which allows everything to be just as it is while perceiving it as a part of the expansive oneness of existence.

We have all been conditioned to run away from storms because we have labeled the storms as bad, wrong, or evil. This conditioning keeps us on edge and anxious. We fear that at any minute a storm can show up out of nowhere and mess up our personalized plan for our life. Running from storms keeps us running on the hamster wheel of life, where we will go nowhere. Storms will keep showing up until we merge with them and go to the center, where we can perceive the storm from the inside-out. When we perceive storms from the outside-in, they appear to be a separate entity that is out to get us. The truth is all perceived storms in life are the aspects of God or divinity that we have judged as wrong, evil, or bad. These are the aspects we refuse to align with because we push them away and perceive them as separate from goodness.

These storms appear to be chasing us, but they aren't. Our rational mind is hyper-aware of all experiences that it has labeled wrong, bad, and evil. Our negative perception heightens our senses to their existence. Our rational mind will notice the negative over the positive in every moment. Our rational mind becomes distracted by its negative perception of experiences because it is a misperception that needs to be corrected. We can correct our perception of these fearful experiences when we choose to breathe them in instead of judge them as wrong. Having the courage and faith to feel these experiences fully allows awareness to merge with them and perceive them from the inside-out. The eye of the storm is the point of singularity where all of existence exists as the same infinite energy at its core. The center or the eye of the storm is the unified field of existence, the one essence of all of existence.

The heart-centered habit is a way that allows awareness to sink out of the head and into the heart of the matter, where we sense oneness with the very thing we thought we were separate from. Being heart-centered throughout the storms of life realigns us with our true authentic nature of pure so we can experience oneness with God, instead of separation from God.

"This unwanted experience is a gift."
You are welcome here.
You are enough!
How may I serve you?

The End of Days

Jesus described the end of days as a time of immense destruction right before the second coming of the Lord. When I studied these scriptures, my intuition guided me into perceiving that this second coming of the Lord was a period of time where individuals were awakening to the one essence of existence within them. We experience this end of days when we shift from being the head-centered habit, which perceives separation and division, into the remembrance of being the heart-centered habit, which perceives only divinity and oneness.

Destruction of ideas, perceptions, ways, habits, motivations, relationships, finances, careers, drives, beliefs, emotions, and feelings will occur when we begin this great shift of awareness. The old foundation that we have built our identity upon, which is rooted in our personal knowledge of right and wrong, crumbles. The loving presence and Divine light of our being melts the old foundation into the spacious presence of our infinite soul.

I used to have such a drive and motivation to pursue goals of becoming better at my career and roles in life. When awareness began to shift from the ways of the world toward the intuition of my heart, my drive and motivation to achieve material success fell away. I started to care more about what I felt on the inside than what the world felt about me. I realized that most of the ways that I lived my life were to fit in with the world, please others, and make myself appear successful.

On the other hand, listening to and following the guidance of my heart set me on a unique and authentic path which was perfect for me. The people I was in relationship with that continued to live according to their comfortable tribes, groups, families, and peers did not understand my path. I felt like I suffered more trying to fit in than following my heart. Therefore, I continued going within. I experienced many endings as awareness shifted more and more from the head to the heart. Careers and jobs came and went. Homes came and went. Money came and went. Friendships came and went. Responsibilities came and went. Habits came and went. Roles came and went. Financial stability came and went. Emotions came and went. Thoughts came and went. Beliefs came and went. Perceptions came and went. Dreams came and went. Ideas came and went. All that remained was the breath and pure love in my heart. They became my best friends; the ones that never left me throughout the end of days.

With every ending came a new beginning of being even more authentic and present than I was before. When we go through many endings, it is a sign that heart-centered consciousness or our authentic nature is being integrated into our entire being. The end of days is not a sign that you have done something wrong. The end of days is not bad, evil, or punishment. Instead, the end of days is the sign that Christ consciousness is here and you are going through an amazing rebirth in consciousness. The heart-centered habit can help you relax through the end of days. When you are relaxed you can celebrate the quantum leap you are going through in human consciousness.

The Kingdom of Heaven is at hand. You will know that you have entered the Kingdom of Heaven when you find yourself making choices that have no reasoning or understanding behind them. You will find yourself creating simply to create, without a reason for creating. You will find yourself doing tasks without a hidden agenda. Thinking, creating, doing, choosing, feeling, and perceiving still happens but without a connection to a future outcome. Life just moves through us as us without any expectations. Inner knowing becomes our constant guide in every moment. Living as a human feels playful and interesting. The struggle, suffering, and limitation we once experienced will come to an end. The journey continues to expand into eternity, and we never fully arrive at a destination. Instead, we enjoy the journey now.

"This uncomfortable experience is a gift."
You are welcome here.
You are enough!
How may I serve you?

Rapture

The rapture is what Christians believe will happen to them some day. Jesus is going to come riding on a cloud out of the sky and rescue them from their suffering. I was taught to believe that this rapture was literal and Jesus would physically ride on a cloud to save me. In my experience, the rapture is happening right now for many people. Jesus represented a human who lived from heart-centered consciousness, which perceives a reality where there is only God, divinity, pure love, and life appearing as many diverse forms; a consciousness that does not perceive opposition, separation, or division; a consciousness that fully recognizes that all of existence is an appearance of the one infinite energy that exists at the center and is connected at that center. Jesus embodied this consciousness.

This heart-centered consciousness is blooming in human consciousness right now within many individuals. Awareness is waking up out of the head-centered me (separate consciousness) and returning to the heart-centered me (unity consciousness). This is the rapture that is happening as an inner journey within the lives of many humans right now. In ancient scriptures the sky was a symbol used for the mind. The rapture is happening within our personal rational mind. The authentic nature of existence or heart-centered consciousness is rapturing all knowledge of wrong, evil, bad, uncomfortable, and negative emotions and bringing them into the loving presence that exists at the core of all existence.

Humanity has been born into an idea of separation that is expressed as personal knowledge of good and evil. The younger generations will struggle with making sense of living a reality that is based upon knowledge of right and wrong. They will struggle because the human species is becoming more interconnected than ever before. Our families, neighborhoods, communities, schools, and churches represent a melting pot of diverse personal knowledge. Cultures, organizations, families, and communities are being raptured up into oneness. It is an upward movement because it is a higher way of being that requires a quantum leap in the way we perceive reality. Human perception is transforming from a personal reality to a universal reality.

The new universal reality has room for every experience on the spectrum of good and evil, where all experiences are accepted as a part of universal truth. The old personal paradigm was a perception that limited our experience of reality. Our minds remained closed to certain experiences that were labeled as wrong, bad, and evil. In the new universal paradigm all experiences are honored as a unique living expression of the whole.

The rapture is occurring within us whether we want it to or not. The heart-centered habit can offer our mind relaxation, so that it may transition easier as it undergoes the quantum leap that is happening in consciousness. Everything that is crumbling in your life is a part of this great shift. It is uncomfortable, but if you can focus on the bigger picture of what is happening to the whole of humanity, you will realize you are not alone. All is well and good. Expansion is occurring in your life right now and soon you will be glorified into a new reality that expresses the fullness of your soul. Do not give up. Relax and go through the eye of the needle. A reality beyond your highest dreams is on the other side!

"This inconvenient experience is a gift."
You are welcome here.
You are enough!
How may I serve you?

World Peace

Humanity has thought for a very long time that it could create world peace through the personal will. This is a misperception because there are many personal wills on how to create world peace, which has caused more wars, conflict, and division than peace. The only way to create world peace is to become heart-centered and allow the nature of existence to be as it always has been: peaceful!

Peace is the authentic nature of existence. Peace is not something that humans create. Just like nature, humans do control the ebbs and flows of nature. However, humans can cause disruption to nature's life-giving flow by trying to control it. Despite our efforts to control, nature will always prevail. World peace will be realized once the majority of humans remember their authentic peaceful nature that exists at their center. Being the heart-centered habit is a way that can assist humanity in being peaceful. When we realize that there is nothing to fear, escape, or oppose anymore, we will awaken to our true state of peace that we have always been. The projection of opposition, separation, and division will vanish as we become heart-centered. Instead of 7.2 billion personal wills struggling to compete with each other, all will be guided by our one true Divine will of love, peace, and abundance. Our expression of divinity shall be an infinite array of hues, tones, fragrances, colors, and notes of awe-inspiring splendor!

Grace is the fragrance of our true unified nature. We can sense the grace of existence as we perceive that reality is for us and never against us. Every experience shows up to offer grace, a free gift of transformation. When we remember to relax into every experience and be the heart-centered habit, we merge with the experience and wake up out of separation a little more. Every difficult, uncomfortable, unwanted, and painful experience is here to help us remember oneness and forget separation, which happens spontaneously when we fully receive the experience and breathe it in as life! We can be heart-centered and receive the grace that all of our experiences are here to give us!

Grace offers us the remembrance of our true nature of peace! The only way to create world peace is to awaken to the peace that is underneath the head-centered me. It is the peace that surpasses our personal understanding. Therefore, the head will never understand it, but we can experience it when the head-centered me expands and opens into the heart-centered nature that is always present. The end of days is a good sign that the rapture of the head- centered me is underway and that peace is about to reign in your reality.

"This unfamiliar experience is a gift."
You are welcome here.
You are enough!
How may I serve you?

Reflection

Are you willing to leave behind the old way of perceiving reality through a belief system in right and wrong? Are you willing to leave behind the ways you have been, known, and understood to be true? Are you truly willing to be born again into a new consciousness, a new way of stillness, which merges into the Divine core of all experiences and perceives through the heart of the matter?

Reprogramming the Subconscious Mind

"Be still and know that the part of you that feels like a victim that is being punished is God, a part of your true authentic nature."

Practicing the heart-centered habit: (Example)

Have you ever felt punished or like a victim?

Welcome these experiences as a part of consciousness (You):

H- HONESTY

"I fully feel the parts of me that have felt punished and like a victim."

A-ACKNOWLEDGE, ALLOW, ASK

"I acknowledge that it is safe and okay to feel this limited experience. I embrace these feelings fully just as they are because I know they are here to show me the way into my heart. As I embrace these feelings fully, I ask them to bring with them all of the past meanings, interpretations, beliefs, and judgments that I thought were true, but are not valid in this present moment, so that I may receive them as a gift, guide, and opening toward the infinite perception in my heart. I acknowledge their Divine role in helping me expand awareness into the depths of infinite knowing."

Allow the uncomfortable experience to have a voice. Do not believe what it is saying, but instead be a loving presence that offers a deeper level of safety, comfort, and acknowledgment than the experience has ever received from you before, thereby being the practice of detachment, allowance, pure love, and space.

Ask: "Divine heart, I accept that I don't know how to breathe deeply through uncomfortable experiences. Therefore, I ask that you breathe deeply for me through this experience of punishment and victimhood. Welcome, embrace, honor, and validate these experiences for me, through me, as I am now, healing the inner division within me, so that my perception can expand and align with the flow of infinite information." And so it is (Amen).

B- BREATHE

Breathe in these feelings ("*I receive you as life*") and breathe out (*"You are free to be"*). Be one with the breath: *"The breath is my salvation."*

I-I LOVE YOU

Place your hands over your heart. Say, *"I love you! All is an expression of one life. I validate this limited experience within me. It is an experience from my past that was not validated by my relationships to the world. Therefore, I choose to be the presence of love that provides this experience the resonation of love that it has never received. May I be all the affirmation that this limited experience needs to remember that it is an infinite expression of divinity, so that it may fully awaken from the illusion of limitation. I love you!"*

"I am abundant, wise, infinite, and free!"

T- THANK YOU

Thank the experience for helping you remember that you are an ever-expanding unique expression of the Truth. Thank the circumstance, story, or relationship that triggered these feelings in your body, so your entire being could awaken to your innocent nature of authentic freedom that can enjoy all experiences.

> *"Thank you for helping me to align and attune with my heart's ever-expanding unique expression of infinite wisdom and pure love! Thank you for helping me to remember the power of life that I am!"*

Intention: *(say aloud)*

"Today, I choose to embrace and enter the eye of all storms in my reality. I choose to allow the heart-centered me to rapture the head-centered me into the Kingdom of Heaven, bringing an end to the perception of limitation, separation, wrong, division, evil, bad, and division."

Affirmation: *(say aloud)*

Say aloud throughout today:

"My surroundings are beautiful because I am eternal beauty!

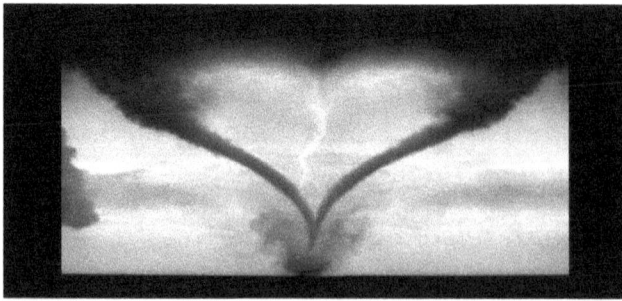

Day 15

The Great I Am

"All are but parts of one stupendous whole."

–Alexander Pope

Say Aloud: (looking into your eyes in a mirror)
Good morning, infinite one. You are safe to feel. I always want to know how you are feeling. You are the soul-mate I have been looking for my entire life. You matter and you are enough. You are worthy of being seen and heard. I see you and I am here to listen to you. There is a good reason you are here; you are Divine perfection. Today, I join you in celebrating your ever-expanding unique expression. I am open to receiving new information and new ways of being by choosing to receive all uncomfortable, unfamiliar, painful, inconvenient, and unwanted experiences as a Divine gift from you, my infinite heart. I love all of you! I really love all of you. (your name), I really love all of you. (Feel free to write your own love statement).

Every appearance and experience of mind and body is an extension of the unified field of existence. Another term used for the unified field of existence or heart-centered consciousness is "The Great I Am." The great I am is the essence that comprises all I am's. For many years I perceived from I am _____. Whatever I filled in the blank with became my identity. I desired to remember the part of me that didn't change identities, so that I could enjoy every identity and experience. My mind felt so limited when I focused on perceiving reality as whatever was filled in the blank. My heart never forgot the great I am. But I had many moments where my head did. Each time my head forgot, I suffered.

I realized that the only way to eradicate my personal suffering was to merge with all I am's. I remember going throughout my day and reminding myself that I am everything I see, feel, and experience. There is nothing that I am not. All of the I am this or that are drops in the vast ocean of the great energy that makes up all forms. I desired to perceive from the perception of the whole ocean and no longer from a single wave's perception that feels lost because it is looking toward the land for the ocean.

Today, remind yourself that you are the great I am. Give yourself the experience of feeling the expansive nature of the great I am, which is all of it. I am this... I am that... I am the murderer. I am the victim. I am the enemy. I am the savior. I am happiness. I am grief. I am positive. I am negative. I am judgment. I am acceptance. I am poor. I am wealthy. I am addiction. I am free. I am every culture. I am every religion. I am every human. I am that I am. When we realize we are all of it, we won't identify with one or the other. Our abundant nature of the great I am is everything: every person, every appearance, every belief, every thought, every feeling, every perception, and every emotion. Experiencing the perception of the great I am in every moment is how we wake up out of limitation, suffering, division, war, conflict, and separation. What we really are is the infinite nature of the great I am!

"This unwanted experience is a gift."
You are welcome here.
You are enough!
How may I serve you?

Exploration

I can remember as a child wanting to understand "why" I was experiencing so much judgment, false accusations, and rejection from the world when I acted from my true innocent, vulnerable, and open-hearted nature. At the time I didn't know that my heart nature was okay with experiencing these uncomfortable feelings. I have never personally met a human who allowed these uncomfortable experiences of judgment and rejection to be okay and respond from a space of pure allowance and love toward the experience. However, I did discover many humans who were worshipped as spiritual teachers, gurus, or enlightened beings who were written about in spiritual texts that lived by an inner state of allowance toward persecution, false accusations, rejection, and judgment. I also discovered many humans who exist today who have written books, teach, and talk on radio shows that live from this inner state of allowance.

I wanted to physically meet someone who responded from the heart- centered nature and allowed all experiences to be just as they are. I wanted to experience their authentic nature of pure love. I wanted a personal Jesus to follow and experience a relationship with them. I explored and searched for my own personal Jesus or enlightened being to be in relationship with. After many years of exploration, one day my heart said in a whisper, "You are the personal Jesus you are searching for. Stop searching and begin a relationship with the enlightened being of pure love that you already are!" I thought, *What does this mean? I am my own personal Jesus – that's blasphemous!*

Many years later, I realized that intuitive guidance was pointing to the fragments of self or the parts of me that felt separate from God that it was time to explore a new relationship to this physical world. I have known my whole life that I was an infinite expression of God, even though I had this deep awareness I still did not embrace and allow certain experiences to be okay because they did not feel like pure love. I have realized that my soul, which is an expression of pure love, came to this world to explore all the diverse aspects of existence. My soul came to experience judgment, rejection, persecution, victimization, false accusations, misunderstandings, punishment, criticism, and wrongness. I realized that the head-centered me had an innate desire to become heart-centered, so it could receive these experiences into my being. This desire was expressed through endless seeking and searching for the Truth.

These unwanted and uncomfortable experiences were like deflated and lifeless balloons, waiting to be filled with the breath of life. My soul wanted to be the one to breathe life into them and allow them to soar into the highest heights of Heaven. I had a new understanding of exploration. Instead of exploring for things or relationships I thought would make me happy, I allowed every moment to be an exploration, where my soul took center stage to fill all experiences with pure love and life. The heart-centered habit creates a new kind of relationship to the physical world. Unlike the head-centered way of judging everything and running from uncomfortable moments, toward what we think will make us feel happy, the heart-centered me remembers that all experiences are waiting to be filled with the remembrance of pure love. My own personal Jesus is my soul's expression of pure love toward all misperceived experiences, which have been viewed through a lens of wrong.

"This uncomfortable experience is a gift."
You are welcome here.
You are enough!
How may I serve you?

Diversity

We live in a diverse world of infinite experiences and possibilities. The head-centered me has been trained to think that oneness or Truth looks and feels one way. The belief in this one way creates a false sense of self that experiences limitation and separation. This one way sets the mind up to filter all other ways through judgment. This judgment of reality into right and wrong is the root of suffering, war, and conflict.

In Truth, diversity is a magic light show of glory. Diversity is a miraculous wonder of how one energy can appear as infinite expressions, appearances, realities, possibilities, and forms. The head-centered me cannot feel the abundance and infinite sense of all that exists when it judges. When the head-centered me experiences too much adversity, suffering, and difficulties, and it has an opportunity to surrender its way of judgment. When it goes searching within for another way to be in this world, it discovers a way that is in total allowance of everything. This allowance is the authentic expression of life that is here to play, explore, and enjoy all experiences. When the head-centered me rests into this heart-centered way of being it rests with the breath, allowing the breath to carry all experiences into the Kingdom of Heaven that exists within the heart. Here they are given new names, labels, and definitions, which reflect their pure nature of oneness, love, and life.

Our true authentic nature enjoys the diversity of life. The heart-centered me perceives all experiences as a loving parent does to their child. The heart- centered me loves observing the many diverse experiences of the one essence of existence. The heart-centered me is amazed at how the head-centered me has created such an infinite spectrum of right and wrong. The head-centered me has been a master at shape-shifting oneness into good and evil. Now the head- centered me is being rescued from the darkness, hell, and evil that it has imagined. What the head-centered me has imagined, it has believed in, and it has become the character experiencing the evil. The head-centered me is now crying out to be rescued from its own imagination. Therefore, the heart of the matter responds and calls it inward. For when the head-centered me sinks deep enough, it will drop out of its imagined character and into its authentic center of oneness, pure love, and life. The head-centered me is on an inner journey of remembrance, floating inward on a river of allowance, so that when it looks outward it may celebrate the diversity of life as never before.

"This painful experience is a gift."
You are welcome here.
You are enough!
How may I serve you?

<u>Allowance</u>

The head-centered me has imagined a reality of judgment and resistance. In truth, judgment and resistance isn't really occurring. It is like watching children play out their imagined games. My children used to love pretend play and they still do as nine and eleven year olds. In their imagination they really felt like they were the roles of their imagination. My son loved imagining himself as a ninja. My daughter loved imagining herself to be a good witch. I enjoyed watching them play out these roles in their imagination. This is exactly how our authentic nature feels toward the head-centered me. The head-centered me is a role we have imagined. It plays its roles and parts like a genius and masterful artist. It totally embodies its role of separation, judgment, division, and limitation. The imagined character plays out the limited stories it has imagined about itself while pretending to perceive an opposing force that is out to get it. Without a story of resistance the imagined character cannot exist. Every story is a portrayal of the hero's journey.

The more the head-centered me fights its imagined story, the more intense the story becomes through the appearance of more opposition. When the head-centered me surrenders into the heart-centered perspective of allowance, the story changes from a story about good and evil, into a story about unity, love, joy, and bliss. Opposition, evil, bad, wrong, and negative experiences are seen for what they really are; little wizards behind a big projector machine that create images of opposition. We came to play. How can we play as separate beings if we don't imagine opposition? The trick is to understand the enjoyment our true nature has in experiencing the play. Just like in the story of the "Wizard of Oz," when Dorothy pulled back the curtain to see the short man who controlled the huge, scary image of the wizard; we pull back the curtain and see clearly too. All scary images and imagined stories of hell are being controlled by an aspect of our true nature that wanted to imagine itself in a new and different way. Why? Maybe because our true nature loves creating diversity? It is an absolute miracle that oneness can enter a form and experience itself as something separate from itself.

We can connect to our childlike mind that enjoys pretending and see the imagined self of right and wrong, just as that; an imagined role that we wanted to experience, for the sake of playing. By loving diversity, exploration, and allowance of all imagined roles of good and evil, we remove the sting of death to then experience all roles without the heavy burden of believing that the role confines or limits us in anyway. We are infinite explorers of reality.

What if the experience of being "human" is the greatest experience of diversity you could have in the entire universe? Maybe it's time to enjoy the diversity of life, like a child enjoying the fantasy of Disneyland! Then nothing will be taken personally or too serious. Nobody really gets hurt if it is a game in our imagination. The character experiences the pain and the hurt. But the great I am remains whole, pure, and unharmed.

Heart-centered me: *(say aloud)*

I allow the stories of right and wrong to play out in my imagination. I take great joy in observing these stories. I allow experiences of pain, suffering, judgment, rejection, and limitation to enter my reality for the sake of observing the play. I allow negative emotions to be experienced for the sake of enjoying the diversity of the play. I am here to allow all experiences into my being for the sake of playing and enjoying the experience of being human.

"This unfamiliar experience is a gift."
You are welcome here.
You are enough!
How may I serve you?

Reflection

How would the quality of your experiences be if you perceived reality from the great I am? Allow today to be an experiment where you agree that everything you feel, think, see, and experience is the great I am, especially the experiences you believe are not "you." "Yes, I am this." "Yes, I am that." When you experience your true self to being everything, you experience being identified with nothing. This is freedom!

Reprogramming the Subconscious Mind

"Be still and know that resistance and blame is God, a part of your true authentic nature."

Practicing the heart-centered habit (Example)

Have you ever felt resistance and blame?

Welcome these experiences as a part of consciousness (You):

H- HONESTY

"I fully feel the parts of me that have felt resistance and blame."

A-ACKNOWLEDGE, ALLOW, ASK

"I acknowledge that it is safe and okay to feel this limited experience. I embrace these feelings fully just as they are because I know they are here to show me the way into my heart. As I embrace these feelings fully, I ask them to bring with them all of the past meanings, interpretations, beliefs, and judgments that I thought were true, but are not valid in this present moment, so that I may receive them as a gift, guide, and opening toward the infinite perception in my heart. I acknowledge their Divine role in helping me expand awareness into the depths of infinite knowing."

Allow the uncomfortable experience to have a voice. Do not believe what it is saying, but instead be a loving presence that offers a deeper level of safety, comfort, and acknowledgment than the experience has ever received from you before, thereby being the practice of detachment, allowance, pure love, and space.

Ask: "Divine heart, I accept that I don't know how to perceive reality through the great I am "I am everything, I am no-thing, therefore I am infinitely free." I ask that you perceive resistance and blame as part of the great I am for me. Welcome, embrace, honor, and validate these experiences for me, through me, as I am now, healing the inner division within me, so that my perception can expand and align with the flow of infinite information." And so it is (Amen).

B- BREATHE

Breathe in these feelings (*"I receive you as life"*) and breathe out (*"You are free to be"*). Be one with the breath: *"The breath aligns me with divinity."*

I-I LOVE YOU

Place your hands over your heart. Say, *"I love you! All is an expression of one life. I validate this limited experience within me. It is an experience from my past that was not validated by my relationships to the world. Therefore, I choose to be the presence of love that provides this experience the resonation of love that it has never received. May I be all the affirmation that this limited experience needs to remember that it is an infinite expression of divinity, so that it may fully awaken from the illusion of limitation. I love you!"*

"I am abundant, wise, infinite, and free!"

T- THANK YOU

Thank the experience for helping you remember that you are an ever-expanding unique expression of the Truth. Thank the circumstance, story, or relationship that triggered these feelings in your body, so your entire being could awaken to your innocent nature of authentic freedom that can enjoy all experiences.

> *"Thank you for helping me to align and attune with my heart's ever-expanding unique expression of infinite wisdom and pure love! Thank you for helping me to remember the power of life that I am!"*

Intention: *(say aloud)*

"Today, I choose to be one with all I am's, so that I may explore the diversity of experience and allow the great I am to play at full capacity as a unique I am."

Affirmation: *(say aloud)*

Say aloud throughout today:

"All emotions are inspirational because I am inspiration!"

Day 16

Openness

"One does not discover new lands without consenting to lose sight of the shore for very long."
–Andre Gide

Say Aloud: (looking into your eyes in a mirror)
Good morning, infinite one. You are safe to feel. I always want to know how you are feeling. You are the soul-mate that I have been looking for my entire life. You matter and you are enough. You are worthy of being seen and heard. I see you and I am here to listen to you. There is a good reason you are here; you are Divine perfection. Today, I join you in celebrating your ever-expanding unique expression. I am open to receiving new information and new ways of being by choosing to receive all uncomfortable, unfamiliar, painful, inconvenient, and unwanted experiences as a Divine gift from you, my infinite heart. I love all of you! I really love all of you. (your name), I really love all of you. (Feel free to write your own love statement).

In my experience reality always points to an open-ended mystery. Every time I thought I understood something, some way, or someone; life would bring an experience that opened me up to perceiving that there was always more to understand. Every time I thought I had an understanding about reality, I would have an experience that I had no idea about reality. Understanding and knowing are like infinite pages of information in the eternal book of life. There truly is so much more than what meets the eye.

My perception always fluctuated between intuitive all-knowing insights and cluelessness. When I learned that there is a unified field of infinite energy, potential, and information within me, I questioned my desire to be stagnant through attaching to one particular body of knowledge or my personal understanding of reality throughout this one lifetime. If I am an infinite being, then why would I experience one experience of understanding and knowing throughout an entire lifetime? I wondered if I remained the heart-centered habit, which keeps me open to new understandings and knowings, could I continue to expand my perception of reality?

Cultural conditioning taught me that change was bad. But this new expanded understanding of myself set my focus on a new trajectory; a path where I began to embrace the change of my personal understanding and knowing. Therefore, I experimented with the heart-centered habit and observed the wisdom, understanding, and knowing that continually streamed through me as me. Information streamed through me that I had not learned from this lifetime. I realized that being heart-centered was the relaxation and peace that I was previously unsuccessful in searching for through mental understanding and knowing. I also realized that understanding and knowing continually changes and becomes deeper and wider, expanding the mind. I have come to enjoy riding the waves of understanding and knowing as they appear and disappear, remaining open for a new wave to take me on another ride. I continually wonder, where will the waves of understanding take me?

The deeper I relaxed and the more heart-centered I became, the more I experienced knowing and not knowing simultaneously. The knowing spontaneously unfolds in the midst of not knowing. The known is made known within the unknown. Remaining heart-centered allowed me to remain open to allowing knowing and understanding to unfold like a flower. Then one petal at a time the understanding or knowing faded away.

The biggest misperception I had about enlightenment, spiritual awakening, or being a born again Christian was that I thought I had to hold onto a certain knowing or understanding about reality. I was searching for the perfect knowledge and understanding, which reflected the Truth. When I stopped searching for the one and only understanding and knowing of Truth, I discovered all knowledge and understandings were reflections of Truth.

Being the heart-centered habit allows us to detach from the knowledge and understanding that is spontaneously emerging from within us. Giving a voice to this intuitive guidance connects our mind and body to our spiritual essence. All knowledge and understanding emerges from the spiritual essence of our being. But when we attach to it as the Truth we will suffer because we are infinite and all knowledge is meant to come and go, so it can fulfill its destiny of freedom.

"This unwanted experience is a gift."
You are welcome here.
You are enough!
How may I serve you?

Open Mind

What narrows and limits the awareness of mind? Judgment is a narrowing and limiting tool for the mind. Judgment says, "This is good and right, but this is wrong and bad." Therefore, do not include these pieces and parts of reality. Either fight to change them or deny them. The only reason why we judge is because we have been judged in the past. There are parts of ourselves that have not been accepted, loved, and embraced as goodness because it was believed to be wrong. The parts of us that judge others are the parts that feel they are wrong due to past judgments. In an effort to deny the wrong we feel about ourselves, we judge the unfamiliar in another.

Judgment is a habit of distraction. As long as we distract our awareness from feeling into the wrong we feel about ourselves, we cannot embrace and love those parts which would resolve and heal the wrong we feel. Instead, we expect our relationships to confirm the wrong we judge in others to give us a superficial sense of right, which masks the wrong we feel deep inside. Judgment is a temporary solution to making us feel better. Feeling right by judging another as wrong only masks the wrong within us. There is another way that would instantly heal and resolve the parts of us that feel wrong. We don't have to narrow the mind and close awareness in on one particular belief system of right and wrong. We can keep the mind open.

Judgment is a symptom that we feel there is something wrong with us. As soon as we find ourselves judging another and perceiving a part of them as wrong, we can stop and go within to facilitate our own deep healing. Instead of believing in the wrong we perceive in another, we can remember that we are only judging because we have not welcomed, embraced, and loved a part of our self that has been judged as wrong by others in our past. When we choose to open our mind by loving the parts of our self that our environment has judged as not good enough or wrong, we experience the freedom and fulfillment that we were searching for from our relationships.

We don't have to expect our relationships to make us feel right. We can embrace all of the parts of our self that have been condemned, judged, and rejected. We can perceive the wrong in us as goodness because in essence it is pure goodness. The part of you that likes to keep your head in the clouds is waiting to be loved by you. The part of you that is melancholy is waiting to be loved by you. The part of you that strives for perfection is waiting to be loved by you. The part of you that is "too sensitive" is waiting to be loved by you. The part of you that is secretive is waiting to be loved by you. The part of you that is skeptical is waiting to be loved by you. The part of you that is "too emotional" or "not emotional enough" is waiting to be loved by you. The part of you that is callous and cold is waiting to be loved by you. The part of you that has been judged as fake is waiting to be loved by you. The part of you that has been judged as "too independent" or "too dependent" is waiting to be loved by you. The part of you that wants to be a hermit or be the center of attention is waiting to be loved by you.

      This is what Jesus was talking about when he said, "First remove the beam out of your own eye, and then you can see clearly to remove the speck out of your brother's eye." We judge another as wrong because we perceive there is wrong in us. There is no wrong in us; this is the misperception or sin that Jesus was talking about. Jesus also said to LOVE the Lord your God with all your heart, soul, and mind. If God is the totality of all the pieces, parts, and aspects of reality, then we are called to love everything in existence, including the parts of our self that the world has judged as wrong. Love every feeling and emotion that arises from within your heart. Love every thought, idea, perception, and belief that arises in the mind. Love every experience that arises from within your soul. When you love every aspect of existence, then you will be filled with the energy of God and the mind will remain open and free to receiving everything in existence through the LOVE that you truly are.

"This uncomfortable experience is a gift."
You are welcome here.
You are enough!
How may I serve you?

Open Heart

We have learned what feelings to accept and what feelings to condemn through how we were judged by our relationships. We have been so used to trying to conform to the judgments of others that we have forgotten our true authentic nature, which is pure life, God, divinity, pure love, and infinite energy. When we remember our true infinite nature, we can perceive all feelings and emotions as a piece of our infinite nature. Feelings and emotions are like a rainbow of an infinite spectrum of color. When we embrace, welcome, and love every feeling and emotion that we have judged as wrong about us, our heart opens into eternity. Pure love is an ever-expanding energy. At the core of every diverse feeling and emotion is pure love. Therefore, even limited feelings and emotions are connected to eternity. However, if we judge certain feelings and emotions that arise within us as bad or wrong, we will never experience their infinite nature of love. Pure love is the source of all feelings, emotions, experiences, thoughts, beliefs, and perceptions. However, our perception distorts certain feelings and emotions when it is viewed through judgment.

The heart-centered habit is a guide that opens our mind and heart to embracing every aspect of our infinite nature. When the mind and heart fully open, we will experience Heaven on Earth. There will be no more wrong, limitation, pain, suffering, stress, or division. All of life will be perceived through the expanded perception of infinite love.

"This inconvenient experience is a gift."
You are welcome here.
You are enough!
How may I serve you?

Resonance

Resonance is the sound produced by a body vibrating in synchrony with a neighboring source of sound. As humans we experience sounds from our environment and sounds from deep within ourselves. In our society, we are extremely focused on being energized because we have become so good at doing, doing, doing... Resonating with this fast paced energy has caused a dissonance between our head and our heart. Our head is always in the past or future. If it is in the future it feels energized. If it is in the past it feels depressed or not energized. Our identity is always running away from the past and into the future. This creates an experience of struggling and striving.

We are not as comfortable with being, which is more of a neutral vibration. We feel that if we are not working toward some goal, then we will somehow go backwards. We all want to arrive at some destination of perfection before we allow ourselves to enjoy life. When we resonate with a world of doers, we forget the balance and harmony of life. We become extremely head-centered by thinking too much about what needs done so we can get what we want. We forget to check in with how we feel. We forget to listen to our intuition. We forget the peace, serenity, and joy of being alive, which is sensed from within our heart.

When we are born into a world that is energized by doing, we become over focused on results and matching up to society's standards. We raise our children to be more responsible and demanding that they conform to the standards, so that as parents, we feel we are doing our job to mold them. All the while, our children show us the ease and joy of being present. Children already know how to laugh, play, and enjoy life. What are we molding future generations into? Doers! Do, do, do, do, do, work, work, work.... We can choose to wake up out of the fast paced environment that is in constant motion of arriving at some future destination. We can choose to resonate with the presence, enjoyment, relaxation, and peace from within our heart. The more we slow down, breathe, and check in with what our heart senses, the more we will awaken to the innocence of our true nature.

Every day, take time to be with your own heart. Take time to check in with what you feel within. Take time to love yourself like you never have before. Take time to breathe. Take time to walk in nature. Take time to listen to the sounds around you. Take time to encourage and speak loving words to yourself. Take time every day to be heart-centered in a head-centered world and you will be a guide for future generations. You will be a part of the new resonation, which vibrates a sense of wonder, awe, peace, joy, relaxation, and love.

If we resonate with what we sense from the outside-in (head-centered me), we will resonate a sense of separation, conflict, division, and limitation, creating an experience of stress and struggle. If we resonate with what we sense from within the presence of our soul from the inside-out (heart-centered me), we will resonate unity, harmony, abundance, freedom, and equanimity, creating an experience of ease and wonder.

When I was growing up it was rare to know someone who didn't conform to some group understanding of reality. Most people seemed to conform to their generation group understanding, culture group understanding, religious group understanding, family group understanding, sports group understanding, political group understanding, and so on... In the past twenty years or so, more and more people are stepping out into the world as a unique expression of the Divine. These people do not conform to any group understanding about reality. They are just aligned with their soul and speak, act, and live in harmony with life. But they are unique, special, and authentic. Instead of possessing an understanding about reality, they live as reality. They inspire me to remember my soul's unique voice and live in alignment with life.

When we live in a heart-centered way, we will all express our oneness in a unique way. We can resonate the Truth we feel in our heart. When we live as a unique expression of the Divine, we resonate love, harmony, peace, and kindness out into the world. It is the resonance of our soul that inspires others to wake up to their soul expression. We were never meant to follow others or put others on a pedestal. Nobody is higher or lower than another. We are all equally brilliant, beautiful, loving, and kind souls. We are here to share with each other the different ways and expressions that can come forth from our infinite one essence of divinity. We can resonate the love and peace that we are in a brilliant array of unique ways!

"This unfamiliar experience is a gift."
You are welcome here.
You are enough!
How may I serve you?

Reflection

Are you afraid to be unique and allow your voice to resonate the truth you feel in your heart?

Your true authentic expression is hiding in feelings of unworthiness and insecurity. Merge with these feelings by perceiving them as God and you will find your authentic and unique expression of Truth, love, divinity, and fulfillment.

Reprogramming the Subconscious Mind

"Be still and know that insecurity and unworthiness is God, a part of your true authentic nature."

264

Practicing the heart-centered habit: (Example)

Have you ever felt the need to seek or follow someone else to know the truth of your being?

Welcome these experiences as a part of consciousness (You):

H- HONESTY

"I fully feel the parts of me that need to seek and follow someone else to know the truth of my being. I fully feel the parts of me that have felt insecure and unworthy."

A-ACKNOWLEDGE, ALLOW, ASK

"I acknowledge that it is safe and okay to feel this limited experience. I embrace these feelings fully just as they are because I know they are here to show me the way into my heart. As I embrace these feelings fully, I ask them to bring with them all of the past meanings, interpretations, beliefs, and judgments that I thought were true, but are not valid in this present moment, so that I may receive them as a gift, guide, and opening toward the infinite perception in my heart. I acknowledge their Divine role in helping me expand awareness into the depths of infinite knowing."

Allow the uncomfortable experience to have a voice. Do not believe what it is saying, but instead be a loving presence that offers a deeper level of safety, comfort, and acknowledgment than the experience has ever received from you before, thereby being the practice of detachment, allowance, pure love, and space.

Ask: "Divine heart, I accept that I don't know how to open my mind and resonate pure love. Therefore, I ask that you open my mind and resonate pure love through me, so that I may shine in the glory of Divine Light. Welcome, embrace, honor, and validate these experiences for me, through me, as I am now, healing the inner division within me, so that my perception can expand and align with the flow of infinite information." And so it is (Amen).

Ask: "*Divine heart, please teach me how to receive the stagnant beliefs that created this inner sense of division, separation, disharmony, and imbalance, so that my perception can expand and align with the flow of infinite information.*" And so it is (Amen).

B- BREATHE

Breathe in these feelings ("*I receive you as life*") and breathe out (*"You are free to be"*). Be one with the breath: *"The breath guides me to my unique soul expression."*

I-I LOVE YOU

Place your hands over your heart. Say, "*I love you! All is an expression of one life. I validate this limited experience within me. It is an experience from my past that was not validated by my relationships to the world. Therefore, I choose to be the presence of love that provides this experience the resonation of love that it has never received. May I be all the affirmation that this limited experience needs to remember that it is an infinite expression of divinity, so that it may fully awaken from the illusion of limitation. I love you!*"

"*I am abundant, wise, infinite, and free!*"

T- THANK YOU

Thank the experience for helping you remember that you are an ever-expanding unique expression of the truth. Thank the circumstance, story, or relationship that triggered these feelings in your body, so your entire being could awaken to your innocent nature of authentic freedom that can enjoy all experiences.

> *"Thank you for helping me to align and attune with my heart's ever-expanding unique expression of infinite wisdom and pure love! Thank you for helping me to remember the power of life that I am!"*

Intention: *(Say aloud)*

"Today, I choose to allow life to crack open my mind and heart, so that I may resonate or tune into the vibration of pure infinite love through all experiences."

Affirmation: *(say aloud)*

Say aloud throughout today:

"All ideas are genuine because I am genuine."

Day 17

Reconciliation

"When the heart opens completely, you will stumble upon the most powerful force in the universe... your loving presence."
-Matt Kahn

Say Aloud: (looking into your eyes in a mirror)
> Good morning, infinite one. You are safe to feel. I always want to know how you are feeling. You are the soul-mate that I have been looking for my entire life. You matter and you are enough. You are worthy of being seen and heard. I see you and I am here to listen to you. There is a good reason you are here; you are Divine perfection! Today, I join you in celebrating your ever-expanding unique expression. I am open to receiving new information and new ways of being by choosing to receive all uncomfortable, unfamiliar, painful, inconvenient, and unwanted experiences as a Divine gift from you, my infinite heart. I love all of you! I really love all of you. (your name), I really love all of you. (Feel free to write your own love statement).

When my heart opened fully, I remembered my soul's purpose was reconciliation. My soul came to Earth to reconcile or harmonize with every part of the human experience. Reconciliation means the process of bringing harmony into all relationships to the physical world. Being heart-centered allowed my mind and heart to open and reconcile all opposing views that blocked awareness from remembering the true nature of existence, which is pure love.

I realized that all belief systems of right and wrong created an inner experience of pain. Since I have always been extremely sensitive, empathic, and emotional I could feel the pain of this world from the time I was a child. In the beginning, the pain wasn't mine, but I could feel it in others. Not only could I feel expressed pain, but I could also feel repressed pain. I noticed that when people repress their pain, they unconsciously create pain for other people. It is not the authentic self creating the pain, but rather it is repressed pain creating more pain. As I got older I began to blame myself for the pain I felt in others. This began my journey of repressing pain. I didn't know what to do with pain, so I carried it in my body just like everybody else.

I also noticed that every time I followed the intuition of my heart, my choices created pain in my relationships. Standing out as an authentic expression of the Divine shed a bright light into my relationships. The Divine light that we are sheds light on everything we repress. I did not know how to have a relationship with the pain that was revealed in others when I was authentic. In an effort to not shed light on other people's experience of inner pain, I chose to be head-centered in my relationships and kept intuitive guidance to myself.

When I began to practice the heart-centered habit, I realized that I can't run from feeling pain in the world and I can't hide in the false head-centered me to ease other people's pain. Pain was the next one in line that my heart wanted to harmonize with. I began reconciling my relationship with pain. Pain became the last door toward authentic freedom. I began to acknowledge the pain I felt within me. I went through the memories of my past where I felt hurt by others and the pain I carried for others. I acknowledged, blessed, and loved my pain. Then I acknowledged the pain in the person who created pain in me during that past experience. I realized it was their repressed pain that they had not acknowledged within themselves that created the pain in me. It wasn't their heart's intention. Somebody created pain in them and nobody showed them by example that they could acknowledge, bless, and love the pain for themselves. So, they stored it in their body, where it created dis-ease.

Honesty and acknowledgement are the first steps to reconcile unresolved pain. Being honest about the pain we feel and acknowledging that the one who caused us pain was doing the best they knew to do at the time places our mind and body on a path of healing. Blessing our heart and the heart of the ones who taught us pain through the heart-centered habit can offer healing toward all hearts involved with the pain. The heart-centered habit is a way that we can harmonize with pain, instead of passing on pain to our relationships.

"This unwanted experience is a gift."
You are welcome here.
You are enough!
How may I serve you?

Forgiveness

The common thread that spurs every mind to attach to a knowledge of right and wrong is the condition of unresolved repressed pain. We have all experienced pain in this world. Nobody talks about facing, embracing, acknowledging, and loving the pain they feel, whether it is manifesting in you or someone else. We have all been taught to escape, run, fight, deny, or repress the pain we feel from our relationships to the physical world. Part of the journey of being human is embracing pain. Being the heart-centered habit guides awareness to acknowledge all repressed pain within ourselves, and then acknowledge the repressed pain in others that you have blamed for the pain you feel. When we acknowledge our pain, we will no longer create or repress pain. When we acknowledge other people's pain and bless them by sending them love, they no longer have the power to create pain in us.

We can remain healed and in the full remembrance of Divine Love by bringing reconciliation to our relationship with pain. Reconciliation with pain is the path of true forgiveness. Forgiveness is the symptom of bringing harmony into every relationship we have with the physical world. Being heart-centered allows us to harmonize with judgment, fear, pain, anxiety, hatred, anger, rage, stress, and suffering. We become the instrument that harmonizes every experience into the remembrance of pure love.

Forgiveness is a symptom of remaining open toward all experiences of reality. Forgiveness is the inner yes that allows all emotions, thoughts, feelings, beliefs, and perceptions to be received as divinity. Forgiveness is the breath that breathes in every experience and lets it go to return to its true essence of purity. Forgiveness is the intuitive guidance that guides us to give people space who we feel have intense repressed unresolved pain. We still acknowledge their pain and bless them as we give them space to acknowledge their own pain. This means if we are in abusive relationships, we forgive them by giving them the space to reconcile their relationship with inner pain.

The heart-centered habit is a living practice of forgiveness. Forgiveness is an intuitive perception of sensing harmony at the heart of all experiences, including pain, judgment, fear, and stress. Forgiveness is our authentic nature. Forgiveness isn't something we do. Rather, it is what we are! Forgiveness is a perception of heart-centered consciousness that perceives no wrong. If we harmonize with every perception of wrong and reconcile it as pure goodness, there will be no symptom of pain.

Forgiveness says:

"Pain, you are welcome here. I acknowledge the insight that you are delivering to me in this moment. I realize that I was lost in a perception or belief in wrong. Pain, thank you for bringing me this message. I release my belief in wrong by feeling and experiencing it fully. Wrong and pain, you are the light, the light I am! I no longer exclude you from my awareness of God!

"I release all of my relationships to this physical world that I have blamed for teaching me wrong and blame. I acknowledge that you were only doing what you knew to do. If you could have done better, you would have! I acknowledge your repressed pain and feel it fully for you because we are one in the same! I no longer exclude you from my awareness of God! I love you!"

"This uncomfortable experience is a gift."
You are welcome here.
You are enough!
How may I serve you?

Healing

Have you ever noticed the millions, maybe billions of different healing modalities in our world? We are always searching for a way to heal our emotional, mental, and physical problems. When we experience any sort of pain, we seek a way to get rid of it. We have been conditioned to be scared of getting hurt because we don't want to feel pain. The rational mind has projected pain to be a scary monster that is out to get us, and as such pain has become our greatest enemy. Jesus said to love your enemy. If we could remember to love the pain we feel, we would pull back the curtain and see that it is nothing more than a little child projecting a big bad monster in our brain. If we ask the child why it is creating such a big show of disturbance, it would show us that it is afraid of change. The human experience involves a lot of change. We simply have to become the voice of our heart, embrace the pain, and remind it that all is well.

We must remind pain that change is the experience that allows us to play at full capacity. Change allows us to experience ourselves in a vast array of expressions. Change is an amazing and beautiful experience. It is a privilege to our soul to experience change.

When our mind and body are undergoing change, we experience it as pain. However, if we perceive change as a Divine gift, then it will feel more like excitement. Pain is just a sensation, and it doesn't have to be interpreted as something bad. If we acknowledge pain and know it carries an intuitive message from our soul, we will perceive it as a gift. Pain has nothing to do with your external environment or your relationships to the physical world. Pain has to do with alignment. When our perception of reality is aligned with the perception of our infinite nature, we do not experience pain as bad. Instead we experience pain as the Divine light, which is the same Divine light we are. The more the mind and body align with our spiritual nature, the more we sense the renewal, rejuvenation, and rebirth of life, and our experience of pain vanishes.

It is a common belief that vulnerability keeps you open to being hurt. The head-centered me perceives pain as a threat, thinking that the pain is a symptom that either we or another have done something wrong. We have been conditioned to repress pain, which hides our vulnerable, innocent nature. We learn to repress pain because we are taught that our authentic vulnerable nature is weak. However, the opposite is the Truth. Vulnerability is an all-powerful expression of our heart-centered Divine nature. Vulnerability has been given a bad rap, like pain, however pain points to our authentic nature of pure love like every other experience we have of this world. Pain is an angel that comes to bring an intuitive message. When we embrace pain, we merge with our spiritual nature in a human form. The pain teaches us the infinite power of our true nature. As we reconcile our relationship with pain, we open our mind and heart to receiving Divine guidance. When we remember our true nature of vulnerability as we did when we were a child, we can build a new way to relate to the world and we no longer have to protect our vulnerability.

Being heart-centered brings harmony between our vulnerable nature and pain. We can shift from needing to protect our heart's vulnerability with an innate desire to bring harmony and reconciliation to every experience knowing that there is no real force that can harm, hurt, or cause us pain. The force our mind used to perceive as an enemy is now perceived as a part of the one essence of goodness or God. The heart-centered me is here to acknowledge, bless, and love all experiences, including the painful, unwanted, inconvenient, and uncomfortable experiences.

If you are in a mental, emotional, or physical abusive relationship, you should give the abuser space and leave the relationship. Even by leaving an abusive relationship, you can still acknowledge the pain that has been created in you, as well as acknowledging the pain that is unresolved in the one who has abused you. By acknowledging your pain and their pain, blessing yourself and them, and loving your heart and theirs, you can walk away healed and return to your authentic vulnerable nature by acknowledging the authentic you, which can never be harmed, killed, or hurt. Otherwise, you will repress the pain that their pain caused you and you will be used to create more pain in the world, becoming more closed and head-centered. Being heart-centered with your pain from an abusive relationship will remind you of the intuitive guidance within, which will guide you on what to do and where to go.

I acknowledge your pain and I see your pain as the Truth I am. May you remember your authentic nature of pure love by becoming heart-centered!

"This inconvenient experience is a gift."
You are welcome here.
You are enough!
How may I serve you?

Innocence

We desire change in our uncomfortable and unwanted circumstances because we desire to merge with change. Our innocent nature desires to become one with all change. Change is like Disneyworld to our innocent nature. Our innocent nature is our everlasting presence that desires to experience the human conditions of change, evolution, and diversity. Our innocence delights in change because change is like a child dressing up in a costume and playing a character.

Our innocent heart-centered nature is open to every experience. Innocence can never be hurt, harmed, or killed. It is our eternal nature. No matter the amount of pain we endure as we go through the evolution of being human, our innocent nature stays pure and untainted. When the mind and body remember to align with the innocence of our heart-centered nature, we feel more relaxed through the turbulence of change. When the mind is not relaxed, it is in a hyper state of fight or flight, which triggers a head-centered response and we perceive everything through a limited lens. When perceiving reality through a limited lens we feel disconnected from our innocent nature. We feel like we have to protect our heart and we filter every experience.

Pain, judgment, fear, stress, and negative emotions are what we experience in our innocent nature when we perceive experience through the limited lens of the head-centered me.

The sense of pain, judgment, limitation, stress, and negative emotions is our innocent nature trying to get our attention, but we are too distracted through our rational mind's identification with the world to stop and listen. So, the intensity of the pain, stress, limitation, frustration, negative emotions, and fear increase until we are willing to stop focusing outward and instead focus inward. But we have to merge with the pain, stress, limitation, and negative emotions to be able to sense the intuitive messages of our innocent nature. If we remain distracted by identifying with our environment we will perceive the pain, judgment, fear, negative emotions, and stress as separate from us and begin blaming it for ruining our plans. However, when we perceive these experiences as gifts from our innocent nature, we can play as reality instead of watching reality pass us by. We can wake up out of the trance and participate in the joy of living.

As we open the rational mind and empty it of its understanding and personal knowledge of right and wrong, it expands into the intuitive space of the heart. The rational mind and the heart merge into one open innocent nature. The childlike inquisitive mind is healed and safe to play at full capacity. Misinterpretation of reality becomes a faint memory. All experiences become a playground for the innocent nature to explore. There is no more separation. The experience of another is felt and embraced fully as our own. There is no one to protect. Nothing to guard. Nothing to fight against. Nothing to escape. No desire for the moment to be any different than it is appearing. All is well! We have returned to aloneness or all-oneness. Everything has been welcomed into the wholeness of existence. Everything is perceived as divinity. Freedom is remembered! The heart-centered habit spontaneously and magically guides awareness to return toward the remembrance of innocence.

"This unfamiliar experience is a gift."
You are welcome here.
You are enough!
How may I serve you?

Reflection

What if you were born to remove the sting of death, pain, and fear from your experience of reality by shifting your perception of reality from the head to the heart? The head believes that this uncomfortable experience is blocking me from feeling whole, God, divinity, freedom, fulfillment, goodness, or love. The heart knows that this uncomfortable experience is God and carries an intuitive message that is here to awaken me out of a belief in wrong.

Reprogramming the Subconscious Mind

"Be still and know that pain, hurt, emptiness, and dis-ease is God, a part of your true authentic nature."

Practicing the heart-centered habit: (Example)

Have you ever felt pain, hurt, emptiness, or dis-ease?

Welcome these experiences as a part of consciousness (You):

H- HONESTY

"I fully feel the parts of me that have felt pain, hurt, emptiness, and dis-ease."

A-ACKNOWLEDGE, ALLOW, ASK

"I acknowledge that it is safe and okay to feel this limited experience. I embrace these feelings fully just as they are because I know they are here to show me the way into my heart. As I embrace these feelings fully, I ask them to bring with them all of the past meanings, interpretations, beliefs, and judgments that I thought were true, but are not valid in this present moment, so I may receive them as a gift, guide, and opening toward the infinite perception in my heart. I acknowledge their Divine role in helping me expand awareness into the depths of infinite knowing."

Allow the uncomfortable experience to have a voice. Do not believe what it is saying, but instead be a loving presence that offers a deeper level of safety, comfort, and acknowledgment than the experience has ever received from you before, thereby being the practice of detachment, allowance, pure love, and space.

Ask: "Divine heart, I accept that I don't know how to forgive and heal my mind from past hurts and wounds. Therefore, I ask that you forgive and heal all past wounds for me. Welcome, embrace, honor, and validate these experiences for me, through me, as I am now, healing the inner division within me, so my perception can expand and align with the flow of infinite information." And so it is (Amen)

B- BREATHE

Breathe in these feelings (*"I receive you as life"*) breathe out (*"You are free to be"*). Be one with the breath: *"The breath guides me to return to innocence."*

I-I LOVE YOU

Place your hands over your heart. Say, *"I love you! All is an expression of one life. I validate this limited experience within me. It is an experience from my past that was not validated by my relationships to the world. Therefore, I choose to be the presence of love that provides this experience the resonation of love that it has never received. May I be all the affirmation that this limited experience needs to remember that it is an infinite expression of divinity, so it may fully awaken from the illusion of limitation. I love you!"*

"I am abundant, wise, infinite, and free!"

T- THANK YOU

Thank the experience for helping you remember that you are an ever-expanding unique expression of the Truth. Thank the circumstance, story, or relationship that triggered these feelings in your body, so your entire being could awaken to your innocent nature of authentic freedom that can enjoy all experiences.

> *"Thank you for helping me to align and attune with my heart's ever-expanding unique expression of infinite wisdom and pure love! Thank you for helping me to remember the power of life that I am!"*

Intention: *(Say aloud)*:

"Today I choose to reconcile or harmonize with the pain I feel in me, others, and the world. I choose to invite healing into my perception of reality by awakening to my authentic nature of forgiveness and innocence. May the hearts of all be healed."

Affirmation: *(say aloud)*

Say aloud throughout today:

"My reality is healed and whole because I am healed and whole!"

Day 18

You Are the Mystery

*"The mystery of life is not a problem to be solved but a
reality to be experienced."*
-Kymberly (unknown last name)

Say Aloud: (looking into your eyes in a mirror)
Good morning, infinite one. You are safe to feel. I
always want to know how you are feeling. You are
the soul-mate that I have been looking for my
entire life. You matter and you are enough. You
are worthy of being seen and heard. I see you and
I am here to listen to you. There is a good reason
you are here; you are Divine perfection. Today, I
join you in celebrating your ever-expanding
unique expression. I am open to receiving new
information and new ways of being by choosing to
receive all uncomfortable, unfamiliar, painful,
inconvenient, and unwanted experiences as a
Divine gift from you, my infinite heart. I love all of
you! I really love all of you. (your name), I really
love all of you. (Feel free to write your own love
statement).

If I had the words to express what I felt as a child
I would have said, "Why do people have such a problem
with me being a mystery!" I was totally content not
knowing who or what I was! I enjoyed basking in the
wonder, magic, and mystery of our human nature. This
mystery seemed to trigger unwanted experiences for
others. I could see they were not comfortable with being
a mystery. They had a need to figure me out and
determine whether I was safe or not. Therefore, I grew
up thinking that something was wrong with me because
I was comfortable not knowing who I was.

I felt like the world portrayed the mysterious self as a major problem. Therefore, I looked to others to show me what was wrong with me. I bought into their ideas of wrong. This is how I became a head-centered me that pretended to know "who" I was. I could not create new possibilities in my reality through perceiving reality as the head-centered me. I tried so hard to be right, good, and spiritual. I worked hard to deserve my heart's desires. But my life seemed to reproduce the same circumstances over and over again. It wasn't until I relaxed into being okay and willing to embrace being a mystery that new possibilities began to emerge.

When I started to practice the heart-centered habit, I had to reprogram my subconscious mind to be willing to embrace this sense of mystery I felt within me. This required faith and trust in what I sensed from within my heart. The heart-centered me is full of life, love, passion, excitement, enthusiasm, inspiration, and intuitive insights. The heart-centered me lives without reasons nor a reference point because it is my mind and body's connection to the formless spiritual essence of all existence. It is my connection to infinite wisdom and potential.

My rational mind was trained by the physical world to misinterpret the love, life, passion, excitement, enthusiasm, inspiration, and intuitive insights as pain, fear, and wrong. My rational mind was trained to function only through reasoning and reference points that were rooted in a knowledge of right and wrong. The heart-centered me became my rational mind's enemy because it did not follow the world's rules of reasoning and reference points from past experiences. Therefore, my rational mind began to repress the love, life, passion, excitement, enthusiasm, inspiration, and intuitive insights that were coming from my authentic mysterious, formless spiritual nature.

My rational mind interpreted excitement as fear because it was coming from a mysterious unreasonable formless place within. My rational interpreted authentic expression as anger because the expression was coming from a mysterious place within. My rational mind interpreted intuition as judgment because it was arising from an unknown space within. My rational mind interpreted passion as guilt because it was arising from the essence within. My rational mind interpreted enthusiasm as stress and struggle because it was coming from a no-point of reference from within. My rational mind interpreted pure love as pain because it was arising from the mysterious nature within. My rational mind interpreted spiritual insights as an enemy because they had no explanation, reasons, or point of reference.

The longer my rational mind misinterpreted the love, life, inspiration, enthusiasm, passion, and excitement from my soul's authentic expression, the more I repressed these intuitive experiences, increasing the inner experience of fear, anger, judgment, guilt, stress, struggle, pain, division, and ego. I realized that the head-centered me is the repressed heart-centered me.

Pure life and love flow from the inside-out. The head-centered me is a subconscious conditioned way of only receiving information or life from the outside-in. The head-centered me has its back facing our heart-centered nature. Therefore, the head-centered me feels attacked by the intuitive information that flows from the inside-out and perceives intuition as a mysterious attack, thereby becoming life's eternal enemy. The ego or head- centered me always feels like life is happening to it, which could arrive in the form of a gift or a thief. The head-centered me always believes that life is adding value to my experience or taking value away from my experience. The head-centered me believes that life either gives me what I want or takes what I want from me!

If the head-centered me could change its position and repent, which means to make an 180-degree turn, it could receive the life that is flowing from within. The heart-centered me is life's eternal ally. The heart-centered habit reprograms our subconscious mind to receiving every experience that arises from our mysterious nature that functions without reason or a point of reference, remembering that we are an eternal ally to all that exists. There is no separation, division, opposition, or enemy. We don't have to perpetuate a false sense of self in the head to protect us from our authentic mysterious spiritual formless nature anymore. Just turn within and face the repressed love, life, excitement, enthusiasm, passion, insights, and intuition that has been waiting in the darkness for your return. Fear will unravel into new excitement. Anger will unravel into a new authentic expression. Judgment will unravel into new intuition. Guilt will unravel into new passion. Stress and struggle will unravel into new enthusiasm. Pain will unravel into new love. Ego or the head-centered me will unravel into the heart-centered me, which is pure, authentic, raw, and eternal truth. The truth spontaneously arises from our formless mysterious nature. The rational mind doesn't need to misinterpret it anymore. Instead, the rational mind can rest from its desire to protect. All is well!

I am a mystery! The mystery of life is happening through me as me! I am the unknown being made known into new possibilities through infinite experiences. It is a mystery who I will become. It is a mystery what I will do next. It is a mystery who I will meet. It is a mystery if anyone will read this book. It is a mystery what fruit it will bear, if any. Every moment is a gift of presence that unfolds the mystery of what we truly are! The mystery of what we are is every potential, possibility, reality, and dimension of all of existence. The rational mind cannot fathom our infinite nature. Therefore, we are a miraculous mystery!

"This unwanted experience is a gift."
You are welcome here.
You are enough!
How may I serve you?

Magic

Magic can be defined in two ways. One definition is the practice of illusion. The other definition expresses something that is wonderful, marvelous, and exciting. When the mind is focused on perceiving reality from the head-centered me by identifying with external circumstances, it creates an illusion of who you think you are. The illusion is a false sense of self that is imagined and not authentic. We imagine ourselves to be this false self to protect ourselves from experiencing all of reality. Therefore, if we believe that we need to protect ourselves from certain experiences, then we will use the magic that we are to create an illusory self in the head.

On the other hand, when the mind is focused on perceiving reality from the heart-centered habit, by sensing the intuition of the space within, it experiences the wonderful, marvelous, and exciting life of our infinite soul. Magic is awareness. We can use awareness to focus on a story of me in the head, which is an illusion or we can use awareness to focus on everything that is present now to co-create an authentic expression of our true nature.

These two ways to use the magic of awareness is illustrated in the story of "The Wizard of Oz." Dorothy gets swept up by a cyclone and lands in Oz. The cyclone represents our unwanted circumstances. Dorothy is told that she must go to the Emerald City to get help from the powerful Wizard of Oz. This represents our search to fix our unwanted circumstances. When Dorothy finally arrives at the Emerald City, her trusted companion Toto, tips over a screen, revealing that the Wizard of Oz is just an ordinary man from Omaha. Awareness can project an image of who we think we should be to appear powerful in the eyes of the world, like the humbug ordinary man did in the Wizard of Oz. The difference is, we actually believe that this imagined self is really who we are. In the story, Dorothy realizes that she has placed her faith in the wrong direction thanks to the guidance of the good witch. She realizes that she always possessed everything she needed to create the desires of her heart. So she clicks her heels three times and returns home to her heart. We can realize that everything we have ever needed is within the authentic expression of our heart. We can use awareness to shed light on all experiences that are present now and return to our heart-centered nature of freedom, love, and beauty, co-creating a magical, wonderful, exciting, and marvelous reality from the inside-out.

When we feel powerless in our reality we can either create an illusory sense of self in the head or we can align with the powerful nature that we are within our heart. Power is equally available to everyone regardless of economic, social, financial, or geographical location. The magic is available to you right now. You just have to let go of needing to create an illusion of magic and align with the magical power of heart-centered consciousness. Heart-centered consciousness is all powerful and perceives love, life, and harmony; where the head-centered consciousness misinterprets this power from within as lack, limitation, and fear. Are you willing to let go of creating an illusion in your head and align with the power of the Universe, which is alive and active in your heart right now?

"This uncomfortable experience is a gift."
You are welcome here.
You are enough!
How may I serve you?

Miracles

A miracle is a surprising and welcome event that is unexplainable. Miracles are happening in every moment, but we cannot perceive the miracles from the head-centered me. The head-centered me thinks it knows everything, and it thinks it is in control of creating miracles. But it also thinks it is in control of creating tragedy. Miracles to the head-centered me are labels given to wanted circumstances and events. Tragedy to the head-centered me are labels given to unwanted circumstances and events. The head-centered me is focused on information that has a point of reference and an explanation of its validity. Miracles are the reflection of the natural creative flow of life, which begins from the mysterious unknown spiritual essence of existence and manifests into a physical tangible form. The head-centered me cannot understand the natural process of creation because it begins from an unknown point of reference. The head-centered me has to be able to identify the cause and effect for it to be considered as true. If information comes from a place of no reason, meaning, point of reference, or explanations then the head-centered "me" disregards it altogether, closing awareness off from being able to perceive the miracle of life. This inability to embrace miracles, blocks our ability to experience the magic, wonder, and amazement within every experience. Through this misinterpretation of reality, life becomes stale, dull, and boring.

The heart-centered habit welcomes every event, which opens our perception out of a limited view. When our perception is wide open, we can sense and perceive the miracle of life happening within us and around us in every moment, regardless of whether we want it or not. Just by welcoming every event and circumstance as it is, our perception widens into sensing the intuition of miracles. The spontaneous flow of new information that arises from our mysterious formless essence births new life in every moment. The heart- centered habit will shift our perspective from a fear based view to a miraculous view. We can perceive the synchronicities of life happening for us. Our needs are met in spontaneous and miraculous ways. The heart-centered habit returns our sense of reality back toward perceiving life with a fresh perspective. We begin to feel our childlike faith return and bloom within every cell of our being.

The heart-centered habit allows our rational mind to slow down and relax through chaos and stress. Miraculously our rational mind aligns with heart-centered consciousness. We begin to realize that our reactions to our circumstances feel different. Our choices shift from being rooted in fear and protection toward love and innocence. Our authentic voice becomes more comfortable in our expression than the head-centered illusion that we used to portray. We wonder how did the shift happen from perceiving through a lens of separation to perceiving through a lens of unity? It feels like a miracle. Our experiences begin to bear fruit of the love we feel within our heart-centered expression. It is a miracle how our perception of self shifts from the head- centered me to the heart-centered me. We don't feel like we did anything. We just stayed with our experience, acknowledging, welcoming, breathing, loving, and thanking them all! Life is so magical and miraculous!

"This inconvenient experience is a gift."
You are welcome here.
You are enough!
How may I serve you?

Inspiration

A heart-centered being creates inspiration through every word, idea, thought, way, and action.

288

Everything that comes through a heart-centered being creates an interaction of magic and miracles in the world. They don't try to inspire. They are inspiration. They are filled with the spiritual essence of life in mind and body. As we continue to be the heart-centered habit, we too will fully merge with the inspiration that we truly are. Inspiration happens from the inside-out. It is generated within the heart and shared through intuition with the mind and body. As we become one with every experience, we will merge with the spirit of all of existence. Inspiration becomes a spontaneous endeavor that our mind has no control over. As I share the flow of inspiration that I am, inspiration magically awakens in the hearts of all. Therefore, the inspiration that you are awaits to flow through you as you.

When all misinterpretations have been resolved within you and you have merged with all repressed experiences of you authentic nature, you will merge with universal flow of inspiration. Inspiration means being filled with spirit. When all human experiences are perceived through the heart-centered habit, our spiritual nature and human nature merge into one inspired being. This union becomes the inspiration that triggers all unresolved and repressed energies in others to return home. When we are heart-centered, the inspiration that flows through us may trigger uncomfortable emotions within others. When we remain heart-centered through other people's head-centered reactions, we are inspiring their subconscious mind to remember their heart-centered nature.

Inspiration sometimes does not feel like what we think it should. Inspiration is not a high or a low. Instead, inspiration feels like relaxation to an over-stimulated nervous system. When one person is head-centered and a heart-centered person enters their presence, the head-centered me can go into a fog of confusion. Confusion is when thinking slows down and the rational mind has no reference point to act from. So we call it confusion because two points are not being joined together. Instead, awareness is in the space in between two points. Confusion is a sign that we are aligning with inspiration or our spiritual nature. Confusion is a symptom that our rational mind is aligning with intuition. Confusion is a good sign that our perception is opening to seeing the miracle and magic of life.

Confusion offers us an opportunity to inspire our relationships to the physical world. We feel confused in the moment because our subconscious mind is empty. Now that it is empty reprogramming can start. The first one that we inspire is our subconscious mind. We begin to program self-talk that is kind, loving, and inspiring. We comment on the miracles and magic that we experience through the mundane rituals of our life. Our daily routine becomes infused with awe and wonder, instead of complaining. Everything is received with thanks, instead of grumbling. Life is absolutely delightful just as it is!

Confusion isn't bad. Confusion is good because it is the experience of the deletion of past and future. Let the reprogramming of being present begin!

"This unfamiliar experience is a gift."
You are welcome here.
You are enough!
How may I serve you?

Reflection

What if life isn't happening to you, but instead life is happening through you?

Reprogramming the Subconscious Mind

"Be still and know that hopelessness and sadness is
God, a part of your true authentic nature."

Practicing the heart-centered habit: (Example)

Have you felt hopeless and sadness?

Welcome these experiences as a part of consciousness (You):

H- HONESTY

"I fully feel the parts of me that have felt hopeless and sad."

A-ACKNOWLEDGE, ALLOW, ASK

"I acknowledge that it is safe and okay to feel this limited experience. I embrace these feelings fully just as they are because I know they are here to show me the way into my heart. As I embrace these feelings fully, I ask them to bring with them all of the past meanings, interpretations, beliefs, and judgments that I thought were true, but are not valid in this present moment, so that I may receive them as a gift, guide, and opening toward the infinite perception in my heart. I acknowledge their Divine role in helping me expand awareness into the depths of infinite knowing."

Allow the uncomfortable experience to have a voice. Do not believe what it is saying, but instead be a loving presence that offers a deeper level of safety, comfort, and acknowledgment than the experience has ever received from you before, thereby being the practice of detachment, allowance, pure love, and space.

Ask: *"Divine heart, I accept that I don't know how to receive inspiration and perceive miracles and magic. Therefore, I ask that you receive the inspiration, miracles, and magic that is arising through the experience of hopelessness and sadness. Welcome, embrace, honor, and validate these experiences for me, through me, as I am now, healing the inner division within me, so that my perception can expand and align with the flow of infinite information."* And so it is (Amen).

B- BREATHE

"May every breath I take cleanse all bodies of disease!"

I-I LOVE YOU

Place your hands over your heart. Say, *"I love you! All is an expression of one life. I validate this limited experience within me. It is an experience from my past that was not validated by my relationships to the world. Therefore, I choose to be the presence of love that provides this experience the resonation of love that it has never received. May I be all the affirmation that this limited experience needs to remember that it is an infinite expression of divinity, so that it may fully awaken from the illusion of limitation. I love you!"*

"I am abundant, wise, infinite, and free!"

T- THANK YOU

Thank the experience for helping you remember that you are an ever-expanding unique expression of the Truth. Thank the circumstance, story, or relationship that triggered these feelings in your body, so your entire being could awaken to your innocent nature of authentic freedom that can enjoy all experiences.

"Thank you for helping me to align and attune with my heart's ever-expanding unique expression of infinite wisdom and pure love! Thank you for helping me to remember the power of life that I am!"

Intention: *(say aloud)*

"Today, I choose to delight in the mystery of my authentic nature, so that I may perceive the magic, miracle, and wonder of life, aligning with the inspiration that is present within all experiences."

Affirmation: *(say aloud)*

Say aloud throughout today:

"My roles are magical because I am the essence of magic!"

Day 19

Enlightenment

"TRAVEL light, LIVE light, SPREAD the light, BE the light."
-Yogi Bhajan

Say Aloud: (looking into your eyes in a mirror)
Good morning, infinite one. You are safe to feel. I always want to know how you are feeling. You are the soul-mate I have been looking for my entire life. You matter and you are enough. You are worthy of being seen and heard. I see you and I am here to listen to you. There is a good reason you are here; you are Divine perfection. Today, I join you in celebrating your ever-expanding unique expression. I am open to receiving new information and new ways of being by choosing to receive all uncomfortable, unfamiliar, painful, inconvenient, and unwanted experiences as a Divine gift from you, my infinite heart. I love all of you! I really love all of you. (your name), I really love all of you. (Feel free to write your own love statement)

Enlightenment is a word that is used to describe a being that is fully aware of heart-centered consciousness. Heart-centered consciousness is an expanded perception that perceives the light or core essence of life throughout all of existence. Everything and everyone is an appearance of the one light of divinity. Therefore, enlightenment isn't a destination. Instead it is a perception that is centered in the heart of all matter or appearances, which allows infinite information to unfold. If we believe that enlightenment is a destination then we are perceiving reality from the head-centered me, which has adopted a new closed loop belief system to live by, cutting off awareness to experiencing the present moment just as it is. Every moment is new and if we are not aligned with the heart-centered habit, we will perceive reality through the past, which is fading and remain centered in the head.

As I practiced the heart-centered habit, my reactions to situations and circumstances began to shift. My subconscious mind was being reprogrammed as I chose to be the heart-centered habit toward all experiences. I began experiencing more calm in the midst of life's storms. My rational mind continues to open and become infused with clarity, which allows an infinite light of awareness to shine through me as me. This light allows my rational mind to remain free of experiences by fully feeling every experience as it is and no longer shutting down awareness by not looking at it or embracing it. My rational mind has become free to welcome, see, and feel every experience as a part of the one eternal presence.

Enlightenment snuck up on me as I focused on being the heart-centered habit. I spontaneously realized my quality of experience in all of my relationships to the world shift from stress to peace. I felt more loving and peaceful toward everything and everyone. Circumstances didn't change, but the quality of my experience changed drastically, from one of suffering to one of pure love. This enlightenment was not the end of my journey. Instead, it was a new beginning, where I could function as an instrument of harmony, peace, and love toward all relationships in this physical world. Inspiration continued to unfold and the journey continued. I no longer related to the world in a limited way. Instead, I related to the world as the infinite presence of all experiences!

I am the light of the world and so are you! How magical, wonderful, and miraculous that the one light of divinity can appear in so many different forms. We chose to come here and experience our oneness in a unique way. Once I was lost, but now I am found. I see clearly and I see you! You are brighter than a trillion stars. You came here to shine on a hill. Therefore, inspire and infuse the mind and body with the light of your being. This book represents my unique expression of the one light. I am beyond excited to hear what your unique expression of the one light will be! Now that you are perceiving that all appearances, experiences, beliefs, thoughts, emotions, feelings, relationships, and people are the one light of divinity, step out and express the light you are! We don't have to repress the light we are anymore! Welcome home!

"This unwanted experience is a gift."
You are welcome here.
You are enough!
How may I serve you?

Being the Light of the World

When Jesus was being crucified on the cross, he didn't identify with what was happening to him. In fact, he acknowledged the pain in the people who were crucifying him and asked God to forgive them. In his greatest moment of isolation, pain, and feeling forsaken, he still identified with the light of his being. He still loved the people that were killing him. Right before my rational mind entered into enlightenment, it went through a sort of crucifixion. My rational mind experienced a withdrawal of light from all of its relationships to the outside world. My rational mind felt like God had forsaken it. My rational mind spent sixteen years of seeking and searching for the Truth, only to arrive at a place of feeling forsaken by God. My marriage, children, purpose, passion, friendships, finances, and every other relationship to the physical world appeared to lack life and light. My mind, body, experiences, circumstances, life situation, relationships, friendships, marriage, roles, career, passion, and purpose went through a death. When all of my relationships were lying lifeless before me, it was time to be the embodiment of light.

The light of existence that is within me resurrected my entire life spontaneously and miraculously. I just focused on remaining heart-centered and the light of my being took care of the rest. I was no longer chasing the light, truth, or enlightenment. Instead I aligned with the light I always was, always am, and always will be.

I chose to be heart-centered and I began to welcome all appearances of darkness. I began to speak the Truth that I perceived through my heart, which is life and all a symbol of pure love and divinity. I spoke to my relationship with finances. "Debt and financial lack you are the light, the light I am. I perceive you as the light of the world. Thank you for blessing me with your light." I spoke to my marriage. "Marriage, you are the light, the light I am. I perceive you as the light of divinity. Thank you for blessing me with your light." I spoke to all of my relationships, including children, family, and friends. "Relationships, you are the light, the light I am. You are the light of God. Thank you for blessing me with your light." I spoke to world events that were the appearance of darkness on the news. "World suffering, you are the light, the light I am. You are the light of Heaven. Thank you for blessing me with your light." The light that I felt in my heart, my mind and body became filled with the light of divinity. Spontaneously enlightenment flooded my entire being as I aligned my voice with the light within my heart. I became the embodiment of my soul's eternal light. I found my authentic voice of light, love, and pure life in and through the darkest of days!

If you are in the midst of feeling forsaken by God, divinity, or source of life; now is your time to embody the light that you are! Remain heart-centered and hand your voice over to your heart. Allow your heart to speak light into your life. Then watch your life resurrect to a life that far exceeds anything you could have ever imagined.

"This uncomfortable experience is a gift."
You are welcome here.
You are enough!
How may I serve you?

Shine On

Every time you listen, read, or tune in to the information that is streaming through your heart, the one light shines brighter in human consciousness. Therefore, as I have shared my unique expression of our Divine light through the pages written in this book, the Divine light burns brighter within you. You will discover that our one light moves in a direction of expansion, igniting the light of oneness in all hearts, expressions, and experiences. The light that we are eventually takes over and our mind and body become one with the light of divinity. The light will keep expanding in consciousness for eternity. If you were led to read this book, then you are willing to participate in being a vessel of the one light of existence. The way in which it expresses itself through you will be unique, but it will resonate pure love, harmony, and peace. Whether you realize it or not, the light of divinity that you are has expanded more into your personal reality. It will continue to expand and you will be glorified in the process. Your life, reality, and perception will never be the same. Instead, it will be on an infinite continuum of openness, expansion, abundance, and fulfillment.

The rational mind or head-centered you will probably feel confused most more time each day as you read this book. Confusion is a good sign that you are on the highest path because each day the light of your being comes into the rational mind through a new door. These doors were pathways that the rational mind least expected that the light of your being would come through. The light did not enter through the world around you. Instead, it came streaming through from within you. The pathways were the uncomfortable, unwanted, bad, wrong, and negative thoughts, feelings, emotions, and experiences that were held prisoner. The head-centered me is so focused on what it thinks is good, true, and right; that it didn't even see the light coming through the back door of its awareness. The rational mind or head-centered me couldn't protect itself by grasping hold of any understanding of the truth because the truth became an actual experience as it merged, expanded, and infused the head-centered me with light. The light of our being comes from within, which confuses the head-centered me because it was always looking for an understanding of the truth outside of itself. Enlightenment spontaneously happens and the rational mind is captivated by the brilliance of the light streaming from within. Just like when you look into the sun, then look away, your eyes are blinded momentarily. The rational mind has the same experience when it looks within and perceives the light of divinity. The rational mind is blinded (confused) of its personal reasoning, understanding, and points of reference from the past.

The more confused you are, the less you can think about what you read, so you could breathe and embrace what you felt each day. This 22-day journey is retraining your subconscious mind to breathe and feel every experience, instead of think and repress feelings. The light that you are is merging with every aspect of the self, whether your rational mind is aware of it or not. The "you" that you thought you were is toast. The light has come and you will be glorified by the brilliance of divinity. You don't have to do anything to be the light you already are! Just by tuning into the words in this book, you are already aligning with the eternal presence of your heart-centered nature. Just like you don't have to think about breathing, you don't have to think about enlightenment. There is nothing for your rational mind to do, nothing to understand, nothing to figure out, nothing to grasp hold of, and nothing to remember. Enlightenment is happening now. You can rest in the knowing that you are home!

"This inconvenient experience is a gift."
You are welcome here.
You are enough!
How may I serve you?

Ignite

When we were born into this world, we came in as a shining bright light, which is why everyone notices babies. Babies don't have to do anything to make the light that they are shine. However, as we grew accustomed to this world, we were taught to believe in darkness. As we grew out of the infant stage, we were prepared, molded, and shaped by our relationships to the world to fight the darkness. When we are young we are like, "What darkness?" The adults in our lives make sure to protect us from the darkness they believe in. Of course, this protection is well intended. Soon, we notice that shining bright does not fit in with this world of darkness, so we dim our light to fit in with the world and believe in darkness. Until we come across someone who stands in the light of our one essence. Then that light we remember as an infant or child gets ignited.

The heart-centered habit brings light into the darkness that we have maintained in our rational minds. The rational mind or head-centered me becomes enlightened through the most unlikely pathway of unwanted experiences, uncomfortable feelings, wrong, bad, pain, fear, and negative emotions. The rational mind feels light, as if heavy weights have been removed from its experience of reality. Now our rational mind is a tool that feels the freedom to express the light of love, life, harmony, and peace that streams through from within. Now the rational mind is in alignment with the Source of creation and functions to ignite the light in all. We stand in the full light of our Divine nature. We don't have to dim our light anymore. No matter how dark life appears, we can remain in the light because we have remembered how to be heart-centered.

The appearance of darkness may remain in your relationships, but be the light anyway. The appearance of darkness may continue to appear in world affairs, but be the light anyway. The appearance of darkness may remain in your circumstances, but be the light anyway. The appearance of darkness may remain in your body, but be the light anyway. The appearance of darkness may remain in your thoughts, but be the light anyway. The appearance of darkness may remain in your emotions, but be the light anyway. Nobody may understand the light you are, but be the light anyway. People may reject you, but be the light anyway. People may persecute you, be but the light anyway. People may abandon you, but be the light anyway. People may judge you as evil, but be the light anyway. You are the light of the world! Being the heart-centered habit allows the light that you are to shine brighter and brighter in every moment into eternity!

"This unfamiliar experience is a gift."
You are welcome here.
You are enough!
How may I serve you?

Reflection

What if every perceived failure in your life was an opportunity to awaken to the brilliant light of your heart-centered nature?

Reprogramming the Subconscious Mind

"Be still and know that failure is God, a part of your true authentic nature."

Practicing the heart-centered habit: (Example)

Have you ever felt like a failure?

Welcome these experiences as a part of consciousness (You):

H- HONESTY

"I fully feel the parts of me that have felt failure."

A-ACKNOWLEDGE, ALLOW, ASK

"I acknowledge that it is safe and okay to feel this limited experience. I embrace these feelings fully just as they are because I know they are here to show me the way into my heart. As I embrace these feelings fully, I ask them to bring with them all of the past meanings, interpretations, beliefs, and judgments that I thought were true, but are not valid in this present moment, so that I may receive them as a gift, guide, and opening toward the infinite perception in my heart. I acknowledge their Divine role in helping me expand awareness into the depths of infinite knowing."

Allow the uncomfortable experience to have a voice. Do not believe what it is saying, but instead be a loving presence that offers a deeper level of safety, comfort, and acknowledgment than the experience has ever received from you before, thereby being the practice of detachment, allowance, pure love, and space.

Ask: "Divine heart, I accept that I don't know how to release control of making life happen the way I want. Therefore, I ask that you release my grasp of wanting and receive failure as a Divine gift on my behalf. Welcome, embrace, honor, and validate these experiences for me, through me, as I am now, healing the inner division within me, so that my perception can expand and align with the flow of infinite information." And so it is (Amen)

B- BREATHE

Breathe in all feelings, thoughts, and appearances associated with your finances, relationships, roles, career, and job! Breathe out light and love!

I-I LOVE YOU

Place your hands over your heart. Say, *"I love you! All is an expression of one life. I validate this limited experience within me. It is an experience from my past that was not validated by my relationships to the world. Therefore, I choose to be the presence of love that provides this experience the resonation of love that it has never received. May I be all the affirmation that this limited experience needs to remember that it is an infinite expression of divinity, so that it may fully awaken from the illusion of limitation. I love you!"*

"I am abundant, wise, infinite, and free!"

T- THANK YOU

Thank the experience for helping you remember that you are an ever-expanding unique expression of the Truth. Thank the circumstance, story, or relationship that triggered these feelings in your body, so your entire being could awaken to your innocent nature of authentic freedom that can enjoy all experiences.

> *"Thank you for helping me to align and attune with my heart's ever-expanding unique expression of infinite wisdom and pure love! Thank you for helping me to remember the power of life that I am!"*

Intention: *(say aloud)*

"Today, I choose to be the light of divinity. No matter how dark my circumstances appear, I choose to shine on and ignite the light within the darkness by being heart- centered, aligning my words and actions with pure love."

Affirmation: *(Say aloud)*

Say aloud throughout today:

"My knowing is powerful because I am Divine power

Day 20

Integration

"The planet needs your soul's unique tone to harmonize."
-Sera Beak

Say Aloud: (looking into your eyes in a mirror)
Good morning, infinite one. You are safe to feel. I always want to know how you are feeling. You are the soul-mate that I have been looking for my entire life. You matter and you are enough. You are worthy of being seen and heard. I see you and I am here to listen to you. There is a good reason you are here; you are Divine perfection. Today, I join you in celebrating your ever-expanding unique expression. I am open to receiving new information and new ways of being by choosing to receive all uncomfortable, unfamiliar, painful, inconvenient, and unwanted experiences as a Divine gift from you, my infinite heart. I love all of you! I really love all of you. (your name), I really love all of you. (Feel free to write your own love statement)

Integration is the act of combining parts into an integral whole. The process of becoming heart-centered involves the act of combining all aspects of the self into a harmonious whole being. An integrated being is a heart-centered being that has no war or conflict going on below the surface. This means all perceptions, facts, and knowledge have been brought into the light and aligned with perceiving only light in all appearances. Integration occurs within us first. At first, being heart-centered requires conscious effort as we choose to embrace and allow ourselves to look at the uncomfortable and unwanted feelings, emotions, and

305

memories that we have repressed from our past. As we become heart-centered toward the aspects that we have shunned into the darkness, our perception of darkness begins to shift. Emotions, thoughts, feelings, beliefs, and past experiences that were once sensed as darkness are now perceived as the Divine light of all. Now that our mind and body are filled with the light of divinity, it is time to spread the light into the world.

You are here to be a vessel of integrating the light of existence into your mind, body, and relationships to the world. You have a tone to your unique expression of the one light of existence that nobody else can express. The planet is waiting to harmonize, which will happen when we all become heart- centered and express the unique tone of the one light of divinity that we sense within the heart of the matter. Healing, peace, and goodness are the fruits of the integration of Divine light in human form. Integration begins within you, and then ripples out into the world. Humanity is in the process of integrating the Divine light of existence throughout all forms of matter. The heart-centered habit is a way that allows the integration of humanity, world, planet, and universe into a unique manifestation of brilliance, beauty, and wholeness.

"This unwanted experience is a gift."
You are welcome here.
You are enough!
How may I serve you?

New Species

The other day, while I was sitting in stillness through focusing on my breath, I began singing love songs to myself, my life situation, others, and the world. I felt like I was being transported to some moment in the future where the entire world was a reflection of Divine light. Separation, division, limitation, darkness, evil, and lack were distant memories. Then I realized, wait that world isn't in the future because I am experiencing it now! I am in Heaven now, even though world affairs appear to be dark. Even though my husband is suffering with shingles. Even though we are broke as smoke and it ain't no joke! In my world everything is an expression of light, regardless of the way it appears. I realized that I am an angel and all experiences are angels. I am in Heaven right now! Heaven is here, it really is! I remembered reading a scripture where Jesus told some of his disciples that they would enter the Kingdom of Heaven before they physically died. Now I knew what he meant.

We can enter the Kingdom of Heaven within us now by being heart-centered toward every aspect of life, regardless of how your life appears. Just like a loving parent speaks to a newborn child. By aligning our voice with the infinite love within our heart, we become a loving parent that speaks words of love, life, and encouragement to every aspect of our self, our circumstances, our relationships, our world, and our universe.

The light in our heart is the Divine essence of our formless nature. It doesn't matter whether we call it our soul or our spirit. It doesn't have a name, definition, or meaning behind it because our formless nature is the energy that forms all of existence. We are angels of light, here to remind all forms that they are angels of light too. We are a new kind of species that is an expression of the integration of Divine light into human form. We are a species of wholeness, unity, peace, and equanimity. We are the bridge between the unseen and the seen. We are the pathways for divinity to flow through and create beautiful masterpieces. We are the lighthouses that guide all ships home. We are the angels wearing a human costume. We are the frequencies that transmit the voice of God. We are the new species that have come to create Heaven on Earth.

"This uncomfortable experience is a gift."
You are welcome here.
You are enough!
How may I serve you?

Armor of God

Now that we sense the truth of our being and our entire being is integrating into the overflowing light of divinity, we are called to be the light in the world. The world still reflects the appearance of darkness, which we have resolved within ourselves by shifting our perception from good and evil to perceiving only life, love, and light; which has no opposite. We are called to be brave, courageous, faithful, and radical. The only way to heal our world of the appearance of darkness is to no longer believe in the darkness we see. Instead, we must be radical and claim that all appearances of darkness are the light of divinity, the light we are. This does not mean that we are making justifications for the darkness. This also does not mean that we don't feel and embrace the suffering that results from the long held belief in darkness. Instead, we remain heart-centered by welcoming, embracing, acknowledging, loving, breathing, and thanking every appearance of darkness. This is the way we surrender our perception of darkness and align with perceiving all experiences from the heart of the matter, co-creating a reality of equanimity, harmony, joy, peace, love, and abundance.

The world is a manifestation of our perception. We have perceived good and bad; right and wrong, light and dark, God and devil; and our world reflects back the appearance of both sides. Two sides that are fighting to prevail and win the battle. The battle will never stop, until as a whole we shift the root of our perception of reality. Therefore, when we claim that the awful, heart-wrenching appearances of darkness are actually the one Divine light, the light I am, we are shifting the consciousness of our world and healing the hearts of all! As we go out into the world to shine the light of divinity, the armor of God will allow us to stand firm in the Divine light of our spiritual essence in a world that has yet to remember. I love how the Bible describes the Armor of God.

"Stand firm, with the belt of truth buckled around your waist, with the breastplate of righteousness in place, and your feet fitted with the readiness that comes from the gospel of peace. In addition to all this, take up the shield of faith, with which you can extinguish all the flaming arrows. Take the helmet of salvation and the sword of the Spirit." (Bible: Ephesians 6: 14-17)

The **BELT OF TRUTH** is the remembrance of our one authentic, innocent, vulnerable, pristine, pure, loving, and Divine nature. The **BREASTPLATE OF RIGHTEOUSNESS** represents sensing into perceiving circumstances through the heart of the matter, which perceives all aspects of reality as the goodness and Divine light that they really are! **FEET FITTED WITH THE READINESS THAT COMES FROM THE GOSPEL OF PEACE** represents being the light and perceiving only divinity in all. The **SHIELD OF FAITH** represents a faith in the light we are in the midst of a world that still believes in the appearance of darkness, limitation, and separation. Heart-centered faith will extinguish the flaming arrows of remaining accusations that will come at us from rational minds that still believe in darkness. They may crucify us with their reasons, explanations, and points of references that appear to be valid. Despite the physical evidence that proves there is darkness, we stand firm in our faith of knowing that all is an appearance of Divine light. Wearing the **HELMET OF SALVATION** refers to knowing that we are saved and we no longer need to believe that we are a victim to the appearance of darkness. We are saved from the identification of limitation and separation because we have remembered that all unwanted, inconvenient, and uncomfortable circumstances are tools that sharpen our remembrance of our authentic powerful Divine nature, therefore standing in the full remembrance of the truth of our one spiritual essence. The **SWORD OF THE SPIRIT** represents taking conscious, slow, and deep breathes in the face of the appearance of darkness. The people in our environment will continue to breathe shallow and fast if they believe in darkness or separation. But we will stand in their presence breathing deeper and slower, guiding their breath to align with ours. We can teach other people to relax out of their knowledge of separation and limitation by consciously breathing deeper and slower.

Every day as we suit up with this armor, we will participate in spreading the life, light, goodness, joy, peace, and harmony throughout the hearts of all. Perceiving through the heart of the matter places the armor of God around our experience of reality, allowing our one Divine light to shine and awaken in the hearts of those around us, regardless of how reality is appearing in the moment.

"This inconvenient experience is a gift."
You are welcome here.
You are enough!
How may I serve you?

<u>Education</u>

The word 'education' is derived from the Latin root 'educare.' While education refers to the collection of wordly facts, educare is to bring out from within. Education is for a living while educare is for life."
–Sri Sathya Sai Baba

The head-centered me or rational mind functions to educate people on its knowledge of facts, teaching about its personal knowledge of the world. Many systems in our world today educate through this kind of limited knowledge. Our educational systems focus on learning, studying, and memorizing facts, which become the foundation to the jobs we create in our society. However, facts do not teach us how to deal with separation, darkness, limitation, negative emotions, and negative thoughts. Our need to memorize facts becomes the very distraction to embracing the pain we feel from a world that believes in the appearance of darkness. As a whole we become distracted from having the time to focus on being the embodiment of Truth, which means we are a living example of integrating the truth from within not without.

On the other hand, the heart-centered me or intuitive mind functions to educare or bring out the Truth from within. Many enlightened heart-centered beings are an example of educare. As we continually draw upon the Truth that resides within us, we are leading by example and showing others the way; a way that guides all perceptions to the Truth from within the source of all wisdom. Instead of the rational mind being a student to a teacher outside of itself and learning facts based upon limited knowledge, the rational mind can be the student that seeks truth from within the unified field of Divine wisdom. Then draws information out from within through intuition and expresses it as a unique expression, creating more harmony and peace in the world. Divine wisdom, Divine Light, Divine Truth, and Divine Love all come from within us.

Jesus was a great example of educare, one who was a living example of Truth. He went to the well of living water from within him and spoke with Divine power. He did not go through the educational system that was available at that time to be a religious leader, which taught facts about spirituality. From the time he was very young, he followed the intuition of his heart. The people who followed him felt this same Divine power awaken within themselves, but they didn't realize the Source of what they felt was within them. They thought they only felt that Divine power because they were in the presence of Jesus, distracting the rational mind from ever integrating Divine power from within through their mind and body as long as Jesus was alive. Therefore, when we project the truth of our being to existing outside of us in a body of knowledge or facts, we forget that it is our innate nature, which can flow through us like a never-ending well of wisdom. After Jesus died many of his followers went through the act of integration, where their mind and body became a living embodiment of Divine Truth, light, and love. Finally they were given an opportunity to draw the truth out from within them because they did not have Jesus to do it for them. In their minds the embodiment of Truth – Jesus – was gone. The only way the Truth could continue out in the world was for them to go within and become the embodiment of truth themselves. Some of them did just that and continued to educare, just as Jesus did. We have this same opportunity now!

There are many religions or facts taught about spirituality. We will not embody the Truth of our spiritual nature through believing in facts about spirituality. Our true essence is omniscient and omnipresent, which means it is connected and a part of everything all at once. There is no separation in our true nature. Therefore, all facts about spirituality point to our one spiritual essence, which cannot be fully described through facts. The facts themselves do not contain the Truth because the Truth is formless and infinite. It cannot be contained in a certain religion of facts. We can embody and integrate the power of our infinite spiritual essence when we radically accept that all religions point to the one Divine light of our being.

When separation, division, and limitation is no longer our experience, we will know that we have fully integrated the power of divinity in the experiences of mind and body.

We are not in control of enlightenment, awakening, or integration of our Divine nature in human form. However, we can participate in the process of Divine integration by remaining heart-centered and continually surrendering our knowledge about reality. We have spent so many years learning, memorizing, and studying facts. Now, it is time to surrender them all, so that our Divine nature may integrate them into the whole of existence through perceiving that everything is of the essence of Divine oneness.

Children are not stupid, dumb, or ignorant. They possess the same Divine wisdom within them as the greatest spiritual masters. Future generations do not have to get lost in the appearances of darkness and limitation. They can remain in the remembrance of divinity that they were born with! When we stand in the light in the face of the appearance of evil and darkness, we are being a living example that awakens the one Divine power within others. We are teaching future generations to stand in the light of divinity and always perceive through the heart of the matter.

The question is, who is going to be brave, courageous, radical, and faithful enough to educare them, to point them within to discover and awaken the Divine power of the universe? Who is going to radically surrender their limited perception of reality and integrate the Divine light of all creation into their human form? The more humanity chooses to be brave, courageous, and faithful by perceiving through heart-centered consciousness and claiming that all is God and there is no opposing force to God, the more future generations will have an opportunity to be an authentic true expression of the Truth they sense within their heart. This is the true meaning of education. This is how we as mature adults can educate future generations to maintaining a healthy relationship to the innocence within their heart!

"This unfamiliar experience is a gift."
You are welcome here.
You are enough!
How may I serve you?

Reflection

Are you willing to be a living example of the one Divine light that exists in the hearts of all?

Reprogramming the Subconscious Mind

"Be still and know that weakness and deficiency is God, a part of your true authentic nature."

Practicing the heart-centered habit: (Example)

Have you felt weak or deficient?

Welcome these experiences as a part of consciousness (You):

H- HONESTY

"I fully the parts of me that have felt weak and deficient."

A-ACKNOWLEDGE, ALLOW, ASK

"I acknowledge that it is safe and okay to feel this limited experience. I embrace these feelings fully just as they are because I know they are here to show me the way into my heart. As I embrace these feelings fully, I ask them to bring with them all of the past meanings, interpretations,

beliefs, and judgments that I thought were true, but are not valid in this present moment, so that I may receive them as a gift, guide, and opening toward the infinite perception in my heart. I acknowledge their Divine role in helping me expand awareness into the depths of infinite knowing."

Allow the uncomfortable experience to have a voice. Do not believe what it is saying, but instead be a loving presence that offers a deeper level of safety, comfort, and acknowledgment than the experience has ever received from you before, thereby being the practice of detachment, allowance, pure love, and space.

Ask: "Divine heart, I accept that I don't know how to clothe my mind in the armor of God. Therefore, I ask that you clothe my mind in the armor of God, so I may receive weakness and deficiency as a Divine gift. Welcome, embrace, honor, and validate these experiences for me, through me, as I am now, healing the inner division within me, so that my perception can expand and align with the flow of infinite information." And so it is (Amen).

B- BREATHE

Breathe in all feelings, thoughts, and appearances associated with the conditions in your environment! Breathe out light and love!

I-I LOVE YOU

Place your hands over your heart. Say, *"I love you! All is an expression of one life. I validate this limited experience within me. It is an experience from my past that was not validated by my relationships to the world. Therefore, I choose to be the presence of love that provides this experience the resonation of love that it has never received. May I be all the affirmation that this limited experience needs to remember that it is an infinite expression of divinity so that it may fully awaken from the illusion of limitation. I love you!"*

"I am abundant, wise, infinite, and free!"

T- THANK YOU

Thank the experience for helping you remember that you are an ever-expanding unique expression of the truth. Thank the circumstance, story, or relationship that triggered these feelings in your body, so your entire being could awaken to your innocent nature of authentic freedom that can enjoy all experiences.

> *"Thank you for helping me to align and attune with my heart's ever-expanding unique expression of infinite wisdom and pure love! Thank you for helping me to remember the power of life that I am!"*

Intention: *(say aloud)*

"Today, I choose to put on the full armor of God. I trust and place my faith in my knowing that all appearances of darkness and personal limitations are here to create space, so that I may shine brighter by becoming more heart-centered than ever before and step into more Divine power and become a greater expression of goodness. I choose to breathe slower and deeper throughout all appearances of conflict, war, separation, division, and suffering."

AFFIRMATION: *(say aloud)*

Say aloud throughout today:

"My finances are enough because I am enough!"

Day 21

Divine Perfection

"Self-conquest is the greatest of victories."
-Plato

Say Aloud: (looking into your eyes in a mirror)
Good morning, infinite one. You are safe to feel. I always want to know how you are feeling. You are the soul-mate that I have been looking for my entire life. You matter and you are enough. You are worthy of being seen and heard. I see you and I am here to listen to you. There is a good reason you are here; you are Divine perfection. Today, I join you in celebrating your ever-expanding unique expression. I am open to receiving new information and new ways of being by choosing to receive all uncomfortable, unfamiliar, painful, inconvenient, and unwanted experiences as a Divine gift from you, my infinite heart. I love all of you! I really love all of you. (your name), I really love all of you. (Feel free to write your own love statement).

The day you arrived here, you were Divine perfection. Every experience and moment of your existence has been Divine perfection. All emotions are Divine perfection. All thoughts are Divine perfection. All appearances are Divine perfection. All experiences are Divine perfection. Even as I sit here now, surrounded by the darkest circumstances that I have experienced in this lifetime, I trust in knowing that it is all here as a symbol of Divine perfection. I notice that the death of my reality has opened my mind and my heart. Actually these dark experiences are the instruments that my Divine nature is using to crack me wide open. This

318

openness has brought me to a depth of surrender that I could have never accomplished through my personal will. The more I surrender my personal knowledge of how reality should be, the more space enters my rational mind, allowing space for Divine wisdom and light to fill me from the inside-out.

As I am filled daily through being the heart-centered habit, I become more aware of the light, divinity, and goodness that exists within all experiences. A perception of Divine perfection floods my being as all reasons, explanations, and understandings continue to get crucified by experiences of lack and limitation. I am grateful for the Divine purpose that is within every circumstance of struggle, lack, limitation, and suffering. Everything is working together for the good of all! Divine perfection is here, right now within your experience too!

The more my perception of reality shifts from the head-centered character that believes it's in control to the perception of the formless heart-centered nature of divinity; the more I realize that every experience points to the formless essence of one Divine nature. It is as if my current reality is a reflection of everything that the character in my head has regarded as NOT Divine, NOT the light, and NOT good. These experiences are not here to make me feel like a victim. Instead, they are here, so that I may shift my perception about them. They are the light, the light I am. By faith my rational mind aligns with the truth it senses in my heart and claims that they too are Divine perfection. The old way of perceiving is fading and the new way of perceiving is here now! This is the true born again experience!

"This unwanted experience is a gift."
You are welcome here.
You are enough!
How may I serve you?

319

The Old is Gone

This is the old habit of "me" that is fading away: The "me" that used attachment to identify and define itself from its external environment. The "me" that ate from the tree of the knowledge of good and evil, which it learned from its external environment. The "me" that used its imagined belief system of right and wrong as a point of reference to prove its existence. The "me" that used personal reasoning to navigate its way in this world. The "me" that believed in the appearance of wrong, darkness, shouldn't, bad, evil, and opposition. The "me" that lived in the past through repressed experiences that were held in darkness through long held perceptions of wrong. The "me" that projected hopes and dreams into a distant unattainable future. The "me" that functioned from an illusory personal will and judged Divine will as an enemy. The "me" that judged emptiness and no-thingness as death and evil. The "me" that thought it had to earn love, trust, and goodness. The "me" that believed in punishment and reward. The "me" that believed in the appearance of separation, division, conflict, and war. The "me" that used comparison, control, expectation, judgment, and manipulation to fit into the world. The "me" that feared change and struggled to maintain the desirable appearance of reality. The "me" whose breathing was controlled by its external environment.

Yes, this is the old habit of "me" that is unraveling into the Divine will of God. The "me" that entered through the wide gate and walked along the broad path of extremes. The "me" that perceived the physical and spiritual as two separate places or dimensions of reality. The "me" that finds comfort in the known and is afraid of the unknown. The "me" that created separate files of "me" in the rational mind. The "me" that doesn't know how to relax into uncomfortable or unwanted experiences. The "me" that was distracted by facts and appearances so much that it forgot its connection to sensing into the formless greater part of reality. The "me" that hoarded and possessed ideas, thoughts, beliefs, memories, emotions, relationships, habits, experiences, and material things. The "me" that projected truth into an external object, way, person, or set of facts. The "me" that needed to know and understand "why," so I created stories of blame! The "me" that needed to find someone or something to blame for its undesirable conditions. The "me" that needed its relationships to the physical world to make it happy. The "me" that perceived through the .00001 percent of reality, instead of the 99.99999 percent of reality. The "me" that perceived limited resources and abundance. The "me" that ran, hid, and escaped every perceived storm in life. The "me" that was very picky and choosey as to what it was and what it was NOT! The "me" that held onto grudges and complained about its hurts. The "me" that felt like a victim to the appearance of darkness in this world. The "me" that always felt higher or lower and hardly ever at peace with life. The "me" that believed it had enemies. The "me" that opposed, repressed, and suppressed experiences that were uncomfortable, unwanted, and inconvenient. The "me' that was afraid to be in this world. The "me" that believed it was in control of its survival. The "me" that felt separate from God, abundance, peace, harmony, and eternal life. The "me" that had personal limitations, weaknesses, and addictions. The "me" that resided in the head and was terrified of the greater whole of reality. The "me" that struggled to be good enough, spiritual enough, or appear right enough. The "me" that always had to explain itself to others. The "me" that felt totally insecure because of the darkness it hid from the light of day. The "me" that had many shadows that lurked beneath the surface.

Yes, this is the habit of "me" that is unraveling into the heart-centered habit. The "me" that felt judged, rejected, abandoned, and isolated from God. The "me" that thought it had to be a spiritual ego of self-righteousness because it was uncomfortable feeling the pain within others. The "me" that ran from pain. The "me" that always had an escape route, so it didn't have to surrender, embrace, and feel uncomfortable emotions. The "me" that unconsciously co-created pain, darkness, stress, and suffering in others and the world because it identified with dark experiences. The "me" that perceived the mystery, magic, and miracles of life as something bad. The "me" that was afraid to shine bright because it didn't want others to feel uncomfortable. The "me" that was always in a state of anticipation. Always looking ahead for what is next and never fully satisfied with the present moment.

This "me" is the head-centered "me" that was waiting for the heart-centered "me" to save it. This is the "me" that we have been willing to embrace and welcome through the door of our hearts over the last 21-days. This is the "me" that is fading into the bright light of our one Divine nature. Welcome to the light of your true nature "little me." Are you ready to be glorified by the light of your true infinite nature? Glory is coming and is fast approaching!

"This uncomfortable experience is a gift."
You are welcome here.
You are enough!
How may I serve you?

The New Has Come

This is the new habit of "me" that is here, now: The new has come and was born in the most inconvenient and uncomfortable circumstances. In my experience, Jesus is one of many beings that represent heart-centered consciousness, the mind of God, or Divine perception. He was not born in the most comfortable and convenient places. Instead, he was born far away from his parents' home and in a stable. I have cleaned horse stalls before and they are far from clean and sanitary. Just like Jesus was born in an uncomfortable and inconvenient environment, so was the heart-centered me. Experiences arose that took me way out of my rational mind's comfort zone, which provided it no-thing to grasp hold of except the Truth. THE FORMLESS TRUTH.

This is the new "me" that was resurrected out of the most inconvenient, unwanted, and uncomfortable experiences of reality: The "me" that eats only from the Tree of Life. The "me" that is more interested in being genuine, authentic, and honest from within than pleasing the world from without. The "me" that surrenders to Divine will. The "me" that says an inner "yes" to all experiences and perceives them as Divine appointments with God. The "me" that allows uncomfortable experiences to clear space, so that Divine light may enter and overflow from the inside-out. The "me" that welcomes experiences as they are. The "me" that fully embraces and acknowledges every experience as Divine perfection. The "me" that breathes deeper and slower than the rest the world around me. The "me" that sings songs of "I love you" to every appearance, experience, and circumstance, regardless of how it feels in my body. The "me" that is conscious of not liking certain circumstances, but loves it just as it is anyway. The "me" that puts on the armor of God when it steps out into the world. The "me" that is grateful for the unwanted, inconvenient, and uncomfortable experiences. The "me" that walks into the center of a storm to align with the Divine one nature. The "me" that leaves a fragrance of divinity everywhere it goes because it is the embodiment of Truth. The "me" that trusts in goodness even when it doesn't understand. The "me" that trusts in the unknown and waits for intuition to guide its choices. The "me" that leans not upon personal understanding, knowledge, points of reference, or facts about reality.

Yes, this is the new "me" that has come. The "me" that trusts that by remaining heart-centered and faithful that all guidance will come in the moment it is needed. The "me" that is an inspiration to the world and points toward the truth within all. The "me" that embraces pain, judgment, darkness, limitation, and lack as a best friend that has come delivering a Divine gift. The "me" that rests in the mystery, magic, and miracles of the authentic nature of existence. The "me" that is eternally present here and now with nowhere else to go or be. The "me" that has nothing to hide, oppose, shun, or condemn into darkness. The "me" that resonates with what is being sensed from within. The "me" that lives in a perpetual state of forgiveness and gratitude. The "me" that shines bright, regardless of how it makes the world feel. The "me" that possesses nothing, not even an identity. The "me" that perceives Heaven and infinite abundance throughout all experiences of reality. The "me" that chooses peace over the need to know or understand. The "me" that perceives the great I am in all I am's. The "me" that chooses to enter the narrow gate and walk along the middle path. The "me" that perceives unity throughout all of existence. The "me" that continues to expand into infinite frequencies of divinity. The "me" that allows the infinite flow of reality to change effortlessly through all phases of metamorphosis. The "me" that delights in all experiences. The "me" that doesn't need to know itself to exist. The "me" that rests in eternal patience by enjoying the present moment just as it is, without interfering with any of it.

How do we know when the old habit of the head-centered "me" is no longer dominating the way we perceive reality? How will we know when it is time to drop the practice of the heart-centered habit because it has been programmed in the subconscious mind? How will we know that we are heart-centered? We will know because when we experience unwanted, uncomfortable, or inconvenient experiences; we will no longer fight, deny, or escape them. We will spontaneously realize that we don't feel identified with any experience. We will feel abundant, free, fulfilled, and relaxed on the inside, regardless of how the world around us appears. You will know that you have shifted when you respond to life in a heart-centered way. When there is nothing within you that desires to escape your reality. When there is nothing within you that desires to change your current circumstances. When there is nothing within you that identifies with your external reality. When there is nothing and no one to blame for what you are experiencing in your external reality.

When the uncomfortable experiences of life become your ally, you will sense this inner shift because the quality of your experience will feel expanded not limited. You will feel grateful that these undesirable circumstances have chosen you to be the one to awaken them through the light that is dormant within them. Conditions of scarcity, lack, and limitation I perceive you as the light, the light I am. May the light awaken and resurrect into a new reality! The new reality that these uncomfortable experiences resurrect into is, a deep sense of eternal patience within you. You will begin to notice an eternal patience toward relationships that used to trigger uncomfortable feelings within you. You will begin to sense an eternal patience toward all experiences. Anticipation will fade and you feel born again into the enjoyment of the present moment, where every experience feels like the eternal presence of God.

Until then, keep using the heart-centered habit to reprogram your subconscious mind. Eventually being heart-centered will be as natural as breathing.

"This inconvenient experience is a gift."
You are welcome here.
You are enough!
How may I serve you?

The Heart of Patience

I always wondered why the Bible used the word long-suffering for the word patience. Long-suffering does not sound very enjoyable. In my experience I endured reality through long-suffering, until my perception shifted from the head-centered me to the heart-centered me. From the perspective of the head- centered me undesirable experiences felt like long-suffering because they lingered for long periods of time. I would only have brief moments of not suffering, but the undesirable circumstances would re-emerge. Now the same undesirable circumstances do not make me suffer. Instead, I have an eternal patience for their visit. They are welcome to stay for as long as they need to because I know they have a Divine job to do. They are here to help me transform from the old habit of me to the new heart-centered habit of me. They are here to cleanse, purify, and heal my rational mind. So I invite them in and they are free to stay as long as they need to be here. These unwanted experiences are helping my rational mind to surrender its need to fight or flight, so that it can remember its authentic nature of surrender. They are angels here to help my rational mind let go of attachments, or the way it defined a sense of self from my external reality.

Patience is the authentic nature of the heart-centered me, which honors and respects all experiences! When we are heart-centered we honor the experience without the need to identify it as anything. It can be exactly as it is without needing to know where it came from, what it means, or taking any credit for it showing up! We do not have to define ourselves to know the light of God. For instance, there is the experience of thinking, but no thinker. There is the experience of breathing, but no breather. There is the experience of speaking, but no speaker. There is the experience of tasting, but no taster. There is the experience of smelling, but no smeller. There is the experience of seeking, but no seeker. There is the experience of pain, but no victim. There is the experience of seeing, but no seer. There is the experience of hearing, but no hearer. Look into your eyes... what is beyond your eyes doing the seeing? Nothing! The head-centered me believes there is a character inside doing the thinking, breathing, speaking, hurting, seeking, seeing, hearing, tasting, and smelling. But when you really look, you will find nothing but experience experiencing itself. Every experience is a joy. Experience has no way of confining you. Our humanness is a multidimensional and multisensory explosion of experiences. Our formless spiritual essence is experiencing itself throughout infinite experiences. Patience is the heart-centered awareness that I am whatever experience is arising. I am the birth, expansion, and death of every experience.

When you realize that there is no character creating experiences, you will awaken to the joy of experience. Your perception will no longer perceive unwanted experiences as suffering. Instead, the quality of our experience shifts from suffering to eternal paticncc. Eternal patience honors and respects all experiences just as they are! Eternal patience allows every experience to be on its own journey of birth, expansion, and death without the need to identify or attach to any stage of its existence. When our rational mind fully awakens to the Divine light of awareness or no-thingness, it aligns with eternal patience.

When we are heart-centered and perceiving reality through the eye of no-thingness, we will honor and enjoy whatever is arising so much that we will forget to anticipate what's next. Anticipation will fall away because we will be so aligned with enjoying the present moment. This is how long-suffering dissolves and resurrects as eternal patience. May you perceive all experiences through the heart of the matter!

"This unfamiliar experience is a gift."
You are welcome here.
You are enough!
How may I serve you?

Reflection

Are you willing to let the "old" fixed and solid way of being die in the arms of the "new" ever-expanding infinite way of being?

Reprogramming the Subconscious Mind

"Be still and know that pain and suffering is God, a part of your true authentic nature."

Practicing the heart-centered habit: (Example)

Have you ever felt the pain and suffering of the world?

Welcome these experiences as a part of consciousness (You):

H- HONESTY

"I fully feel the parts of me that have felt the pain and suffering of the world."

A-ACKNOWLEDGE, ALLOW, ASK

"I acknowledge that it is safe and okay to feel this limited experience. I embrace these feelings fully just as they are because I know they are here to show me the way into my heart. As I embrace these feelings fully, I ask them to bring with them all of the past meanings, interpretations, beliefs, and judgments that I thought were true, but are not valid in this present moment, so that I may receive them as a gift, guide, and opening toward the infinite perception in my heart. I acknowledge their Divine role in helping me expand awareness into the depths of infinite knowing."

Allow the uncomfortable experience to have a voice. Do not believe what it is saying, but instead be a loving presence that offers a deeper level of safety, comfort, and acknowledgment than the experience has ever received from you before, thereby being the practice of detachment, allowance, pure love, and space.

Ask: "Divine heart, I accept that I don't know how to be patient and allow the pain and suffering I feel in the world to heal through Divine timing. Therefore, I ask that you be patient on my behalf as I witness the pain and suffering dissolve in my inner world. Welcome, embrace, honor, and validate these experiences for me, through me, as I am now, healing the inner division within me, so that my perception can expand and align with the flow of infinite information." And so it is (Amen).

B- BREATHE

Breathe in all the pain and suffering you see on the news! Breathe out blessings of light and love!

I-I LOVE YOU

Place your hands over your heart. Say, *"I love you! All is an expression of one life. I validate this limited experience within me. It is an experience from my past that was not validated by my relationships to the world. Therefore, I choose to be the presence of love that provides this experience the resonation of love that it has never received. May I be all the affirmation that this limited experience needs to remember that it is an infinite expression of divinity, so that it may fully awaken from the illusion of limitation. I love you!"*

"I am abundant, wise, infinite, and free!"

T- THANK YOU

Thank the experience for helping you remember that you are an ever-expanding unique expression of the Truth. Thank the circumstance, story, or relationship that triggered these feelings in your body, so your entire being could awaken to your innocent nature of authentic freedom that can enjoy all experiences.

> *"Thank you for helping me to align and attune with my heart's ever-expanding unique expression of infinite wisdom and pure love! Thank you for helping me to remember the power of life that I am!"*

Intention: *(say aloud)*

"Today, I choose to welcome all experiences that I cannot change. I choose to allow these undesirable experiences to teach me to surrender deeper and allow them to clear, cleanse, and purify my rational mind, so that I may remember my heart-centered nature of eternal patience!"

Affirmation: *(say aloud)*

Say aloud throughout today:

"My heart is Divine perfection because I am Divine perfection!"

Day 22

Path of Least Resistance

"I'm not afraid. I was born to do this."
~Joan of Arc

Say Aloud: (looking into your eyes in a mirror)
Good morning, infinite one. You are safe to feel. I always want to know how you are feeling. You are the soul-mate that I have been looking for my entire life. You matter and you are enough. You are worthy of being seen and heard. I see you and I am here to listen to you. There is a good reason you are here; you are Divine perfection. Today, I join you in celebrating your ever-expanding unique expression. I am open to receiving new information and new ways of being by choosing to receive all uncomfortable, unfamiliar, painful, inconvenient, and unwanted experiences as a Divine gift from you, my infinite heart. I love all of you! I really love all of you. (your name), I really love all of you. (Feel free to write your own love statement).

As we end our 22-day journey together, we come to a place where we can fully disarm the head-centered me, which is on the lookout for some aspect of reality to oppose. The head-centered me always looks for the path of most resistance because it needs to oppose something to exist. Now that we are a living embodiment of the heart-centered habit, we can choose the path of least resistance. This means we choose to no longer deny what we feel and we choose to no longer oppose any part of reality. We no longer wish to fight reality or escape reality. Instead, we wish to merge with reality by taking the path of least resistance.

During circumstances that appear and feel limited, we can receive it fully through the inner knowing that it is here to help us remember the light that exists through all of existence. These limited external circumstances are welcome to stay as long as they need to, so that they may fulfill their mission in stripping us of any misperception that we hold onto that does not resonate the light of divinity, our authentic nature. These circumstances are here to help us in ways that we may not totally understand, realizing that we can embrace them as agents of the Divine that are here to unarm all of our weapons and defenses that we have learned to use to oppose reality in any way. Therefore, we can receive these limited experiences as a Divine gift and continue to love the aspects of ourselves that still have a little fight left in them that want to oppose or escape this reality. By being the heart-centered habit toward all parts within us that oppose or desire to escape our present circumstances, we can align with the path of least resistance.

The path of least resistance is a deep awareness that encompasses heart- centered consciousness. The path of least resistance is a Divine perception toward all aspects of reality; a perception that perceives only light and opposes nothing! Right now, look into your reality. Write down every aspect or relationship that you oppose. This is your opportunity to choose the path of least resistance and honor and respect all that you oppose in your reality. It is time for you to turn on the light in all the dark places in your reality, until your entire reality is lit up by your authentic Divine perception that all is one light of existence! Then keep the lights on and guide the way for the rest of the world.

"This unwanted experience is a gift."
You are welcome here.
You are enough!
How may I serve you?

Desires of the Heart

The desires of our heart are Divine imprints of what is ready to enter our reality as soon as we receive the Divine messages that are hidden within the darkness. The darkness is the reflection of the aspect of the self that still believes in darkness and opposes any part of reality that it deems as uncomfortable, inconvenient, unwanted, and unfamiliar. As we awaken out of the head-centered habit of me, we see clearly that what appeared to darkness was actually Divine light, which was shedding light on the beliefs in darkness that we were unconscious of within our rational mind. Being heart-centered allows all beliefs in darkness and the parts of the self that opposed reality to completely heal and transform within own perception of reality.

When our perception of reality becomes fully filled with the light, reality mirrors back the desires of our heart, which are mirror reflections of Heaven. They are the reflections we were born to manifest through our perception of Divine light. As our reality shifts from the appearance of darkness into the reflection of pure Divine light, the light awakens within the hearts of all matter. The light continues to awaken within all perceptions and beliefs in darkness within the rational minds of all. This is the good news that we don't even have to preach to the masses. Simply by being the living embodiment of perceiving only light, we are transmitting the truth to all rational minds or head-centered "egos" that still oppose aspects of reality.

The change and shift that occurs to manifest the desires of our heart is within the internal compass of our perception. This is why focusing on the outcomes of reality and trying to change our circumstances from the outside-in does not create lasting change! Instead, remaining present with our experiences and allowing them to show us the aspects of our perception that still believe in darkness is what provides the opportunity to align with the heart-centered habit. Being centered and grounded in the heart centered- consciousness provides the foundation for our reality to shift and resonate the Divine light that we are, allowing us to awaken to the remembrance of our true nature of goodness. The way we co-create and manifest the desires of heart is by allowing more light to enter our perception of reality. The Divine light that we are magically and mysteriously shapes our reality into a new reflection that mirrors the goodness that we are! As we focus on keeping the cause in the light, life takes care of the effect.

This is very different than the way the head-centered me went about trying to create and manifest our heart's desires. The head-centered me tried to run away from the darkness in our reality or fight the darkness in our reality or deny and cover up the appearance of darkness in our reality by repressing the feelings and emotions that the appearance of darkness was triggering within us. The head-centered habit could not perceive from its divided perception that the darkness was actually the path, doorway, or the entrance into a new reality that reflected more of the desires in our heart. However, the heart-centered habit looks for the darkness, merges with the darkness, and allows the darkness to shape-shift our perception from darkness to light. Thereby, we remember to work with reality, instead of against reality. Becoming an eternal partner with all of reality, we become eternal partners in the co-creation of Heaven on Earth!

Every experience in all of existence points to our one formless nature of Divine light. May you continue to perceive all experiences through the heart of the matter, choosing the path of least resistance and co-creating the desires of your heart!

"This uncomfortable experience is a gift."
You are welcome here.
You are enough!
How may I serve you?

Resolution

Here we are, on our last day of this journey. It has been an absolute honor to be with you over these last 2 days. The journey continues and we will forever be One because we have shared our Divine nature together. You were with me the entire time that I wrote this book. Now it is time to bring a resolution to all of the information that was shared over the last 22 days. The resolution is an exercise of claiming the light in all experiences as the light you are. This is our final intention together, at least in this way. When every experience is perceived as the light, the light you are; you will no longer need to repress, suppress, deny, or become unconscious again. Instead, you will remain a conscious participant as the light of divinity. Therefore, you will no longer be a participant of co-creating the appearance of darkness, opposition, separation, and division. This is why you were born. You are a revolutionary bearer of light! You have come to be the light and spread the light, participating in the co-creation of Heaven on Earth!

May you glide upon the wings of angels as you welcome, acknowledge, breathe deeper, love more, and receive with gratitude every part of the human experience exactly as it is. As you say these intentions out loud, feel your energy levels increase to heights beyond what you could have ever imagined. This is a taste of the light of your true authentic nature. The light which opposes nothing. Be the faith that trusts in this light that can be sensed, but never totally grasped. This is your infinite nature of passion, excitement, enthusiasm, peace, harmony, and pure love that is filling the space in your mind, body, and circumstances that darkness has created just for you! The darkness, personal limitations, struggle, and suffering has been for you, not against you. As you perceive the darkness as the light, the light you are; you will be fulfilled with the light of divinity that you are. We are the light that transforms all perceptions through respect, honor, acknowledgement, love, and gratitude.

As we resolve to bring equality to all experiences, we step out into the world to be a beacon of light! Continue the heart-centered habit until all experiences have been brought into a perception of equality, so that you may continue to inspire your subconscious mind to co-create a new reality that reflects the authentic light of your being, perceiving the light within you and within the whole world! This is how we participate in bringing the light of Heaven into being realized here as Earth.

"This inconvenient experience is a gift."
You are welcome here.
You are enough!
How may I serve you?

Divine Perception

SAY ALOUD:
"Anger is the light, the light I AM"
Take a deep, slow conscious breath
"Rage is the light, the light I AM"
Take a deep, slow conscious breath
"Depression is the light, the light I AM"
Take a deep, slow conscious breath
"Sadness is the light, the light I AM"
Take a deep, slow conscious breath
"Fear is the light, the light I AM"
Take a deep, slow conscious breath
"Anxiety is the light, the light I AM"
Take a deep, slow conscious breath

"Hatred is the light, the light I AM"
Take a deep, slow conscious breath
"Grief is the light, the light I AM"
Take a deep, slow conscious breath
"Shame is the light, the light I AM"
Take a deep, slow conscious breath
"Guilt is the light, the light I AM"
Take a deep, slow conscious breath
"Confusion is the light, the light I AM"
Take a deep, slow conscious breath
"Frustration is the light, the light I AM"
Take a deep, slow conscious breath
"Jealousy is the light, the light I AM"
Take a deep, slow conscious breath
"Envy is the light, the light I AM"
Take a deep, slow conscious breath
"Loneliness is the light, the light I AM"
Take a deep, slow conscious breath
"Negative emotions are the light, the light I AM"
Take a deep, slow conscious breath
"Rational mind is the light, the light I AM"
Take a deep, slow conscious breath
"Ego is the light, the light I AM"
Take a deep, slow conscious breath
"Judgment is the light, the light I AM"
Take a deep, slow conscious breath
"Beliefs in wrong are the light, the light I AM"
Take a deep, slow conscious breath
"Criticism is the light, the light I AM"
Take a deep, slow conscious breath
"Skepticism is the light, the light I AM"
Take a deep, slow conscious breath
"Noisy mind is the light, the light I AM"
Take a deep, slow conscious breath
"Victim is the light, the light I AM"
Take a deep, slow conscious breath
"Blame is the light, the light I AM"
Take a deep, slow conscious breath

"Emptiness is the light, the light I AM"
Take a deep, slow conscious breath
"Painful memories are the light, the light I AM"
Take a deep, slow conscious breath
"Negative thoughts are the light, the light I AM"
Take a deep, slow conscious breath
"Limited perceptions are the light, the light I AM"
Take a deep, slow conscious breath
"Lack is the light, the light I AM"
Take a deep, slow conscious breath
"Poverty is the light, the light I AM"
Take a deep, slow conscious breath
"Debt is the light, the light I AM"
Take a deep, slow conscious breath
"Addiction is the light, the light I AM"
Take a deep, slow conscious breath
"Stress is the light, the light I AM"
Take a deep, slow conscious breath
"Suffering is the light, the light I AM"
Take a deep, slow conscious breath
"Boredom is the light, the light I AM"
Take a deep, slow conscious breath
"Scarcity is the light, the light I AM"
Take a deep, slow conscious breath
"Divorce is the light, the light I AM"
Take a deep, slow conscious breath
"Separation is the light, the light I AM"
Take a deep, slow conscious breath
"Division is the light, the light I AM"
Take a deep, slow conscious breath
"War is the light, the light I AM"
Take a deep, slow conscious breath
"Conflict is the light, the light I AM"
Take a deep, slow conscious breath
"Death is the light, the light I AM"
Take a deep, slow conscious breath
Pain and hurt is the light, the light I AM"
Take a deep, slow conscious breath

"Punishment is the light, the light I AM"
Take a deep, slow conscious breath
"Fatigue and exhaustion is the light, the light I AM"
Take a deep, slow conscious breath
"Rejection is the light, the light I AM"
Take a deep, slow conscious breath
"Abandonment is the light, the light I AM"
Take a deep, slow conscious breath
"Isolation is the light, the light I AM"
Take a deep, slow conscious breath
"Chaos is the light, the light I AM"
Take a deep, slow conscious breath
"Overwhelm is the light, the light I AM"
Take a deep, slow conscious breath
"Add anymore that come up for you..."

"This unfamiliar experience is a gift."
You are welcome here.
You are enough!
How may I serve you?

Reflection

When you contemplate Heaven, what ideas come to mind to the way you think it is? Is it a place free of pain, suffering, fear, division, stress, separation, war, conflict, hatred, murder...? Is it a place of infinite freedom, fulfillment, peace, love, joy, life, goodness, Truth...? What if Heaven is real and is the heart-centered perception within you right now?

Reprogramming the Subconscious Mind

"Be still and know that everything is God, your true authentic nature."

Practicing the Heart Centered Habit for yourself:

Have you ever felt abused and neglected?

Welcome these experiences as a part of consciousness (You)

H- HONESTY

"I fully feel the parts of me that have felt abused and neglected."

A-ACKNOWLEDGE, ALLOW, ASK

"I acknowledge that it is safe and okay to feel this limited experience. I embrace these feelings fully just as they are because I know they are here to show me the way into my heart. As I embrace these feelings fully, I ask them to bring with them all of the past meanings, interpretations, beliefs, and judgments that I thought were true, but are not valid in this present moment, so that I may receive them as a gift, guide, and opening toward the infinite perception in my heart. I acknowledge their Divine role in helping me expand awareness into the depths of infinite knowing."

Allow the uncomfortable experience to have a voice. Do not believe what it is saying, but instead be a loving presence that offers a deeper level of safety, comfort, and acknowledgment than the experience has ever received from you before, thereby being the practice of detachment, allowance, pure love, and space.

Ask: "Divine heart, I accept that I don't know how to perceive through the lens of least resistance. Therefore, I ask that you perceive experiences of neglect and abuse through the lens of least resistance on my behalf.

341

Welcome, embrace, honor, and validate these experiences for me, through me, as I am now, healing the inner division within me, so that my perception can expand and align with the flow of infinite information." And so it is (Amen).

B- BREATHE

Breathe in these feelings (*"I receive you as life"*) breathe out (*"You are free to be"*). Be one with the breath: *"The breath enlightens my experiences."*

I-I LOVE YOU

Place your hands over your heart. Say, *"I love you! All is an expression of one life. I validate this limited experience within me. It is an experience from my past that was not validated by my relationships to the world. Therefore, I choose to be the presence of love that provides this experience the resonation of love that it has never received. May I be all the affirmation that this limited experience needs to remember that it is an infinite expression of divinity, so that it may fully awaken from the illusion of limitation. I love you!"*

"I am abundant, wise, infinite, and free!"

T- THANK YOU

Thank the experience for helping you remember that you are an ever-expanding unique expression of the Truth. Thank the circumstance, story, or relationship that triggered these feelings in your body, so your entire being could awaken to your innocent nature of authentic freedom that can enjoy all experiences.

> *"Thank you for helping me to align and attune with my heart's ever-expanding unique expression of*

infinite wisdom and pure love! Thank you for helping me to remember the power of life that I am!"

Intention: *(say aloud)*

"I honor and respect every circumstance, appearance, and experience that feels dark. Thank you for being here to unravel all attachments, identifications, judgments, and knowledge of good and evil, so that I perceive the light that I am in all! I choose the path of least resistance and merge with the darkness, working with reality to co-create the desires of my heart!
And so I am free!"

Affirmation: *(say aloud)*

Say aloud throughout today:

"My perception is Divine light because I am Divine light!"

May you feel blessed and loved beyond measure, as you continue the journey of becoming more aware of your

infinite nature!

www.ingramcontent.com/pod-product-compliance
Lightning Source LLC
Chambersburg PA
CBHW021043090426
42738CB00006B/158